THE SCHOOL ON THE BLUFF

A History of the University of Albuquerque

THE SCHOOL ON THE BLUFF

A History of the University of Albuquerque

JOHN TAYLOR

© 2022 by John Taylor
All Rights Reserved
No part of this book may be reproduced in any form or by any electronic or mechanical means including information storage and retrieval systems without permission in writing from the publisher, except by a reviewer who may quote brief passages in a review.

Sunstone books may be purchased for educational, business, or sales promotional use. For information please write: Special Markets Department, Sunstone Press, P.O. Box 2321, Santa Fe, New Mexico 87504-2321.

Book and cover design › R. Ahl
Printed on acid-free paper

WWW.SUNSTONEPRESS.COM
SUNSTONE PRESS / POST OFFICE BOX 2321 / SANTA FE, NM 87504-2321 /USA
(505) 988-4418 / FAX (505) 988-1025

Dedication

Michael L. and Margaret Keleher.
(courtesy of the Keleher family)

This work is dedicated to Michael and Margaret "Peggy" Keleher. On occasion the Sisters would consult Albuquerque attorney William A. Keleher. After his son, Michael, joined his father's law office in March 1962, he would be called into meetings pertaining to the University. In time the Sisters called on Michael. His files were retained by Keleher & McLeod PA until removed to a family storage, and later loaned to John Taylor who arranged for a gift to the Center for Southwest Research and Special Collections at the University of New Mexico. Without Michael's interest in preserving the history of the school as contained in these files, this work would not have been possible.

Contents

Acknowledgment ~ 8
Foreword ~ 9
Introduction ~ 11
1: Background ~ 13
2: Early Years ~ 20
St. Francis Normal School for Catholic Sisters of St. Francis ~ 20
Catholic Teachers College of New Mexico ~ 27
College of St. Joseph on the Rio Grande ~ 38
3: Crossing the Rio Grande ~ 40
4: A Long-Term Gamble ~ 61
5: From Problem to Crisis ~ 86
6: From Crisis to Recovery ~ 104
7: Community College Issues ~ 133
8: Multiple Administrations ~ 144
9: Out of the Frying Pan and into the Fire (again) ~ 164
10: A Civil War on the West Mesa ~ 184
11: Peace and Progress ~ 209
12: Inevitability ~ 219
13: Demise and Disposition ~ 227
14: Retrospective ~ 242
Presidents of University of Albuquerque and its Predecessors ~ 250
Notes ~ 251
Bibliography ~ 283
Index ~ 287

Acknowledgment

The author wishes to acknowledge the help provided by Sister Stephanie McReynolds, Order of St. Francis; Richard Melzer, PhD; Ray John and Rosa de Aragon; Chris Geherin and Jennifer Eggleston from the Center for Southwest Research and Special Collections at the University of New Mexico; Elsie Scott; and Mary Engel, Frankie McCarty, Susanne Burks, Arturo Sandoval, Susan Landon, and other newspaper writers who documented the ups and downs of the University of Albuquerque over the years.

Foreword

The University of Albuquerque expired in August 1986. We had heard that it was seriously ill, but we had heard spurious stories of its demise many times before. Like an old, ailing friend, it had always rallied, and most of us thought it would rally again. But it didn't. The school that had gone through so many illnesses and attempted cures, finally succumbed. Finding it hard to imagine the city without its small college on the West Mesa, all of Albuquerque mourned its passing.

Sadly, the University of Albuquerque died without a proper obituary, eulogy, or funeral. Without an active alumni association, graduates seldom gathered or made contact beyond occasional postings on a Facebook page. In fact, so many years have gone by that most of the University's graduates have now retired as nurses or teachers or whatever field they entered after completing their studies. Former faculty and staff have also retired or, increasingly, passed on. The sixty-acre campus still exists, but it has long served as Albuquerque's only Catholic high school, St. Pius X, with little trace that it was once a post-secondary institution.

It is time to remember the University for its many contributions to education in New Mexico and its impact on thousands of lives. It is time for a historian to write its obituary, depicting the school's true character and interesting history. It is also time for such a historian to conduct a thorough autopsy on the college so that other schools can learn not only what the University did well, but also what it did poorly and led to its demise. Only by studying deceased schools like the University of Albuquerque can the leaders of other colleges and universities avoid the illnesses that killed the UofA and might well threaten their own school's health and continued existence.

Fortunately, historian John Taylor has accepted the challenge of writing the University of Albuquerque's colorful, often compelling history. Employing the same investigative tools that have helped him produce nearly twenty award-winning books, Taylor has interviewed many former students, faculty, and staff. He has combed through countless newspapers in search of relevant articles, large and small. He has researched private collections and delved into the University of Albuquerque's considerable records, housed at the Center for Southwest Research and Special Collections at the University of New Mexico. Remarkably, he has accomplished all this in the midst of the COVID-19 pandemic that has impeded progress on many other worthy projects. Only a historian with Taylor's energy, skills, intelligence, and determination could have attempted, no less completed such a daunting task in these troubled times.

What is true of humans is also true of institutions: Our earthly lives are only forgotten when no one is left to remember what good we did or what lessons we taught, albeit by either good or bad behavior. Thanks to John Taylor's excellent new book, the University of Albuquerque will not be forgotten or have died in vain, especially if our wisest educators heed its still-important lessons.

—Richard Melzer, PhD

Introduction

On June 1, 1966, the first graduates of the University of Albuquerque (UofA) proudly walked across the new stage at the nearly completed University Center to receive diplomas from Sister M. Viatora Schuller, OSF.[1] There were cheers, hugs, tears, and perhaps even a few mortarboards flung into the air.

On May 17, 1986, the last graduate of the University walked across the stage of the Kiva Auditorium at the Albuquerque Convention Center to listen to a commencement address by Representative Manuel Lujan and to receive a diploma from University President Father Alfred McBride. O.Praem.[2] Once again, there were tears and hugs, but this time the mood was much more somber with few if any mortarboards thrown into the air. The University was closing its doors, culminating a 66-year journey from a small Catholic teachers college to a full-fledged university.

The story of the University of Albuquerque is one of dedication and faith, as well as struggles and contrasting visions. There are many players who participated in this endeavor—the Sisters of St. Francis Seraph, a series of presidents, the Archdiocese of Santa Fe, dedicated members of the Board of Trustees, and, of course, many students and faculty. This volume will trace that story from its earliest roots in early Spanish New Mexico through the closure of the institution in August 1986.

A note on the title—the phrase "The School on the Bluff" came from a 1973 statement by Senator Pete Domenici, a former student (and star athlete) at the school when it was still named the College of St. Joseph on the Rio Grande. In addition to the obvious physical reference to the location of the school, it is also is an apt metaphor for many aspects of the school's history including its unique Catholic-Christian principles as stated in Jesus's reference to "the City on the Hill" in the Sermon on the Mount, as well as the brinksmanship suffered by the school through much of its life.[3]

1
Background[4]

Francisco Vasquez de Coronado.
(New Mexico Photo Archives, negative 20206)

Catholicism came to New Mexico with the earliest explorers and colonists. Franciscan priests and brothers from the Franciscan Province of the Holy Gospel, headquartered in Mexico City, accompanied Coronado in 1540. Two of these Franciscans, Fray Juan de Padilla and Fray Luis de Escalona, remained behind and are generally credited as being the first "teachers" in the area.[5] Padilla set up a school in Quivera (thought by some to be located somewhere near the present-day location of Salina, Kansas) and Escalona established one at Cicuye, present-day Pecos. Both priests were killed within a few years of the start of their missionary work.[6]

The principal mission of these Franciscans was to Christianize the Native Americans. In fact, this was more than a mission—it was viewed as their sacred duty.[7] In order to convert the Native Americans, the Franciscans first had to provide basic education, both in the catechism of the Church and in rudimentary language skills. These friars and brothers were New Mexico's first Catholic educators.

By 1598, the Franciscans had established five mission schools where they taught reading, writing, and singing, as well as practical crafts such as shoemaking, carpentry, blacksmithing, metal working, weaving, and painting.[8] In fact, Avant asserts that New Mexico can claim to have had the first schools in what is now the United States.[9] Brother Basil from the Catholic Teachers College referred to the Franciscans as "the founders of education in New Mexico."[10] In 1630, Fray Alonso de Benavides reported that the Indians were "dexterous in reading, writing, playing all musical instruments, and as craftsmen for all trades."[11]

Throughout the Spanish period (1598–1821), the status of education waxed and waned. There were basic schools teaching Christian doctrine, reading, writing, and basic arithmetic at the pueblo missions and in some military garrisons, but the political and military turmoil, coupled with the distance from the seat of power in Mexico City, meant that education often took a back seat to more pressing issues.[12]

In the late Spanish and early Mexican period, education became more of an issue, with public schools being established across the territory. For example, in 1827, a set of 23 formal *estatutos* (regulations) was published for a school in Santa Cruz de Cañada, a village about 25 miles north of Santa Fe.

Throughout this period, there were arguments in legislative bodies about how to establish and fund schools. In many cases, the teachers were still Catholic priests, but there are also examples of non-clerical teachers.[13] Many of the wealthier families chose to either home-school their children or send them to schools outside the territory to further their education. For example, Civil War Governor Henry Connelly hired Harriet Shaw, the wife of Methodist minister, John Milton Shaw, to tutor his children, and the wealthy Luna family of Los Lunas sent their sons east to St. Louis for their education.[14]

In 1826, Presbyter Don Antonio Jose Martinez, commonly known as Padre Martinez, established a primary school in Taos. In 1833, he established a college preparatory school for prospective seminarians. He also established a press and printed textbooks for his schools. Although later in his career he ran afoul of the Catholic bureaucracy, he was one of the prominent early educators in Mexican-era New Mexico.[15]

Padre Don Antonio Jose Martinez.
(courtesy Dora Martinez de Armijo)

As diocesan priests from Durango, Mexico, began to take over parishes from the Franciscans, the mission schools began to suffer. Despite the best efforts of the Diocese of Durango, the shortage of priests and the general poverty of the area meant that educational mission faltered.

In 1850, Pope Pius IX designated part of the territory acquired from Mexico after the Mexican-American War as the Vicariate Apostolic of New Mexico and assigned it to the westernmost archdiocese in the United States—the Archdiocese of St. Louis. He appointed Jean Baptiste Lamy, a French-born priest then serving in Kentucky, as bishop. In 1853, the area was detached from St. Louis and designated as the Diocese of Santa Fe. The diocese was elevated to an archdiocese in 1875, and Lamy continued as archbishop until his death in 1888.

Lamy's influence on the new diocese was profound. When he arrived in 1850, he found the status of Catholic education deplorable. In a later recollection, Lamy's secretary, Reverend James Defouri wrote, "through want of care of both the Mexican government and the Mexican clergy, the province was destitute of educational establishments of any kind."[16]

Jean Baptiste Lamy, first Archbishop of Santa Fe.
(collection of the Archdiocese of Santa Fe)

In order to remedy the situation, Lamy recruited nuns from the Sisters of Loretto and the Sisters of Charity, as well as seeking help from the Christian Brothers, to assist him. Lamy's endeavors were so successful that by the early 1860s, Catholic schools were essentially the only educational institutions in the Territory. Lamy's educational outreach was further helped by an influx of Jesuit priests starting in the late 1860s.[17]

The success of Catholic education in the Territory proved to be a two-edged sword. On the one hand, the grand tradition of Catholic education served both the Catholic and non-Catholic populations. On the other hand, the largely Protestant opponents of New Mexico statehood noted the Catholic Church's influence on public education as one of several reasons to oppose statehood for New Mexico.

Catholic schools continued to grow and flourish through the middle of the twentieth century. At its peak, Albuquerque's Catholic community had elementary schools in almost every parish, three high schools, and a university. However, by the beginning of the twenty-first century, as budget woes forced many of the parish and mission schools to close, there were only eight elementary schools, one middle school, one high school, and no Catholic colleges in the Albuquerque area.

The story of the University of Albuquerque not only has deep roots in Catholic New Mexico, but also traces its roots to nineteenth century Prussia. In 1830, Aline Bonzel was born in the small town of Olpe in the Prussian Province of Westphalia. She grew up in a period of religious revival in Germany and entered the religious life in 1860.[18]

In 1859, together with several other nuns, Bonzel founded the Sisters of St. Francis and Daughters of the Most Holy Hearts of Jesus and Mary, a Franciscan order which was devoted to care for the sick with particular attention to the physical and educational needs of children. As the mother superior of the new order, she adopted the name of Mother Maria Theresia. In 1865, the name of the order was changed to the Congregation of the Poor Sisters of St. Francis Seraph of Perpetual Adoration.

The name of the order was taken from Christian angelology. In that discipline, the seraphim (plural of seraph) are a group of angels that surround the throne of God, offering Him perpetual praise and adoration, chanting "Holy, holy, holy is the Lord Almighty; the whole earth is full of his glory." Pope Gregory I (540–604) declared that the seraphim were the highest of the nine orders of angels.[19]

When Otto von Bismarck succeeded in the unification of Germany in the 1871, he instituted Kulturkampf, an organized suppression and persecution of Catholicism throughout Germany. The Sisters of St. Francis managed to survive because of the care they provided for wounded soldiers during the Franco-Prussian War (1870–1871), but Mother Theresia saw the handwriting on the wall and, at the suggestion of Bishop Joseph Gregory Dwenger of Fort Wayne, Indiana, sent some of the Sisters to the United States. The Sisters in the United States changed their name to the Sisters of the Third Order Regular of St. Francis.[20]

Mother Maria Theresia Bonzel, OSF. (en.wikipedia.org)

The transplanted Sisters had an immediate impact—first in Indiana, then in Nebraska, then spreading throughout the West with 21 hospitals, 52 schools, and four orphanages. In 1932, the Congregation of the Sisters of Saint Francis of the Perpetual Adoration was split into two provinces—the Immaculate Heart of Mary Province with headquarters in Lafayette, Indiana, and the St. Joseph Province with headquarters in Denver, Colorado. Between 1953 and 1959, the Sisters in the St. Joseph Province relocated their headquarters to Colorado Springs.[21]

The Sisters first came to New Mexico in 1904 at the request of Reverend Alfred Daeger, OFM (later the sixth Archbishop of Santa Fe).[22] Father Daeger recognized the need for Catholic education in the territory and asked the Sisters to establish a mission and school in Peña Blanca, a small village between Albuquerque and Santa Fe. At some time, the order changed its name once more to Sisters of St. Francis of the Perpetual Adoration. Over the next few years, several additional schools were established in New Mexico by the Sisters of Saint Francis.

Alfred Thomas Daeger, OFM, Sixth Archbishop of Santa Fe.
(collection of the Archdiocese of Santa Fe)

2
Early Years[23]

ST. FRANCIS NORMAL SCHOOL FOR CATHOLIC SISTERS OF ST. FRANCIS (1920–1940)

As their ministry in the territory and, after 1912, the state of New Mexico expanded, the Sisters recognized a need for providing continuing education for their fellow teachers. Initially, they held summer institutes or conferences among themselves. At the August 1920 conference, James W. Searson, PhD, a well-known Nebraska educator and the co-author of the Searson-Martin reading series, suggested that a more formal summer school, similar to one that had been started in Columbus, Nebraska, be established for the teaching nuns. The New Mexico State Superintendent of Public Education, John V. Conway, agreed with Searson's idea. With their encouragement, the St. Francis Normal School for Catholic Sisters of St. Francis, also referred to as the St. Francis Summer College, officially opened in 1921.

The school grew and expanded through the decade of the 1920s with support from the Archdiocese of Santa Fe. Although initially envisioned as a school for nuns teaching throughout the state, lay teachers were also admitted beginning with the summer session in 1922. Both teachers and students stayed in the dormitory section of St. Anthony's Orphanage, located at 1500 Indian School Boulevard NW, in Albuquerque. Classes were held on the first floor of the building in the orphanage's classrooms.

St. Anthony's Orphanage, the first orphanage in New Mexico, was founded in 1913 by nuns from the Order of St. Francis Seraph of Lafayette, Indiana. The Albuquerque Catholic community, led by Father Alphonse Mandalari, SJ, the Jesuit priest at Albuquerque's Church of the Immaculate Conception, had solicited support and financial contributions.[24] The Jesuit fathers of Albuquerque donated 50 acres for the facility, and the new adobe structure was dedicated by Archbishop John Baptiste Pitival on October 25, 1914.[25]

John Baptiste Pitival, Fifth Archbishop of Santa Fe.
(collection of the Archdiocese of Santa Fe)

The building included a chapel, a kitchen, classrooms, offices, and dormitories that could house 150 boys and 15 girls. A three-story dormitory/classroom structure was added between 1920 and 1924, along with a 700-seat auditorium. A new chapel was added in 1931.

St. Anthony's Orphanage.
(Library of Congress)

In the early 1920s, the facility had 175 children. The emphasis had always been on making the facility as self-sufficient as possible. In the 1930s, the Sisters purchased an additional 41 acres to expand the ability of the residents of the orphanage to raise their own food. This also provided the opportunity for the young men of the orphanage to work on the "farm." In an undated Albuquerque newspaper article, the work was described as:

> Each boy old enough to work is assigned a specific job around the home or farm. Assignments are changed each month in order to break the monotony and so the boys can learn to do numerous things. Among the assignments are work in the dining room and laundry, bakery, chicken house, main building hall, chapel, vegetable room, kitchen, school building, the yards, nursery, barn, basement, boiler room, incinerator, library, sewing room, playground, and others. Livestock maintained on the farm to furnish food for the home now includes 40 milk cows and calves, two goats to provide milk for the nursery, about 100 rabbits, around 900 hens, 70 turkeys, and 10 hogs.[26]

In June 1922, the St. Francis Normal School for Catholic Sisters of St. Francis opened its second annual summer session at St. Anthony's Orphanage with a Mass celebrated by Archbishop Daeger.[27] Sister M. Mathias Boyle, OSF, of Jemez was the superintendent for this session which was open to both Sisters and lay teachers from across the state. The Sisters, both faculty and students, stayed in the dormitory at the orphanage and taught in the classrooms at the facility.[28]

The class of 1921 with faculty in the first row.
(CSWR/UofA photo archives)

One of the school's faculty members was the highly regarded Franciscan priest, Father Claude Mindorf, OFM, who was the Chair of Philosophy at St. Francis Seminary in Cincinnati and who was called to chair the philosophy department at the International Franciscan College in Rome. In addition, the State Superintendent of Public Education, John V. Conway, one of the original supporters of the school, was scheduled to speak to the students and faculty of the college.

In June 1925, St. Francis Summer College opened its fifth session with enrollment of more than 60 teaching Sisters from around the Southwest. It was now a recognized center for Catholic education in the Southwest. The State of New Mexico gave students and graduates full college credits.[29]

The school was now affiliated with St. Bonaventure College in New York. Its faculty consisted of Catholic clergy and Franciscan Sisters who held college degrees from around the country. The overall operation was controlled by the Poor Sisters of St. Francis Seraph from their Colorado headquarters. The school had three superintendents or principals in the mid-to late 1920s. Sister Mathias Boyle, OSF, of Jemez served in 1922 and may have headed up the summer school both earlier and later. Father Albert O'Brien, OFM, ran the school as early as 1927 and was there until his untimely death in 1937. Father Bernard Espelage, a principal aide to Archbishop Daeger and the future first Bishop of the Diocese of Gallup, managed the school in 1928 and may have been there at other times as well.[30]

Father Albert O'Brien.
(CSWR/UofA photo archives)

Annual college sessions began in June with a 10-day institute for those who were unable to stay for the full session. Although the student body was primarily nuns assigned as teachers in parochial schools around the region, lay teachers were also admitted. Two new orders of Sisters, Grey Nuns and Sisters of Mercy, were admitted in 1925.

The school traversed its second decade with about 160 students, 12 full-time professors, classes offered in English, Latin, Spanish, psychology, history, philosophy, sociology, psychology of methods, library methods, physics, chemistry, biology, college algebra, religion, fine arts, and observation of teaching. High school classes were also offered in in English, Latin, Spanish, history, algebra, and plane geometry. Classes were held from mid-June to late July, six days per week. Students who came to five consecutive summer sessions could earn a Bachelor of Arts. Master of Arts and even PhD degrees could also be obtained. In August of 1927, three students received BAs. As the school closed its 1928 session, it was recognized as "one of the most successful educational courses offered in the state."[31]

The impact of the stock market crash of October 1929 took some time to move West. Eventually, however, banks and businesses in Albuquerque began to suffer and, in some cases, fail altogether. Robert K. Barney noted, "To New Mexico in general, the Great Depression was something that arrived late, lasted briefly, and exited rapidly."[32] This was largely because the state had never really experienced prosperity.[33] The orphanage and school managed to avoid the brunt of the financial collapse and continued to operate successfully through the 1930s.[34] The first lay graduate was Beatrice Sanchez in the class of 1935.[35]

On July 12, 1937, Father Albert O'Brien, OFM, one of the founders and the current president of St. Francis Summer College died rather suddenly at the orphanage. His body was transported to St. Bonaventure, New York, for burial. Colleagues said that his self-sacrificing spirit, loyalty to the college, and untiring zeal for the furtherance of the institution were outstanding.[36]

While the death of a single priest may not seem overly significant, it may actually be the first indication of a change in the course of the school. Archbishop Daeger, the only Franciscan Archbishop of Santa Fe, had died in an accident in 1932, and Father O'Brien represented the strong tie to St. Bonaventure in New York, a Franciscan college. With the loss of these two Franciscan stalwarts, the link to the Franciscan heritage of the School was at least temporarily broken. Despite these losses, the school continued to grow with an enrollment of 265 in 1938.

Both the new Archbishop of Santa Fe, Rudolph Aloysius Gerken, and the new head of the Summer School, Reverend Doctor Hyacinth Barnhardt, were secular (i.e., non-order) priests. Barnhardt came from the prestigious Belgian University of Louvain, and Gerken had been educated at the University of Dallas and at Kenrick Seminary in St. Louis.[37]

Rudolph Aloysius Gerken, Seventh Archbishop of Santa Fe.
(collection of the Archdiocese of Santa Fe)

CATHOLIC TEACHERS COLLEGE OF NEW MEXICO (1940–1949)

In 1939, the Archdiocese of Santa Fe reevaluated its relationship with the college. In private conversations with Roy Deferrari, PhD, Secretary General of Catholic University in Washington, DC, Archbishop Gerken decided that several changes should be made. It appears, at least on the surface, that differences of opinion as to the management of the college may have arisen between the Archbishop and the Sisters of St. Francis. This is hinted at by the fact that the conversations between Gerken and Deferrari did not include any representatives from the college or from the Sisters.[38]

Deferrari and Gerken decided, among other things, that the school would no longer be operated and staffed by the Sisters of St. Francis, but would be run by the Archdiocese. Gerken himself would head the faculty; a secular priest, Father William Bradley, would be the head of school; and the name would be changed to the Catholic Teachers College of New Mexico. The reason provided for the change in management was that it was "in response to wide demand for its services on the part of the general public, as well as on the part of the religious, both teachers and others."[39] In addition, the school would operate on a year-round basis and would now accept male students.[40] The faculty would consist of members of 23 religious orders, including representatives from Franciscans, Jesuits, Christian Brothers, and 14 communities of nuns.[41]

This arrangement was formalized in a certificate of incorporation dated March 19, 1940, for the Catholic Teachers' College of New Mexico with the incorporators being Archbishop Gerken and the Reverends Jules Stoffel, Julius Hartmann, William Bradley, and Clarence C. Schoeppner.[42]

In 1940, a ruling from the New Mexico State Board of Education said that in order for graduates of the college to be accredited to teach in New Mexico, the college could no longer operate under the umbrella of St. Bonaventure. Archbishop Gerken initially suggested that the institution could be affiliated with the University of New Mexico, and that university agreed to provide oversight for at least one year. However, after consultation with Reverend Hyacinth Barnhardt, the Archbishop decided to ask Catholic University in Washington, DC, to perform the oversight function.[43]

In June 1940, the summer school opened with an enrollment of 220, down from the previous high of 350. There were 100 students from Catholic teaching orders and 120 lay students. These students came from New Mexico, Kansas, Nebraska, Colorado, and Arizona. The school was declared to be open to "Catholic young men and women who intend to follow the teaching profession." The school, still at St. Anthony's Orphanage, welcomed its first freshman class of 50 in September 1940.[44] The librarian reported that the school's library was stocked with 3,748 books and subscribed to 40 periodicals.[45]

During 1940, some of the Sisters at the school approached local attorney William A. Keleher and asked him if he would help them find some land for a permanent home for the college. Keleher took the Sisters on a tour of town so that they could examine potential properties. They were particularly interested in a piece of land north of the University of New Mexico near Girard and Lomas. However, before any transaction could be completed, the war intervened, and the search for a new location was put on hold.[46]

William A. Keleher.
(courtesy the Keleher family)

The United States entered World War II in December 1941 following the attack on Pearl Harbor. Historian Marc Simmons observed, "the strong trend toward economic recovery ... blossomed into full prosperity."[47] The war years were slow but steady for the school. The reduced summer enrollment (135 in 1943) was attributed to teachers working in defense industries during the summer. Despite the fighting in the Pacific theater, the students put on a Japanese cultural program in 1942, following Pope Pius XII's admonition that "we can love our enemies even while fighting them."[48]

The prospective teachers met their recommended student teaching practice by teaching various subjects to the boys at the orphanage. Grading was stringent with multiple requests to the faculty to give out more "Cs" than the total of "As" and "Bs."[49] In order to work more efficiently, the faculty asked to have a typewriter to be made available to them.[50]

During 1945, the student teaching recommendation was elevated to a requirement for a full summer of actual classroom experience and was expanded to include schools from Bernalillo to Tome and even as far away as Grants and Nambe.[51]

As the war drew to a close, soldiers, sailors, and airmen returning from overseas were pleased to find that the college had been approved for them under the Servicemen's Readjustment Act of 1944, commonly known as the GI Bill of Rights or just the GI Bill. These returnees and the influx of scientists, engineers, and executives, changed the character of Albuquerque from a "slow-paced railroad town" to a "booming metropolis."[52] The newcomers "hungered for, demanded, and expected a program of higher education that would meet their needs."[53]

In June 1945, the registrar announced that a large enrollment was expected including students and veterans from the previously mentioned states plus California. In fact, the number of students who elected to take advantage of the GI Bill caught educators by surprise. By 1946, there were more than two million students enrolled in colleges and universities across the nation, and half of them were veterans.[54]

Archbishop Gerken died on March 2, 1943, and was succeeded by Edwin Vincent Byrne. Byrne was originally from Philadelphia and had been ordained in 1915. A socially conservative bishop (no dating in high school, no Catholic girls in bathing suits in the Miss New Mexico pageant, etc.), Byrne had served in a number of locations, most recently as Bishop of San Juan, Puerto Rico.

Edwin Vincent Byrne, Eighth Archbishop of Santa Fe.
(collection of the Archdiocese of Santa Fe)

During the first three years of Byrne's office, the school continued to operate as a "diocesan institution."

In 1942, Reverend Jules Stoffel replaced Reverend William Bradley as the college's acting president with Bradley returning in 1944. In 1944, Archbishop Gerken had written letters to all of the orders of teaching Sisters in the state, encouraging (essentially mandating) them to send their teachers to the Catholic Teachers College:

> As you well know, the degree of stability attained by our college will be measured by its ability to establish a satisfactory full-time and summer student body. Consequently, we expect each community teaching in the schools within the Archdiocese to send us students ... we trust that each community will make a special effort to fulfill our wishes in this regard.[55]

He had earlier asked the orders to provide Sisters with Masters degrees to come and teach at the college.⁵⁶ The Archbishop's "encouragement" seems to have made a difference since the summer enrollment increased by almost 50 percent from 1944 to 1945, and overall enrollment also showed a substantial increase from 1944 to 1946.⁵⁷

Felicita Sachs Baca and Nika Salazar, two graduates of the class of 1944.⁵⁸
(courtesy Matt Baca)

In the 1940s, Archbishop Gerken had purchased a property on South Second Street that had been developed in 1929 by the Congregational Church as a missionary school for boys. Initially, farming, manual arts, and various trades were taught. Later a preparatory curriculum toward the priesthood was added, and it became a high school renamed Our Lady of Lourdes.⁵⁹

In order to allow the college and its programs to expand, Archbishop

Byrne moved it from the orphanage to the new property, renamed Our Lady of Lourdes Seminary, in the fall of 1946. Sister Agnes de Sales was dean of the college during the move. The displaced seminary was moved to the Santa Fe Inn which had been purchased by Byrne.[60, 61]

Our Lady of Lourdes chapel.
(courtesy Ron Tabor)

Our Lady of Lourdes High School. (courtesy Ron Tabor)

Between 1938 and 1944 there was an ongoing discussion between the State Board of Education and the school over teacher certification. Kathleen Jennings, Director of Certification for the State Board, had notified the teachers graduating from the College that they were required to submit their credits to "some New Mexico college approved by the North Central Association of Colleges and Secondary Schools" before they would be approved. In addition, the University of New Mexico said that it would not approve transfer credits from a non-accredited school.[62]

The accreditation issue resulted in a flurry of correspondence between Jennings, Grace Coniga of the State Board of Education, J. C. Knode, Dean of the UNM College of Arts and Sciences, Roy Deferrari from Catholic University, and Reverend Bradley. This issue was resolved by recognition that the oversight by Catholic University would be sufficient to certify the credits. This certification was reaffirmed in 1950.[63]

In January 1946, the Reverend Edward T. McCarthy replaced Reverend Bradley as the head of the college. Byrne noted that McCarthy "had had a distinguished career in educational circles, having studied in Europe and spent many years as a professor of philosophy, history, and languages." Bradley remained in the Archdiocese as director of all Catholic charities and superintendent of all Catholic schools.[64]

In the school catalog for the 1946–1947 school year, the school laid out its purpose:

> Catholic Teachers College of New Mexico has for its aim the preparation of teachers, both religious and lay, capable of advancing the physical, intellectual, and spiritual well-being of their pupils in the elementary and secondary schools of the state.[65]

Although this seems to omit the Catholic Christian emphasis of the school, it should be remembered that most of the students and all of the faculty were Catholic, so the religious focus of the institution would not need to be emphasized.

The graduating class of 1947, one of the last classes to graduate from the Catholic Teachers College at St. Anthony's Orphanage.
(CSWR/UofA photo archives)

In 1946, the school established its first Board of Trustees. The Board was headed by Archbishop Byrne (*ex officio*) and was composed of five priests—Jules Stoffel, William Bradley, Daniel Krahe, and Clarence Schoeppner.[66] The new Board congratulated 59 graduates in commencement ceremonies in August 1946.

In the spring of 1946, Reverend McCarthy became quite outspoken about a scandal involving two University of New Mexico sociology students. These students were participating in a study on racial attitudes and had substituted the phrase "Spanish-Americans" for "Negroes" on a standard University of Chicago questionnaire. McCarthy railed at the University of New Mexico's handling of the affair, accusing the institution of trying to "whitewash the whole dirty business." The negative publicity apparently put him crosswise with the Archbishop.[67]

Nineteen forty-six was also the first time that the college experienced some financial hardship. Archbishop Byrne noted that the Archdiocese was "too poor" to finance a college, and Monsignor Garcia, pastor at San Ignacio parish in Albuquerque, said that "the college has no place in the Archdiocese, since it takes funds from the various parishes."[68]

According to Sister M. Viatora Schuller, OSF, a future president of the college, writing in 1976, Byrne "urgently appealed" to the Sisters of St. Francis to reassume responsibility for running the college. Mother

M. Basilia Kugler, OSF, Provincial Vicar for the Sisters of St. Francis, heard rumors of the possibility of the closure of the college and agreed to take over responsibility.[69] The "transfer of power" occurred on August 1, 1947. At their request, Reverend Robert Wilken, OFM, a Franciscan priest, picked up the reins with Sister M. Honora Hau, OSF, appointed as Dean and Sister M. Rayneria Willison, OSF, taking on the registrar's job.[70]

Father Wilken came from Duns Scotus College in Detroit. He was described as a "boyish, red-haired padre," and had a deep interest in labor and social justice issues.[71]

Reverend Robert Wilken, OFM.
(CSWR/UofA photo archives)

Under Wilken, the fall term began on September 16 with 65 full-time students, 100 part-time students, plus students attending Saturday and evening classes.

An activity program under the direction of Rudy Cordova was begun in 1947 at the request of Sisters Rayneria and Honora. By the summer of 1948, Cordova was teaching First Aid, Safety, Playground Activities, and Health Education, all to prepare the prospective teachers for certification.

Another milestone for the college occurred in November 1947, when Coach Cordova, with the help of Nick Madrid from Los Lunas, fielded the school's first basketball team, christened "The Dons," a name which had been selected by the Student Assembly.[72] The team consisted of 20 men and competed in a regional junior college league. The team was composed of players who had come to the college from many local towns including Los Lunas, Belen, La Joya, Estancia, Cuba, both Albuquerque public high schools, and St. Mary's in Albuquerque.[73]

Dr. Rudy Cordova.
(CSWR/UofA photo archives)

The Don masthead.
(CSWR/UofA, Box 15, *The Don*, vol. 2, No. 2, 11/48)

Throughout the remainder of 1947 and through 1948 and 1949, the school maintained a robust academic program, and Reverend Wilken was a sought-after speaker across the community and the state on a variety of social issues, including the proposed closed-shop amendment to the state constitution and on the proposal to end rent control.[75]

Biology Class, 1949–1950. (CSWR/UofA photo archives)

COLLEGE OF ST. JOSEPH ON THE RIO GRANDE (1949–1965)

In the spring of 1949, the name of the college was changed to the College of St. Joseph. However, this moniker led to confusion at the Post Office, so the name was informally revised to the College of St. Joseph on the Rio Grande to avoid confusion with the other local institutions bearing the St. Joseph name, especially St. Joseph Hospital.[76]

The 1949–1950 school catalog still assumed that the students who were applying knew of the Catholic nature of the institution. It also reflects a new focus on community outreach which would become more and more important later in the school's history. Its goal statement read:

> Catholic Teachers College assumes to play a modest role in redirecting the philosophy of a regional community, the Southwest, by conservation of human and natural resources, broadening of social and political perspective, and deepening the spiritual vision of man's dignity and destiny. These, in descending order, sum up the larger aims of the liberal and vocational education offered by the Catholic Teachers College.[77]

In September 1949, Mother M. Basilia Kugler, OSF, former Provincial of the Sisters of St. Francis Seraph of the Perpetual Adoration, was named the new president of the college. The renamed college was now accredited by the state as a liberal arts college offering both Bachelor and Master degree programs.[78]

Mother M. Basilia Kugler, OSF.
(CSWR/UofA photo archives)

3
Crossing the Rio Grande

The decade of the 1950s was a great time in the United States, a great time in Albuquerque, and a great time to be associated with the College of St. Joseph on the Rio Grande. The nation had recovered from the Great Depression and World War II in excellent financial shape. Earnings were up, gross domestic product (GDP) was up, and the American dream of family homes was being realized all over Albuquerque. The growth of Sandia Laboratories and Kirtland Air Force Base brought thousands of well-educated engineers and scientists, along with millions of federal dollars, into the Duke City.

On the other hand, the Korean War was ramping up, and issues related to Civil Defense were on the minds of some of the students. In an article in the December 1950 issue of *The Don*, a case was made for Civil Defense preparations at the college. It was pointed out that no one at the campus had heard the warning siren from Albuquerque when it was tested on December 14. The article went on to say:

> No attack by an enemy air force armed with the atomic bomb is going to wait until the students of St. Joseph safely reach their houses and come under the protection of the Civil Defense organization of Albuquerque.[79]

In his celebrated encyclical on Christian education, *Divini Illius Magistri*, Pope Pius XI made clear the need for Christian over secular education. In that encyclical, he said:

> The proper and immediate end of Christian education is to cooperate with divine grace in forming the true and perfect Christian ....

[T]he true Christian, the product of Christian education, is the supernatural man who thinks, judges, and acts always and consistently in accordance with right reason illuminated by the supernatural light of the example and teaching of Christ.

The 1949–1950 school catalog once again restated the purpose of the institution. This time, the statement took into account the Pope's admonitions and was much more focused on the religious goals of the school:

The College of St. Joseph on the Rio Grande is a coeducational college of liberal arts whose purpose is the moral, intellectual, and physical development of students according to the principles of Catholic philosophy of education as laid down by Pope Pius XI.[80]

Since the 1920s, the school in its various forms had either shared facilities or moved into "hand-me-down" locations. After the war, and in keeping with the rosier economic outlook, Sister Honoria and Sister Rayneria had resumed discussions about building a new, permanent home for St. Joseph. When Mother Basilia took over in 1949, she, too, pushed for a new campus. Once again, the Sisters approached William Keleher and asked for help in identifying a suitable property. Keleher showed Mother Basilia several potential locations, including one on the West Mesa. Mother Basilia was impressed with the West Mesa property and asked Keleher to work on obtaining it for the school. The property consisted of 50 acres owned by local realtor E. H. Sloan and his wife, Maxine, and by Mildred White, wife of local businessman, Fred White. With the encouragement of Keleher and his wife, Loretta, Sloan and White agreed to donate the land plus an additional 10 acres to the Sisters of St. Francis. The deed transferring the land was filed with the Bernalillo County clerk on April 7, 1950. The deed included a Possibility of Reverter clause that stated that if the land was not developed for at least $250,000 within two years, it would revert to the donors.[81]

Plans for the new campus, drawn for the Sisters by Denver architect John K. Monroe, envisioned a co-educational institution for up to 1,000 education and business administration students. Buildings were to be constructed in brick with mission-style exteriors. The plans included a science building, classroom buildings, a library, a cafeteria, a gymnasium, a chapel, an auditorium, and housing for resident students and some faculty. Services such as a power house, water and sewer systems, etc. were also in the plans.[82]

The entire project was to be funded by the Sisters and was estimated to cost in the neighborhood of two million dollars. The first actual construction, a 12-inch-bore well, was drilled on the site by Howard Sheets, a local driller, in 1949.[83] Michael Keleher, later the attorney for the school, was working as a "grunt" for Public Service Company of New Mexico and dug post holes for the power poles for the well.[84] Charles Lemke, an Albuquerque contractor, was chosen to do the major construction work. Ground was broken on June 15, 1950; the corner stone was laid on May 1, 1951; and first occupancy was later in May for the 1951 summer session. Completion of the entire campus was projected to take between five and ten years.[85]

Michael L. Keleher.[86] (courtesy Keleher family)

At the ground-breaking, Archbishop Byrne said:

Godless heresy has made its diabolical way across Europe, across Asia, and down to the heart of Africa. This institution will help combat the menace. Its primary objective will be to give the students a philosophy of life based on the best thought of the greatest men that have ever lived. The student of a Catholic college at graduation knows what is right and what is wrong, and almost as important, why certain things are right and why certain other things are wrong.[87]

In keeping with the major transitions, the Student Council published the first student constitution in the fall of 1951. A complete rendition of the document was provided to the student body in *The Don*.[88]

One of the major issues associated with the new location was access. There was only one road from Central Avenue/Route 66 north along the West Mesa to Corrales Road in the far North Valley. This road, aptly named Mesa Road, was unpaved and was noted as being "so sandy that two cars could not meet without getting stuck while pulling out to pass."[89] The road was later renamed Coors Boulevard to honor a 1940s and 1950s district attorney and judge, Henry George Coors III. In July 1952, a paving contract was let to Wylie Brothers for their low bid of $56,388. The paving project began in September 1952. Even before the road was paved, bus service to the campus for students, faculty, and staff was operated by the Albuquerque Bus Company from downtown Albuquerque along the sandy dirt road.[90]

In a sarcastic article in *El Luminario*, the renamed student paper, the editor reflected on the benefits of the new four-lane paved road:

Now students can drive to school without having a wrecker follow behind like a vulture .... After a little research, editors found out why some students in first period class were a little dopey-looking. After that last quarter mile of washboard, one would alight and shake all through English II.[91]

The editor added, tongue in cheek, that prior to completion of the road, students had used somewhat circuitous means of getting to school including horseback, hopping on the (non-existent) ferry across the river, parachuting onto campus, and taking a helicopter. He also noted that "Dr. Romero has junked his Stanley Steamer and now uses his new Studebaker."

The site of the new campus was an oasis of grass in an otherwise barren desert landscape along old Mesa Road. Ruth Hall recounts an incident when horses and cattle from a nearby ranch discovered the grass. Sister Catherine Ann Bintner, OSF, the school's registrar, raced out of her quarters with "her black robes flying" to try to chase the hungry beasts off the lawn. Although her efforts to save the grass were temporarily successful, the animals would not be deterred, and eventually the sheriff had to visit the ranch to ask the owner to please keep his pasture gate shut.[92]

The fall semester of 1951 showed a 20 percent increase in enrollment with 550 students and fifteen new faculty members. Because of the new facility on the west side of the river and the paving of Coors Boulevard, real estate expansion began in the area. The *Albuquerque Journal* was filled with ads for property "near St. Joseph College" with "choice views" and "never-again prices."

Campus with volcanoes in the background, 1950s.
(CSWR/UofA photo archives)

The new campus was formally dedicated on October 15, 1952, by Archbishop Byrne. In his remarks, the Archbishop said:

> We need men and women in New Mexico who are well informed ... but history is filled with men who are well informed but who lacked character that would have made them really great men.... The Catholic College of St. Joseph has a basic objective. Chemistry, physics, and social sciences will be taught, but the primary objective is to give to the students a philosophy of life, based upon the best thought of the greatest men that have ever lived. That philosophy is a perennial philosophy that stems from Plato and Aristotle and was Christianized by Augustine and Thomas Aquinas .... The student is given an orderly understanding of life.... For men and women of New Mexico who seek happiness within the laws of God, the Church in New Mexico offers a new college.[93]

A special feature of the campus was a statue of St. Joseph, a gift of the class of 1951, the first class to graduate from the new campus. It is an imposing 10-foot-tall, 3,500-pound white marble statue that had been carved in Pietrasanta, Italy, from a single piece of Carrata marble under the supervision of Joseph Piccirilli, a member of the noted Piccirilli family of sculptors.[94] In 1980, an arched adobe bell tower was added in front of the statue by the Chi Gamma Iota fraternity to be a symbol of faith and the survival of the school.[95]

Statue of St. Joseph. (CSWR/UofA photo archives)

Bell arch.
(CSWR/UofA, Box 17, folder 7, undated brochure)

A temporary chapel had been built in St. Francis Hall (in what is now St. Pius X High School, Room 114). It was soon replaced by a permanent chapel, named St. Joseph Chapel, in Assumption Hall when that building was completed. As the other buildings were being completed, a small network of utility tunnels was included to connect them—St. Francis Hall was connected to Assumption Hall, etc. Students and faculty occasionally used these tunnels to go from one building to another, especially during inclement weather.[96]

When the school was completed and began instruction in 1951, it had the distinction of being the only private accredited college in either New Mexico or Arizona. It also gave Albuquerque the distinction of being one of the few cities in the West with two fully accredited institutions of higher learning.[97]

The school had had a successful basketball program under Rudy Cordova since 1947. However, the Korean War wreaked havoc with the team, as several of its members chose to "don the khaki." In January 1951, Cordova said that he was determined to finish the 1951 season, even if he had to "put on his old jersey." However, in February, with only six players left, the school suspended all interscholastic athletics "for the duration of the national emergency." In his announcement of the suspension, Cordova promised, "After the end of the national emergency, the Dons will be back!"[98]

As with many new (and old) schools, initiation traditions became a part of welcoming new students. One of these was "refreshing" the painted stone "J" (for Joseph) on Volcon, one of the nearby volcanoes.[99] The "J," initially whitewashed in 1951, was 176-feet tall and 60-feet wide. It had been laid out by an engineer from Sandia Base and was placed on a 45-degree incline on the center volcano so as to be visible for miles around.[100]

The "J" on Volcon. (CSWR/UofA photo archives)

Controversy over the "J" arose almost immediately. People said that it was "rash" and "unartistic." One nearby resident complained that "one of our views has been cheapened. I refer to the painting of the 'J' on the center volcano by the freshman of St. Joseph College."[101]

There was some discussion in the mid-1960s about the fate of the "J." Sister Marilyn Doiron, OSF, the school president, favored blocking it out entirely to "further community relations," while others favored changing it to "U of A." In 1967, "J day" was not held because no one could find the key to the gate in the fence that surrounded the monument. In the end, the "J" was kept, largely because the West Mesa Community Association favored it as a "symbol and landmark."[102]

Matt Baca, a 1957 graduate of St. Joseph, recalled joining other freshman in their trek up the volcano to paint the "J." He said that once the task had been completed, the crew was given a picnic at the Doc Long picnic area in the Sandias. Baca, a country boy from Belen, said that they served potato salad, a dish he had never seen before.[103]

When presidential candidate John F. Kennedy visited Albuquerque during his 1960 campaign, he noticed the "J" while he was being chauffeured to the University of New Mexico's Newman Center for Mass. There are two stories about his reaction. In one, he apparently turned to his host and asked, "Did they do that for me?"[104] In the other he "expressed astonishment at the prominent "J" and supposed it had been the work of Senator Lyndon Johnson's sympathizers to dampen his own spirits."[105]

Sometime during the late 1950s a group of St. Joseph students commandeered a large number of car tires and clandestinely drove them to the west side of Volcon, where they proceeded to set them on fire. The black smoke billowed up and was noticeable all across the area. Local residents, fearing that the long quiescent volcanoes were about to erupt, fled to the foothills of the Sandias, wearing whatever they had on at the time—some apparently still in their pajamas![106]

Two other traditions began in 1951 and 1952. Lieutenant Lee Scoggins, a naval officer and junior at the school, wrote a poem that became the school song on November 28, 1951. The melody was provided by Edmundo Hernandez.

Beside the winding sleepy water
Of the silvery Rio Grande,
On the desert-flowered mesa,
Stands St. Josephs proud and grand.

Proud of knowledge to be given,
Grand in concept of its goal,
Grand the rays of western sunset,
On our waving blue and gold.

May the centuries weave the legend,
'Round the statue on the square.
That St. Joseph guards in wisdom,
Scholars of the true and fair.[107]

The other tradition was the creation of a logo for the school.

Logo of St. Joseph on the Rio Grande.
(CSWR/UofA photo archives)

The design of the logo was created by Father Roger Hoehn to reflect the identity and dignity of the school. The "J" topped with the cross reflects the holy faith and patronage of St. Joseph and the Christian nature of the school. The open book with the Latin words *Pro Dei et Patria* (For God and Country) indicates a constant striving for knowledge, and the torch symbolizes the open light of truth.[108] The school conferred degrees on 86 graduates in May 1952.

The colors were changed from Blue and Gold to Blue and White in 1968. In 1971, the school also created a flag, but it stayed in storage for 13 years until 1984.

In September 1953, Mother Basilia decided to retire and return to the Sisters' motherhouse in Denver.[109] She was replaced by Sister M. Viatora Schuller, OSF. Sister Schuller was born and attended grade school and high school in Nebraska. She entered the order of the Poor Sisters of St. Francis Seraph in Lafayette, Indiana, and obtained a Bachelor's degree from Indiana State University in 1934 with majors in social studies, English, and commerce. She went on to obtain a Master's from Creighton in 1948 and a Doctorate in history from Loyola University in Chicago in 1953. Her dissertation was entitled "A History of Early Catholic Orphanages in the United States." Although it might appear that she came to St. Joseph right out of school, she had taught high school and college for nearly 19 years while getting her various degrees.[110]

Sister M. Viatora Schuller, OSF.
(CSWR/UofA photo archives)

In an effort to improve recruiting and retention, a survey was conducted in March 1954. The results were reported in the *Mesa Messenger* showing, to no one's surprise, that most of the students had chosen to go to college to further their education, receive degrees, and gain better employment opportunities. They had chosen St. Joseph because it was close to home, and they wished to be instructed from the Catholic point of view for their chosen professions, most of which were in the field of education. One respondent noted:

> An education without the spiritual factor is incomplete; a true education must never lack fundamentals of Christianity which are essential in today's world of modernism, materialism, and secularism.[111]

A 1954 article in the *Clovis News-Journal* noted a nearly 15 percent increase in college enrollment across New Mexico. This was attributed to higher birthrates in 1936/1937, more New Mexicans attending college, more college-bound students attending in-state schools, and more women going to college. Sister Viatora said that she anticipated an enrollment of about 400 for the upcoming fall term.[112]

In 1954, the school contacted the North Central Association of Colleges and Secondary Schools to explore the possibility of formal accreditation. This organization, founded in 1895 with headquarters in Tempe, Arizona, and Chicago, Illinois, was one of six regional accreditation bodies in the U.S. recognized by the United States Department of Health, Education, and Welfare as a regional accreditor for higher education institutions. As a part of that process, the school conducted an in-depth self-evaluation. One of the important parts of this self-evaluation was a statement of purpose:

> The College of St. Jospeh is a Catholic liberal arts college, its principal concentration being its Department of Education. As a Catholic college, St. Joseph's basic aim is the formation of the whole man. This man we conceive to consist of body and soul in fundamental union ... to further this general purpose, we offer courses in religion and insist that our whole program be permeated with those principles.[113]

Note that, despite the use of the word "man" in the mission statement, the school had been co-educational for many years.

Also in the self-assessment was a report on enrollment—of the 357 students, 306 were from New Mexico and 14 were from Colorado. Of the New Mexico students, 219 were from Bernalillo County.

The report from the North Central examiners to its Board of Review noted that the physical plant was excellent, the library was excellent, but much of administration and services were provided rather informally. Perhaps most seriously, however, were the serious faculty "gaps." The educational staff was reported to be enthusiastic but not qualified. Several had only Masters degrees, one professor had an Italian doctorate which was considered inadequate, and the psychology courses were taught by a priest who had no psychological training. Because of these shortcomings, accreditation was denied.[114]

Despite the lack of accreditation from the North Central Association, in December 1955, the school renewed its affiliation with Catholic University for the years 1956 through 1961.[115]

Up to this point, the school had been entirely financed by the Sisters in Colorado Springs. In November 1954, the Sisters embarked on a fund-raising campaign for the first time in the school's history. They intended to raise $60,000 from various sources to underwrite a prefabricated auditorium/gymnasium. The long-term vision called for a permanent facility, but the Sisters noted that they would need to retire the $2 million debt for the existing facilities before starting a major new project. Both the fund-raising and debt-retirement efforts were completed by 1955, and the permanent gymnasium (now the St. Pius auxiliary gym) was completed in that year.[116] The first game was played in the new facility on February 20, 1955.

It is perhaps a sign of the good times that much of the newspaper coverage of St. Joseph during the 1950s focused on athletics. Basketball was a principal sport with baseball close behind. In fact, a 1952 baseball score had the Dons defeating St. Michaels 18-0 in a mercy-rule-shortened game with future U.S. Senator Pete Domenici pitching a shutout for St. Joseph.[117] (Domenici would go on to pitch one season for the Albuquerque Dukes, a minor league farm club of the then-Brooklyn Dodgers.)

Prior to the 1950s, the school's athletic programs in tennis, volleyball, and basketball were conducted outside on asphalt courts.

Basketball games with other teams were played on temporary courts set up in the Albuquerque Civic Auditorium. The use of a "fine portable floor" at the Civic Auditorium was continued into the 1970s. It was noted that the floor could either be used at the Civic Auditorium with a capacity of 7,000, or moved to Tingley Coliseum on the State Fairgrounds where the spectator capacity was 12,000.[118]

During this period, Marcia Garihee started a women's athletic program, called the Women's Recreational Association, which included cheerleading, volleyball, and archery. In the 1955–1956 school year, the college joined the National Association of Intercollegiate Athletics (NAIA).[119]

In addition to athletics, there are numerous mentions of concerts, art exhibitions, and dramatic presentations, either by or in support of the school's fund-raising campaign. One particularly notable concert was an October 1958 event featuring famed jazz trumpeter Louis "Satchmo" Armstrong.[120]

The school considered itself to be a four-year, co-educational, liberal arts college, although it still maintained a stress on teacher training. It was the only Catholic, co-educational college in New Mexico and the surrounding area.[121] The Committee on Curriculum, chaired by James McGrath, presented results of the ongoing discussion on integrating curriculum with the Catholic mission of the University at a February 1956 faculty meeting. Sister M. Richardis, OSF, a member of the committee, noted that the proposed integration of curriculum and mission was:

> To produce the perfect Christian. The student, on graduation, should take his place in society as "priest, prophet, ruler, and maker," and he should excel in all four roles. The most perfect Christian will be produced by the most perfect education.[122]

In this regard, Committee Chair McGrath weighed in on recent criticism of Cardinal John Henry Newman who differentiated between knowledge and virtue.[123] McGrath cited Father Edward Bernard's assertion that "theology should have its rightful place among the intellectual disciplines" and that "the object of a university is to be the cultivation of intellectual excellence."[124]

Throughout the decade of the 1950s, issues of student dedication and motivation were problems faced by the faculty. Absences were a particular problem that were discussed in faculty meetings throughout the decade. In addition, the reason that students attended in the first place were raised. Some faculty members, citing the liberal arts focus of the college, expressed the concern that students "do not want to learn for the sake of knowledge but for the sake of a job .... Students do not enter college with a 'will to know.'"[125]

Sister M. Catherine Ann Binter, OSF, another committee member, said that integration with the social sciences was also essential, "Although a reasonable amount of specialization is encouraged, capable teachers are a *sine qua non*. History should be integrated with philosophy and religion and these with other social sciences."[126]

Fifty-nine classes were offered during the summer of 1956, including a special music program for local parochial school students. The University had opened a branch on Sandia Base (the eastern end of Kirtland Air Force Base) in 1951. In the fall of 1956, 106 courses were available, including adult education classes held on Kirtland Air Force Base (which had expanded to include Sandia Base in the mid-1950s) for the convenience of the large and expanding workforce on the base. The 1956 enrollment was 480, and Bachelor's degrees were offered in liberal arts, education, and science. In 1966, the Director of Education for the Air Force specified that the long-assumed purpose of on-base university extensions was to "secure complete college status and curriculum at those permanent Air Force bases which are adjacent to colleges."[127]

Considering the affiliation with some of the nation's highest technology on Sandia Base as well as modern communication technology, a note by Sister Viatora is noteworthy. She pointed out to faculty members that slips were available in the office for those who make long-distance calls or send telegrams through the college switchboard.[128]

The college had been informally referred to as St. Joseph on the Rio Grande for several years in an effort to minimize confusion with other "St. Joseph" entities in the area, especially St. Joseph Hospital in downtown Albuquerque. The name was officially changed in 1957. Also, in 1957, the college began another year-long process to obtain accreditation from the North Central Association of Colleges and Secondary Schools. Accreditation was denied again in 1958, and an editorial in the *Yucca* noted the many shortcomings with the caveat that "There are 120 non-accredited colleges in the United States."[129]

One of the deficiencies noted by the accreditation team was the size and breadth of the library collection. In 1956, the librarians reported that they had added 1,675 volumes to the collection for a total of 15,335 volumes. In addition, the library subscribed to 144 periodicals. They also set a goal of having a collection of 20,000 by 1960.[130] In 1958, the library was bequeathed over 2,000 books from the library of Joaquin Ortega, PhD, a UNM professor who was one of the pioneers of Latin American and borderland studies in New Mexico.[131]

As Sister Viatora observed, this accreditation process, which was eventually successful in 1960 and greeted with a banner headline in the *Yucca*, was a significant factor in helping small colleges to obtain funding from corporations and foundations.[132] At the same time, the New Mexico Independent College Association, a non-profit corporation, was formed to encourage support for the state's two independent colleges—St. Michael's College in Santa Fe and St. Joseph on the Rio Grande.

In 1956, the City of Albuquerque celebrated the two hundred fiftieth anniversary of its founding by Don Fernando Vasquez de la Cueva, Duke of Alburquerque.[133] In conjunction with that city-wide celebration, St. Joseph celebrated the thirty-sixth anniversary of its founding, noting that it had become much more than just a summer school for local nuns at St. Anthony's Orphanage.

Matt Baca, a student from 1953–1957, has very fond memories of his time at St. Joseph. He characterized the school as a "wonderful place to be" with a "strong theological basis" and a Marian spirituality based on the precept that one should "pray, stay pure, reject evil, and welcome God." He also recalled that in his last year, he needed a few more credits and thought it would be fun to join the choir. However, after hearing him sing, the choir director politely, but firmly, told him that he should probably try the art classes in a room right across the hall. In fact, to this day, he is known in the Belen area for his art.[134]

Matt Baca, PhD.
(courtesy Matt Baca)

The fall semester of 1958 welcomed its largest freshman class—90 students—plus part-time students and transfers, giving the school its largest enrollment to date.

In 1959, Albuquerque annexed the portion of the West Mesa that included the St. Joseph campus. The impetus to get this property within the city limits was two-fold. First, the city was concerned that several of the small villages that were contiguous to Albuquerque in the north and south valleys would separately incorporate, as Los Ranchos de Albuquerque had done in December 1958. Secondly, realtor Clyde Shambaugh was exerting pressure on the city to get many of his west side properties within the city limits so that they could have access to city utilities. Of course, both Sister Viatora and the rest of the St. Joseph administration were very supportive of this effort.

The first two months of 1959 were also notable for two more reasons. The first of these was a significant increase in the availability of federal funding support. In January, students at the school became eligible for Operation Bootstrap, a program under which the federal government would pay up to 75 percent of a veteran student's expenses. In February, the school also received $2,155 from the federal government as a part of the $6 million National Defense Student Loan Program.

The second early-1959 development probably seemed small at the time, but was a harbinger of things to come. The spring 1959 semester offered a course entitled Principles of Punched Card Accounting which included four hours of data-processing instruction. Unbeknownst to them at the time, St. Joseph on the Rio Grande had cracked open the door to the computer age.[135]

In its nearly 40 years the college had grown to an enrollment of 480 offering Bachelor's degrees in science and education as well as a Bachelor's degree in science education. It was a fully accredited, four-year, liberal-arts institution with a brand-new campus. A new salary schedule was announced in March 1959: for a nine-month year, instructors received between $4,400 and $5,600; assistant professors received between $5,400 and $6,600; associate professors received between $6,200 and $7,400; and full professors received $7,200 with no upper limit specified.[136]

In the spring of 1959, Father Sullivan, head of the Philosophy Department, noted the importance of using a Thomistic approach to education at St. Joseph or any other Catholic university. Thomism, the form of scholasticism embraced and advanced by St. Thomas Aquinas, held that reason can, in principle, lead the mind to God.[137] Father Sullivan specifically insisted:

> Apart from any purely theological consideration, there are certain natural laws evident in any investigation of reality, and these laws may not be denied. It is not expected that a teacher be a fully trained philosopher and, at the same time, have mastered his own special field of knowledge—life is too short, knowledge is too long. But the teacher is expected to accept Thomistic principles and to teach nothing in contradiction to them.[138]

This point of view was generally accepted by the rest of the faculty.

In preparation for an upcoming visit by the North Central Association of Colleges and Secondary Schools, the faculty put together a self-study program which laid out some of aims and objectives for the school.[139] The evolution of the school since the first application in 1954 was obvious. No longer was this just an institution to train educators; professional training for business was also a major objective. Where the school previously aimed to "produce the perfect Christian" who would "consist of body and soul in fundamental union," the school noted that it was not primarily an institution of moral formation. Rather it was an institution of intellectual formation:[140]

—We are a liberal arts college: we are in agreement with the Aristotelian-Thomistic synthesis.[141]

—We are a Catholic college: we accept as true the great body of Judeo-Christian revelation.

—We support both intellectual and professional training: we hold that society is served best not only by training for competency in the professional arts but also by developing broadly and deeply the intellectual purposes which constitute the college's reason for being.

—We serve our clientele. An examination of our lists of students reveals that a great majority have been Catholic New Mexicans, many of whom are of Spanish-American descent ... for those who show ability, the College proposes to provide an opportunity for higher education.[142]

Aquinas and Aristotle agreed on several key philosophical points including the nature of man as a rational animal, the nature of the soul, the definition of happiness as an "operation of perfect virtue," the fact that something is true when it conforms to an external reality, etc. Importantly, Aquinas added the concept of God to Aristotle's philosophy. This philosophy was summarized in the statement that noted that the mission of the school was "training of the intellect which will aid the student in attaining the truth, and in appreciating intellectually the fundamental principles of morality and beauty."[143]

So, as the decade of the 1950s ended, the school was projecting an enrollment of 1,100 by the mid-1960s, with most of the incoming freshman from one of the Albuquerque high schools, including Albuquerque High and St. Mary's. This would require a doubling of the faculty to nearly 80 in order to maintain a teacher-student ratio of 10:1. Plans were also in place for construction of Madonna Hall, a new women's residence. The $434,000 dorm would be financed through a trust bond between the Saint Joseph on the Rio Grande Development Corporation and Albuquerque National Bank.[144] Construction of the facility to house 92 women, 12 faculty members, and two counselors was slated to begin in April 1960.

Very importantly, the library had exceeded its 1956 goal of 20,000 volumes. In the report for 1959–1960, the librarians reported a total collection of 21,705 volumes and subscriptions to 184 periodicals.[145]

The future certainly looked bright.

4
A Long-Term Gamble

The population of Albuquerque had nearly tripled during the 1940s and doubled again from 1950 to 1960. The post-war boom in federal funding at Kirtland Air Force Base and Sandia Laboratories (Sandia National Laboratories after 1979) brought well-paying jobs and educationally-oriented workers to the area.[146] The decade of the 1950s had also ended on a high note for the University. The school was firmly ensconced on its new campus; enrollment was increasing; funding seemed solid; and projections were for a student body of 1,000, nearly double the current enrollment, by the mid-1960s.

As icing on the cake, on April 22, 1960, the North Central Association of Colleges and Secondary Schools notified the college that, after a detailed, multi-year investigation, it had been fully accredited. The accreditors made several important observations:

1. The college has made a definite departure from a teacher-training institution to one of liberal arts.
2. The college is in an enviable position of being financially supported by the Motherhouse, although
   —faculty pension benefits are inadequate,
   —the library budget is insufficient,
   —more financial help is needed for cultural programs and scholarships,
   —there is a need for better public and alumni relations.
3. The physical resources are good.
4. The quality of personnel is above average, although the faculty is young but devoted, and the administration is devoted but lacks experience,

—there is a need for more PhDs in non-scientific fields,
—the maintenance and cafeteria staff need more help.
5. The library is well balanced in acquisitions but needs more holdings in foreign languages.
6. The administrative organization is adequate but needs more input from lay personnel.
7. The college takes care of its needs in liberal arts.
8. Isolation and finance have been limiting factors in faculty procurement.
9. Administration policy is well-defined.
10. The college provides a type of education suitable to student needs in later life.[147]

Their report concluded with the following complimentary observations:

The college appears to be very effective in fulfilling its objective to provide its students with a liberal arts education within the framework of Christian tradition ... [the college] has put considerable money into its physical plant which is one of its great strengths ... the faculty of the college is young, enthusiastic, dedicated, devoted, and very capable ... a definite family spirit permeates this institution .... The potential of this college is great ... this institution has the opportunity to be a citadel of learning in the geographic area in which it is located.[148]

Sister Viatora and the administration were extremely gratified by the findings of the accreditation association, and, in light of the current and projected growth patterns, described ambitious plans to further expand the physical plant and the academic programs. Madonna Hall, built by Bradbury and Stamm, opened in the fall after a $600,000 construction program (a $170,000 cost overrun from the initial estimate); four tennis courts were added; and new bleachers were installed in the gymnasium. In 1960, the expanded academic program now included more than 150 courses from art to medical technology and 20 evening and Saturday classes. By 1962, the number of courses had grown to 175.

A statistical summary of the school in November 1960 noted that the total enrollment was 411, although only 277 were full-time, a situation that would lead to financial hardship for the school during the 1970s and 1980s. Sixty-six percent of the students were male and 107 of the students were married. There were 26 nuns from various orders. The major interests of incoming freshmen were teaching, engineering, and business. There were 52 Korean War veterans, three disabled veterans, and two war orphans.[149]

Athletics, particularly the basketball program, continued to flourish under Coach Rudy Cordova. In a 1960 presentation to the Board, Coach Cordova made an interesting observation that is suggestive of the racial tenor of the 1960s. He reported that he was going to have a new experience during the Fall 1960 season because he had to arrange for travel and overnight stays for "three Negro boys" on the team. He did say, "Apparently they have been accepted by the team and the other students at the college."[150]

As one might imagine, social activities such as dances were an important part of student life. The administration, especially the Sisters, felt a strong need for chaperones at these events. Although police were occasionally recruited to help maintain order, the school felt that representatives of the faculty needed to be present at all dances, especially to see to it that there was no drinking on campus. There was some concern over female chaperones, and the requirement was set that men and women should serve together. One important point made by the faculty was that no girl was permitted to sit with a boy in a parked car.[151]

The University Scholars Program, begun in 1962 and led by Eugene Brown, a professor of Humanities, would remain one of the touchstone programs at the University. This offered:

> The scholarly-inclined student interested in world culture an integrated, four-year program of seminars ... beginning with classical antiquity, the world of the Greeks, and ending with the contemporary scene, twentieth-century technological society.[152]

The four-year program totaled 24 semester-hours and fulfilled the general Humanities requirement. Seminar size was limited to 20 or so students, and seminar topics included Homer, Plato, Dostoevsky, Chaucer, Shaw, Frank Lloyd Wright, Bach, and Beethoven. This program elicited enormous praise from all of its attendees. Particularly ebullient praise came from Judy Maloof:

> The University Scholars Program at the University of Albuquerque is unrivaled in academic excellence. I can honestly say that I would rather be right here, in this program than at any other university in the country![153]

Graduate programs were being considered in education and social work, and a new cancer research foundation, the Hygein Foundation, was announced in collaboration with Samuel Klein, PhD, a St. Joseph alumnus and New York pharmacist.[154]

In August 1960, Director of Admissions Sister M. Catherine Ann Bintner, OSF, projected a freshman class of between 175 and 200 and a total enrollment of over 500 with the hope of doubling to 1,000 "within the next few years." All of these programs were to be accomplished while maintaining a student-teacher ratio of 10:1.[155]

These ambitious goals seemed achievable to both the Sisters and to Archbishop Byrne. The school was self-supporting, meaning that between income from tuition, underwriting by the Sisters, and a scholarship program from the Archdiocese, no additional funding was solicited. This was important because, as noted by Mr. Zens during a February 1960 Faculty meeting:

> —Because the school was young, it could expect little help from graduates.
> —The Catholic church has never supported colleges.
> —Most New Mexico Catholics don't support anything, even their own parishes.
> —The local community does not support projects.[156]

As a further positive indication of the image of the college, both the *Albuquerque Journal* and the *Albuquerque Tribune* were filled with ads for property on the west side of the river. In addition to the view, these ads frequently touted the proximity to the college as a selling point. In fact, the lion's share of articles about the college in the local papers in the early and mid-1960s were about the successes, and some not-so-successes, of the school's athletic teams.

The many offerings of drama and music that were performed both at the college and elsewhere in the community were also featured. Dramatic offerings included *The Tempest, John Brown's Body, Under Milkwood,* and *The Lark.* The drama department was significantly enhanced in 1962 when Jim Morley joined the faculty. Morley had been a stage actor in London and New York and had had a broad career in both drama and radio, most recently at Albuquerque's classical radio station, KGGM. Over the years Morley would produce and direct numerous dramatic offerings, making the University's drama productions local go-to events.

In 1962, the enrollment was 472, on track with the growth projected earlier. However, there were only 366 full-time-equivalent students, once again demonstrating the specter of financial burden since tuition and fees, which were based on credit hours, represented the school's principal income source.[157]

The school's February 1963 annual report noted that the demand for higher education in New Mexico "greatly outruns the supply" and that the business aspects of the college—enrollment, spending, and investments—have "increased at a rate triple that of the gross national product."[158] This demand was encouraged by the national trend that followed the passage of the Higher Education Facilities Act, signed by President Lyndon Johnson in 1963. Johnson noted:

> This legislation is dramatic, and it is concrete evidence of a renewed and continuing national commitment to education as the key to our nation's social, technological, economic, and moral progress.... President Kennedy fought hard for this legislation. No topic was closer to his heart.[159]

Although the school had transitioned from a strictly teacher college format to liberal arts, the education profession was still one of the top choices for incoming students. In 1962, the teacher candidates were given a glimpse of the future when they were introduced to the use of "machines in teaching." It was pointed out that "machines" would never replace the classroom teacher but could assist the classroom teacher by performing some "ditch-digging" instruction such as teaching elementary students multiplication tables.[160]

Perhaps in some contrast to this rosy economic picture, the school launched its second public funding campaign in April 1963. In a general report issued in the spring of 1962, the administration reported:

> The income from tuition and a few small gifts pays slightly more than half of the total operating expenses. The difference has been met annually by the motherhouse. Unlike many other colleges, it has no endowment, nor have the Sisters heretofore appealed for fund-raising support.[161]

Led by honorary chairman Senator Clinton P. Anderson (a Presbyterian), the aim of the campaign was to raise $750,000 in a six-week period. The money would provide funds to increase the faculty, to build a new library, to provide a convent for the resident nuns (currently housed in the women's dormitory), and to build a new chapel and student center.[162]

Senator Clinton P. Anderson.
(courtesy Richard Melzer)

Archbishop Byrne died unexpectedly in July 1963. James Peter Davis, who had succeeded Byrne as Archbishop of San Juan, Puerto Rico, again succeeded him, becoming the ninth Archbishop of Santa Fe in January 1964.

James Peter Davis, Ninth Archbishop of Santa Fe.
(collection of the Archdiocese of Santa Fe)

The new archbishop gave the June 1964 Commencement address, urging the graduates to consider public service. He said, "May you be leaders of the world, not followers, but doers of the Word."[163]

As the 1963–1964 term opened in September 1963, Sister Viatora announced the start of a $400,000 men's dormitory to house 110 students. This was to be the first part of the multi-year, multi-million-dollar physical plant upgrade. The new dormitory, built on the south campus and named Davis Hall in honor of Archbishop Davis, was financed through a loan with the Housing and Home Finance Administration.[164] Sister Viatora remarked that the Sisters insisted on having it well away from the main campus because "those German nuns would never allow men and women to live on the same campus."[165] She also proudly announced the appointments of the first two full professors: James McGrath, PhD, from the History Department and Simon Kao, PhD, from Mathematics.[166]

The optimism expressed in the 1960 accreditation report and the 1963 annual report continued to be justified in the fall of 1963, as enrollment hit an all-time high of 620, a 30 percent increase over the previous year. About three-quarters of the students were full-time with a male-female ratio of 2:1. Thirty students were in graduate programs, and students hailed from 50 New Mexico communities, 23 states, and five foreign countries. The students were served by 60 faculty members for a student-teacher ratio of 10.3:1. In January 1964, the enrollment jumped again when 799 students registered for the spring semester.[167]

In October 1963, St. Joseph became the first college in the nation to start a Theresian chapter. This organization had been founded in Pueblo, Colorado, in 1961 by Monsignor Elwood C. Voss to provide an opportunity for lay women to come together in community to experience intellectual and spiritual enrichment. It was named for St. Therese of Lisieux, the patroness of the Pueblo diocese.[168] In particular, the chapter at St. Joseph was established to "pray for and foster vocations to the Sisterhood."[169]

In the spring of 1964, an issue that had been bedeviling the school since 1961 finally came to a head. The issue was cheating. In 1961, the faculty discussed evidence of cheating in an April meeting. It was noted that mimeographed tests had been stolen, that professors were missing keys, and that they had evidence of "prowling" in their offices.[170] In December 1962, the Student Council formally asked the faculty to pass a resolution on cheating, saying that there was "an excessive amount of cheating" and suggesting that the faculty should "refuse to allow books and notebooks in classrooms during major examinations." In addition, they asked that faculty "patrol the classroom during tests."[171]

Several of the faculty members pushed back on what they perceived to be police tactics in favor of working to "influence the student body to form a right attitude toward the basic immorality of cheating." After some discussion, the faculty turned the issue over to the Committee on Honors and Discipline for further study. In April of 1963, the committee recommended a two-fold punishment for students found guilty of cheating. Initially, there would be academic/classroom censure—the teacher would fail the student for cause. Secondly, there would be institutional censure. The student would be brought before the committee to receive his/her punishment, usually, but not always, dismissal.[172]

Despite these efforts, cheating continued to plague the school. In May 1964, an entire faculty meeting was devoted to the issue. One student noted that she was "shocked at the amount of cheating at the college, to say nothing of the flippant attitude taken by the students and the apparent indifference by some professors." Another student reported that:

> ...he felt cheating to be a challenge in certain circumstances, particularly when he felt he was being watched so closely that his integrity was antecedently forfeit in the mind of his teacher: he was assumed dishonest. At that point, cheating furnished a means of protesting; it became kind of a game in the clever use of crib-notes to outwit and triumph over a disliked professor and his systems.[173]

Father Morrison noted that "police methods encourage dishonesty—individuals will receive justice from a responsible teacher and before God." The problem remained essentially unresolved with the punishments still in place. However, the issue did seem to subside.

At the same time, changes were occurring in the Archdiocese and at the college; the West Side was expanding around it. Many people had answered the ads promoting the new area, and the city of Albuquerque was reacting. Annexation of the area from Central Avenue (U.S. Route 66) to the north side of the college was formally approved by the City

Commission in December 1964.[174] The population of the newly annexed area was estimated to be 30,000, and the Albuquerque city planners estimated that it would climb to nearly 300,000 by 1985. This projected growth meant that utilities, parks, and other services would have to expand, both between U.S. 66 and St. Joseph on the south and between St. Joseph and Paradise Hills Boulevard on the north. D. W. Falls, a local developer and future member of the college's Board of Trustees, noted:

> There is simply no other place for Albuquerque to grow in the years ahead. It will not be long before the area between the volcanoes and the Rio Grande is as heavily populated as the Northeast Heights.[175]

D. W. Falls.
(courtesy Falls family)

Recall that a data-processing class in 1959 had opened the college to the digital age. In the summer of 1964, the National Science Foundation furthered this process by approving a $10,000 grant, which had been prepared by professors Andrew Imrik and Simon Kao, together with IBM engineer Gene Trivett, to be used toward the purchase of an IBM 1620 main-frame computer with an IBM 1622 card-reading and punch system for the computer science program. IBM also donated $60,000 toward the purchase of the new machine.[176] In particular, the 1620, which could read punched cards at a blistering 200 microseconds per card, was to be used to teach numerical analysis and mathematical statistics.[177]

The fall of 1964 also found the college in the midst of its physical growth spurt. The men's dormitory, named Byrne Hall in honor of the late archbishop, had been funded through a trust indenture with the Bank of New Mexico for $450,000.[178] It was not yet completed, and 62 men, including the basketball team, were being housed in two motels—the El Mac Court on Coors and the Royal Court on Central. There were seven new full-time faculty members, and the gymnasium had been enlarged. In addition, a new women's dormitory, named St. Clare Hall, was under construction with financial help from CIT Corporation, a financial holding company headquartered in New York City that specialized in both commercial and consumer loans. St. Clare would be completed in time for occupancy in the Spring 1965 semester.[179] In addition, the school had awarded 70 scholarships to incoming freshmen, varying in value from $125 to $3,200. Awards were given to students from New Mexico, based on their ACT (American College Testing) scores.[180]

In November 1964, another fund drive was started—this time the goal was $300,000 to qualify for matching funds under Title 1 of the Federal Education Facilities Act of 1963. The funds raised by the drive, coupled with the $125,000 match, would go toward the completion of a $500,000 library. One of the driving factors behind this project was the need for an appropriate archive facility, planned for Assumption Hall, to house the papers of the late Senator Dennis Chavez Jr. Chavez's wife had donated the output of his 27 years as a U.S. senator to the college in 1963.[181] Congressman Tom Morris said, "I can think of no finer tribute to the late Senator Dennis Chavez and his long and distinguished career of public service for New Mexico than to establish a Dennis Chavez Memorial Library."[182]

The Chavez collection, which dated from 1932, had been microfilmed by Yale University in 1967 but had not been cataloged. There was considerable discussion about whether the school could afford the approximately $30,000 that historian Myra Ellen Jenkins estimated would be required to catalog and archive the collection. The State Records and Archives Center did not have the resources to perform the necessary work, so the collection continued to reside at UofA.[183] In 1981, the Chavez collection was transferred to the Center for Southwest Research at UNM in exchange for $50,000 in library materials.[184]

Senator Dennis Chavez, Jr.
(courtesy Richard Melzer)

In January 1965, St. Clare Hall, the new dormitory, was opened for 64 women who had completed their freshman year. Freshmen resided in Madonna Hall which had been completed in 1961.[185] This was part of an ambitious building program which included the completion of the new men's dorm, Byrne House, in August. Sister Viatora announced that the college's Ten-Year Development Program included the construction of a library, a student union, a convent, an administration building, and a science building.[186] Although the movie "Field of Dreams" would not appear for another 21 years, the expansion of facilities and programs at the University was largely reflective of the "if you build it, he will come" philosophy espoused by the character of Ray Kinsella, a corn farmer from Iowa, who builds a baseball field in the middle of his cornfield to attract Shoeless Joe Jackson from the infamous 1919 White Sox.[187] The gamble paid off in the movie, but would eventually lead to significant problems for the University.

Sister Viatora also raised the issue of smoking, saying that it was restricted to common areas (where more ashtrays would be provided) but that there should be no smoking in classrooms or "in the tunnels where there are gas lines."[188]

In April 1965, the college celebrated its forty-fifth anniversary with a Mass led by Archbishop Davis and a banquet for faculty and staff. Governor Jack Campbell proclaimed Friday, April 30, as "College of St. Joseph Day" throughout New Mexico.

In November 1965, the faculty's General Policies Committee recommended that the name of the college be changed from the College of St. Joseph on the Rio Grande to Albuquerque University. The principal reasons for the request were:

—To more closely identify with the community,
—To eliminate confusion with the seven other St. Joseph colleges across the country, and
—To acknowledge that the addition of substantial graduate programs was more clearly signified by the status as a university rather than just a college.[189]

The faculty agreed with the request and forwarded it to the Sisters and to the State Corporation Commission. The name change request was granted on January 7, 1966, and the school was identified as a domestic, non-profit corporation, with a slight modification: the institution would, from now on, be known as the University of Albuquerque.[190]

In May 1966, the faculty organized a representative body called the Faculty Senate. This group, chaired by Professor Lawrence Desaulniers and designed to provide the faculty an opportunity to have a voice in overall policy, drafted a constitution that was approved by the Board of Trustees.[191] In addition, the Board approved the non-voting membership of a member of the Faculty Senate.[192] The Senate established four standing committees: Faculty Affairs, Academic Affairs, Records, and Executive Management.[193] However, the new organization was not always particularly useful or active. For example, some meetings in 1967 and 1968 lasted as little as ten minutes.[194]

The school's ambitious expansion plans continued into 1966 and 1967. There was a considerable discussion among the Academic Affairs Committee about establishing an Institute of Southwestern Studies, as well as undergraduate programs in Sociology, Social Work, and either a Masters or Associates degree in Business Administration.[195] In addition, an African Studies Institute was proposed in early 1968.[196]

Nursing programs were also a focal point. The University of New Mexico had opened a four-year nursing degree program in 1955.[197] A two-year degree program for nurses, first contemplated in April 1952, supported by a survey of high school seniors who showed "great interest" in 1963–1964, and requested by St. Joseph Hospital in 1966, was scheduled to begin at UofA in 1967 to take the place of the Regina School of Nursing at St. Joseph Hospital which was being phased out.[198] Sister Alma Rihm, the director of the Regina program, agreed to stay on as the director of the University of Albuquerque program.[199] Eventually the nursing students would do their in-service training at the Vista Sandia Hospital in the Far Northeast Heights.[200]

Regina Hall, headquarters of the Regina School of Nursing. (author's collection)

Also, in 1966, financing totaling $2 million had been obtained for three new buildings—a student union, a men's dormitory, and a women's dormitory.[201]

A major administrative and philosophical change occurred in the springs of 1966 and 1967. In 1966, the Certificate of Incorporation was modified to permit lay members on the Board of Trustees, and lay members Concha Ortiz y Pino de Kleven, Hugh Funk, and D. W. Falls were added to the school's Board of Trustees.[202]

Concha Ortiz y Pino de Kleven.[204] (www.timetoast.com)

As the Fall 1966–1967 term began, there were ten new faculty members, several new course offerings, and Sister Viatora expected an enrollment of about 1,100. One driving force for increased enrollment was the quest for the much sought-after college draft deferments as the Vietnam War was demanding more and more conscripts.

Lourdes Hall, a new $500,000 dorm for 132 women and the $1.2 million University Center building were under construction. All of the construction projects were being funded on a lease basis with insurance companies providing the up-front capital, and the school taking on 25-year repayment programs.[203]

In December 1966, the University of Albuquerque athletic program was admitted to the National Collegiate Athletic Association (NCAA). This had been a long-term goal of athletic director Rudy Cordova. The Dons' basketball program was ranked first in the National Association of Intercollegiate Athletics (NAIA) District 7 and was one of the top

20 small college basketball teams in the country, so the Albuquerque Athletic Committee and the UofA Student Senate agreed to maintain membership in both the NAIA and the NCAA. Coach Cordova said, "This was a great Christmas present!"[205]

As the school continued to expand, Sister Viatora recognized the need to initiate long-term planning. The first workshop was held in October 1966 under the leadership of Charles Lanier. The third workshop was held in January 1967, and the group hammered out a purpose statement for the school:

> The purpose of the UofA is the intellectual, moral, and physical development of the student according to the principles of Christian education.... The *raison d'etre* for the UofA is to impart knowledge, intellectual awareness, and moral commitment to her students. It follows that most fundamental concerns are with teaching and with an environment that supports and encourages both the learning process, the commitment of men to the common good, and the Christian impulse of Love.[206]

This statement demonstrates a softening of the strict Catholic tradition as enunciated in the early 1950s that the purpose of St. Joseph on the Rio Grande was "the moral, intellectual, and physical development of students according to the principles of Catholic philosophy of education as laid down by Pope Pius XI."[207] This softening, with roots in the Thomistic traditions that had been a part of the school's Christian commitment since its transition from a teachers' college, is consistent with the conclusions of the Second Vatican Council, which had been in session from 1962 to 1965.[208] This philosophy would eventually be codified as Christian humanism in some of the school's Christian commitment statements.

There are three basic approaches to humanism— Christian humanism credits God for morality, for our right to take ethical responsibility, and for our possession of reason. Religious humanism puts our ethical responsibilities first, and then asks intelligence to judge religion/spirituality for its potential guidance. Secular humanism judges everything religious/spiritual as worthless and starts over from just reason.[209]

A follow-on planning study was completed in March 1967. This study included contacts with a number of other colleges across the country seeking information on topics such as dress policy and the advantages/disadvantages of using trimesters versus semesters.[210]

One of the new initiatives proposed in 1966 was the formation of an Institute of Southwestern Studies. Under the direction of Robert Martinez and Assistant Dean of Students Jose Garcia, the center was intended to provide facilities for research, creative production, and academic studies of the Southwest. The Institute also sponsored art shows featuring works from representatives of the various cultures.[211] In addition to Pueblo Indian representatives, Doria Purcell, an Algonquin, was active in both the Institute and in both the Red Power and Black Power movements.[212] The institute was also to be a repository for collections of southwestern materials and a means of providing future teachers an understanding of the cultures and traditions of the Southwest.

Of major concern to UofA faculty and to the accreditation organization was that faculty salaries were substantially below other schools. For example, a UofA instructor would receive between $5,400 and $6,200 per year, an assistant professor received between $6,200 and $8,400, an associate professor received between $7,200 and $10,000, and a full professor received between $9,200 and $12,000. Comparable ranges for the public University of Massachusetts at Amherst were: Instructor—$6,000 to $10,100, assistant professor—$7,500 to $14,700, associate professor—$9,900 to $17,000, and full professor—$11,600 to $21,100.[213] The University of New Mexico's salaries in 1966 were: instructor—$6,000 to $8,250, assistant professor—$7,000 to $12,000, and associate professor—$10,000 to $13,000. (Information on full professor salaries was not available.)[214] UofA faculty did receive some fringe benefits including a 50 percent subsidy for hospitalizations, a five percent match to their retirement account with TIAA-CREF, 50 percent of the TIAA-CREF life insurance premium, and an 80 percent tuition payment for dependents who attended UofA.[215] Despite these fringe benefits, it was clear that UofA faculty were significantly underpaid.

As a part of Lanier's master planning project, a Christian Commitment Committee was established in March 1967. The purpose of the committee was "to bring a unity of perspective to the total Christian context within which the various phases of master planning could achieve coherence." In their report, presented in January 1967, they identified seven issues:

—How (or whether) to translate long-standing essential definitions of Catholic education into terms relevant to contemporary society.
—How to define an appropriate emphasis on the "status of truth."
—How to balance teaching methodology between authoritarian catechesis and eclecticism.
—How to manage student attitudes—anxieties, difficulties, doubts.
—How to balance specific Catholic traditions and other relevant traditions.
—How to establish an appropriate relationship of theology and philosophy with other subjects.
—How to make a distinction between academic/community aims and freedom/control.[216]

The committee deliberated on solutions to these issues throughout the remainder of 1967 and into 1968. Faculty member Eugene Brown wrote the committee several letters, the first, written in March right after they started their deliberations, said:

Unless one is prepared to define the meaning of Catholic education, there is little point in discussing ways to improve it.... The external but imminent crisis in Catholic education is the secularization of the social order.[217]

He ended this letter by quoting British cultural historian Christopher Dawson:

The vital problem of Christian education is a sociological one: how to make students culturally conscious of their religion. Otherwise, they will be divided personalities—with a Christian faith and a pagan culture which contradict constantly.

Professor Brown wrote another lengthy letter in January 1968:

That a Catholic university should have need to form a committee to define its commitment to Christ is another sign of the crisis in Christian education ...with Christian humanism a Catholic university could begin its own regeneration .... A Christian university should be in ferment over something other than student rights and faculty welfare.[218]

As noted earlier, this movement toward Christian humanism is evolutionary rather than revolutionary and in keeping with the earlier Thomistic principles as well as those espoused by the Second Vatican Council.[219]

In May 1968, the Committee submitted its final report. They made seven recommendations:

—Keep the University relatively small.
—Evaluate the mechanics of academics: grades, course structure, and admission standards.
—Establish explicitly remedial programs.
—Establish a faculty enrichment program.
—Discontinue programs which "dissipate the liberal arts emphasis."
—Liberal arts programs should "take on a more interdisciplinary character."
—The Theology Department should become the Department of Ecumenical Studies.[220]

The transition of the Theology Department to the Department of Ecumenical Studies represented a significant step away from the historical Catholic roots of the school. This decision was partially in response to the current requirement that all Protestant students take 12 hours of theology "unless conscience forbids."[221] Some members of the faculty were pushing back on the requirement, noting that for non-Catholic students "past experience suggests that a good many non-Catholics are extremely sensitive to what they regard as the authoritarian aspects of Catholicism."[222]

In May 1967, Sister Viatora had announced that she was retiring from her administrative duties, effective September 1, in order to return to full-time teaching as president emeritus in the University's History Department. In a Board meeting, Board Chair Sister M. Barbara Ann Braun, OSF, noted the accomplishments that Sister Viatora had overseen during her 14-year tenure as president:

—The school had grown from a small liberal arts college with an enrollment of about 200 to a nationally recognized university with 1,200 students and a rapidly expanding physical plant.
—Five new dormitories had been constructed.
—A prefabricated gymnasium had been acquired.
—A theater had been acquired.
—The University had been fully accredited by the North Central Association of Colleges and Secondary Schools.[223]

Sister Viatora was succeeded by Sister M. Marilyn Doiron, OSF. Sister Marilyn was a native New Mexican. She was born in Gallup and received her Bachelor's degree from St. Joseph on the Rio Grande. She had both a Master's and a Doctorate from Fordham University, a Jesuit university in the Bronx, New York. She had also done advanced study at Oxford University in England. Her doctoral thesis was a translation of a Middle English book entitled "The Mirror of Simple Souls."[224] She had come to the University's English department in January 1964.[225]

When told that she, an assistant professor of English at the school, had been appointed president, she remarked, "I think there has been a mistake!" As events unfolded, her prescience would prove largely correct.

Sister M. Marilyn Doiron, OSF.
(CSWR/UofA photo archives)

The Second Vatican Council (1962–1965) made significant changes in several aspects of Catholicism, including allowing Mass to be celebrated in the vernacular with the priest facing the congregation, and removal of some altar fixtures such as the altar rail. These changes were perceived as an increased "informality" in Catholic practice and may have helped with the concerns over Catholic authoritarianism. They were also reflected in several aspects of life at UofA. For example, a dramatic offering in the spring of 1967 had skits that included a nun's fashion show, a bingo party, and an LSD party.[226]

One of Sister Marilyn's first actions was to re-establish the Master Planning Committee to look at the future of the University over the next decade. The committee was chaired by Richard Heim, former Bernalillo County manager and current president of Albuquerque Savings and Loan Association, and included a wide-ranging membership of faculty, administrators, trustees, and community leaders. Heim stated that the job of the committee was to "establish goals for the University of Albuquerque including purpose, construction, and enrollment so the program will complement the rest of this state's higher education over a long-range period."[227]

Sister Marilyn noted that as a Catholic institution, the UofA must keep sight of its objectives, both theoretically and practically. Father Dunphy argued that:

> A university liberal arts curriculum is hardly what it professes to be if it is not committed to providing all Christians enrolled in it with a formal intellectual and academically respectable inquiry into the God/man relationship and that a Catholic institution, *a fortiriori*, should recognize and implement this commitment. [228]

The student body had formed a Student Council (later renamed Student Association and then Student Senate) in 1965.[229] Most of their deliberations had to do with rather mundane subjects—preparations for activities such as dances and athletic events, discussions of protocols for dormitories, noise abatement, etc. In 1967, they proposed a dress code which provided for casual dress (dresses for women and slacks and shirts for men) for most occasions, dressier attire for Mass and Sunday evening activities, and sportswear (slacks or Bermuda shorts) from 4:30 p.m. on Friday through Saturday night.[230]

The school did not have an Activities Director, so Ray John de Aragon, a student and member of the student government, was named as Student Senate Activities Vice President. As such, he set up entertainment activities for the student body. He recalls hiring local bands for dances and arranging for speakers such as Reies Lopez Tijerina and Sabina Ulibarri. An event that featured the band Zozobra was attended by over 500, due in part to publicity offered by well-known Albuquerque DJ Bobby Box.[231]

Occasionally, a more serious situation confronted the Student Senate. For example, in the spring of 1967, the issue of intoxication, both on and off campus, arose. Prior to this time there had been no written rule regarding alcohol, although it had been tacitly permitted in the men's dorms in 1966. Because of several instances of students overindulging both on and off campus, the Senate passed a rule that outlawed alcohol on campus and intoxication either on or off campus.[232]

Sister Marilyn had inherited a college with a substantial financial problem. Barely one year after she took over the reins, the Board was told that the 1967–1968 school year would show a deficit of $340,000 with teacher salaries being nearly 59 percent of the total expenditures. A significant part of the problem was that the dormitories were only 50 percent full because many students lived off-campus. During that meeting, the Board agreed to raise room and board from $75 per semester to $120 per semester and to raise tuition from $450 to $475 per semester.[233] Board member D. W. Falls noted, "The crucial problem at the moment is how do we pay our bills?"[234]

The school had managed to obtain several grants during the decade of the 1960s. Ravel Brothers Feed Store set up a $250 scholarship fund in 1960. The CIT foundation pledged $5,000 if the school could raise matching funds within two years. Household Finance Corporation pledged money to both St. Joseph and St. Michael in Santa Fe as a part of a nationwide program, and Sears Roebuck renewed its $500 scholarship fund for the third consecutive year.

The university also received $121,000 in federal research and development money in 1967 plus a $221,000 grant from the Federal Office of Equal Opportunity to help children from migrant and seasonal worker families complete their high school equivalency with the goal of admitting them to Albuquerque's Technical-Vocational Institute.[235]

In the spring of 1967, another issue surfaced that would bedevil the University in later years. Tom Popejoy, soon-to-be-retired president of the University of New Mexico, said that there was a real need for a junior college in the Albuquerque area. He opined that such an institution would permit high school graduates whose grades were not quite up to par to determine whether or not they could make it at the university level. He noted that this would allow UNM and UofA to concentrate on the upper classes and graduate work, "the real job of a state university."[236] What he failed to note, and what would become as major issue in the future, was the potential impact that such an institution would have on enrollment, particularly at UofA.

On the athletic front, an NCAA rule change which banned dunking in college basketball was enacted at the 1967 spring rules meeting. This changed the Don's basketball tactics and disappointed many UofA fans who were used to raucous cheering when players like Argentinian All-American Zoilo Dominguez, would slam the ball home. This rule change would be in effect for ten years until rescinded by the NCAA for the 1976–1977 season.[237]

Potentially offsetting the troubling financial news, in August 1967, Director of Admissions, Sister M. Catherine Ann Bintner, OSF, announced that she expected another year of record enrollment with over 1,300 students between the full-time programs, the part-time programs at Kirtland and on the main campus, and the new two-year nursing program at Regina Hall. Sister Catherine Ann's estimate proved to be on target with a total of 1,334 students, of which 310 were enrolled at Kirtland and 300 were incoming freshmen.

A new department of Urban Development was added under the direction of Professor Andrew Imrik, and seven new musicians from the Albuquerque area joined the Music Department Staff headed by George DeFoe. In total, 231 courses were offered, taught by 90 faculty members. In addition, the long-awaited $1.2 million University Center was now open for business.[238]

In a September breakfast meeting with the Albuquerque Chamber of Commerce, academic vice-president James McGrath made a strong argument for more community support for the University:

Albuquerque does not have to push big bond issues for the UofA plant. It's already here. An outstanding faculty is already here. Is there a place for the University of Albuquerque? Here we stand, ready and able. We're at the limit of what we can charge for tuition. Government and foundation aid is no problem—it's available. But without community support it's hard to get. The government and foundations want to know if a community is supporting a school before they'll put money into it.... We don't want to become too big, but we want to know how we can best serve the community. And we're asking for your help.[239]

5
From Problem to Crisis

Nineteen sixty-eight began on a cautionary note. Frank Mazzio, the Vice President for Business and Finance, informed Sister Marilyn that the budgeting and financial planning information that she had been provided was, in fact, significantly flawed. He detailed a laundry list of revenue problems:

—The 1967–1968 enrollment had been projected to be 780 but was only 739.
—The projected dorm occupancy was 400 but only reached 346.
—Projected miscellaneous income was $25,000 but had only reached $11,000.
—Scholarship funding and donations had been projected at $37,000 but had only reached $7,500.
—It had simply been assumed, without consultation or planning, that the Sisters would "pick up the tab" for any deficit.

Thus, the revenue stream was short over $130,000.[240]
Expenses had also been significantly underestimated:

—No provisions had been made for faculty salaries at the Kirtland center.
—No provisions had been made for additional faculty salaries after the initial budget workup.
—No provisions had been made for the custodial department.
—No provisions had been made for principal payments on Byrne House.
—No provisions had been made for outstanding accounts payable from the 1965–1966 school year.

—No provisions had been made for the cost of installing a new water line from Coors Boulevard to University Center.
—There had been no accounting for expenses associated with the use of facilities for summer school, workshops, retreats, seminars, etc. It was estimated that these events cost the school approximately $2.85 per-person-per-day.
—There had been no control over the bookstore. Cash was received and doled out from a cigar box. It was estimated that the bookstore had lost about $600 per month.

This led to a total of unrecorded expenses of about $168,000. The bottom line from this accounting nightmare was that the deficit for the coming year had more than doubled from the projection of $159,000 to an actual figure of $327,000.[241]

Mazzio made several recommendations to deal with the revised financial situation.

—Use realistic estimates for dorm occupancy—50 percent to 70 percent instead of assuming 100 percent.
—Increase the fees for dorm occupancy from $1.50 per day to $2.15 per day.
—Require scholarship recipients to live in the dorms.
—Deal more realistically with the Sisters' contribution instead of assuming that they would "make up the difference."
—Evaluate all departments from a cost-benefit point of view.
—Carefully examine the scholarship program, and perhaps reconsider the policy that "no deserving student will be refused because of lack of funds."
—Evaluate the Grant-in-Aid program for student-athletes.
—Better coordinate the Grants and Projects program.
—Establish a Budget or Fiscal Policy Committee.

The last recommendation was immediately enacted, and a proposal for consolidation of the dormitories was put forth. This proposal suggested reserving some dorm space for students and converting some to apartments for married students. Other space would then be used as rental space for organizations that were using university facilities for workshops, retreats, etc.[242]

Enrollment was an ongoing problem and the school endeavored to address this by understanding its demography. In 1968, the survey showed that 69 percent of the 1,436 students were from New Mexico with 62 percent from Bernalillo County. Sixty-two percent also identified as Roman Catholic. In keeping with the financial problems, the school was working hard to keep the student-teacher ratio at 20:1 rather than the financially untenable 10:1 that was previously sought.[243]

A significant problem with attrition had also been observed. Students reported that they had chosen UofA because of its intellectual reputation. However, 56 percent of the incoming freshman had left prior to their senior year, citing money problems and a desire to go to school closer to home.

In October 1968, Sister Marilyn made a presentation to the faculty in which she outlined the challenging situation facing the school:

> The fact is that the Western Province of the Sisters of St. Francis Seraph is in deep financial straits ... in fact, the order is on the verge of bankruptcy ... in short, the University is in financial straits by virtue of the religious order being in financial straits.[244]

When this news was presented to the alumni in a November letter from Sister Marilyn, the alumni were taken aback. Noting that, because the University was a private institution, it did not qualify for direct federal or state assistance, her letter said, in part:

> The University of Albuquerque needs you. Whether you attended while the name was St. Joseph on the Rio Grande or since the change to the University of Albuquerque, we wish you to know that our university needs financial aid more now than at any time in its 48-year history. To use a very old cliché, "We need your help." .... We have become the victim of our own success. We find ourselves at the mercy of conditions of rapid expansion and rising costs which threaten to absorb all our hard-won gains.[245]

Part of this problem stemmed from the decrease in dollars from federal programs such as support for nursing programs from the National Institutes of Health and the President's veto of funding for the Department of Health, Education, and Welfare. The war in Vietnam was increasingly costly and unpopular, and the Great Society movement, supported by Lyndon Johnson, was fading in importance as Congress reduced appropriations for domestic programs in favor of supporting the war effort.[246]

In a letter to Donald Klene, the Director of the Motherhouse in Colorado Springs, President Doiron had written:

> I believe every college and university is afflicted with good advice, and so it has always been. The fact is that we, like all but a few private institutions, face a declining market.... I believe we still lack a complete picture of our financial situation. As a management team we "see through glass darkly."[247]

Earlier in 1968, the University had hired Francis A. "Frank" Kleinhenz to take on the job of vice president for administration and development. Kleinhenz, a World War II veteran, came to Albuquerque from his alma mater, John Carroll University in Cleveland, Ohio. He had served as Director of Continuing Education at Carroll after receiving both his Bachelor's and Master's degrees.[248]

Francis "Frank" Kleinhenz. (CSWR/UofA, Box 18, yearbook collection)

Upon arrival in Albuquerque, Kleinhenz observed:

> If the University was a business corporation, it would be bankrupt! .... There are hundreds of colleges like us, and if these private schools were businesses, they would all be bankrupt. Fortunately, education is not an ordinary market commodity. Thus, most private schools can continue operation despite financial problems. Yet many get so far in debt they must either close down or become state-owned.... They [UofA] had begun two major programs—one in sports and other a building program—which had taken them under financially. They hired much too large a faculty for the size of the student body. They were simply going broke.[249]

He also blamed some of the financial woes on the fact that the University was only 20-years-old. "Since most of our alumni are young and not far along in their professions, they aren't able to help us financially." His concern was born out by an assessment of gift-giving in 1968. Gifts to the university totaled $147,500, but the alumni contribution was only $4,000.[250]

In 1969, the University made another attempt to involve its alumni by publishing a quarterly newsletter entitled *The Ambassador*. In the inaugural volume, Sister Marilyn said, "During the last several years, the university has become deeply involved in the affairs and business of Albuquerque, as evidenced by some of the reports in the first issue of our [alumni] newsletter."[251]

It took a few more years for the alumni to react, but in 1973, they formed an organization led by James R. Gonzales. The goal of the organization was to "support the efforts of the University of Albuquerque and involve the alumni and total community in the activities of the school."[252] Shortly thereafter, the school hired Loretta Salazar, a former wage and salary administrator at Sandia Laboratories, as Director of Resource Development and Alumni Relations.[253]

In a memo to Sister Marilyn, Kleinhenz reemphasized the necessity for long-range planning. He suggested 13 short-range goals which included a reconstitution of the Board of Trustees and tightening controls on expenditures. In addition, he mentioned 16 long-range goals which emphasized community involvement and an ongoing program of fund raising.²⁵⁴ The last of these was acted on by the formation of a fund-raising committee under the direction of Roger Lattanza. The campaign was to run from November 1969 through February 1970, and would include the potential sale of parcels of land near the State Fair grounds and in Paradise Hills.²⁵⁵

Another significant contributor to the red ink was the scholarship and financial aid program. This program represented about 14 percent of the University's outlays. Kleinhenz said, "We must either reduce our financial aid or find more donors for our scholarship funds." A particular concern in this regard was athletic scholarships. Kleinhenz noted:

> Unfortunately, our athletic department is not self-supporting and is quite large for a school this size (1,500 students). We are wondering if the amount of money used for athletes is in accord with our institutional objectives.²⁵⁶

It was further pointed out that the Sisters had loaned the University $485,000 at seven percent interest in order for the University to keep operating. Although no firm date for repayment of the principal was given, the annual interest would have to be added to the cost side of the University's ledger. Furthermore, this loan was noted as a "one-shot operation."²⁵⁷

In July 1969, the Board took these warnings to heart and issued a paper entitled "University of Albuquerque Development of Alternatives." The introduction to this paper summarized the challenging state of affairs at the University:

> The University of Albuquerque is passing through a period of change prompted by a too rapid construction of certain kinds of facilities without supporting enrollment and finances and by the lack of development of other necessary facilities and services. In addition, the religious order which has, for so many years, provided a substantial subsidy for University operation finds that it can no longer bear alone the financial burden of support. Indeed, the Order has instructed the University to support itself. Either new sources of revenue must be found if the University is to move forward toward the objectives it has set for itself, or other forms of control and development must be sought if the University, in

its present form or in some modified form, is to persevere as an institution of higher learning for the Albuquerque community.

Five alternatives were presented for discussion:

Alternative I—Complete phase-out and closure.
Alternative II—Joint operation of a public junior college and a private university.
Alternative III—Establishing a community college as a replacement for the University.
Alternative IV—Reorganization of the corporate structure of the University under lay control.
Alternative V—Modified reorganization of the Board of Trustees.[258]

In an attempt to identify solutions to the looming financial crisis, a large amount of correspondence occurred in the fall of 1969. Letters flew back and forth between the Motherhouse attorney, Motherhouse Director Klene, Motherhouse Director of Management and Planning William Ryan, UofA attorney Michael Keleher, and Sister Marilyn. In addition, letters were sent to a number of private colleges—Fordham, Creighton, Baylor, Webster Grove, and Loyola of New Orleans—asking for advice based on their individual experiences.[259]

The general consensus that came out of these discussions had several components. One was that the Board should be restructured. Enrollment was recognized as an issue. Local recruiting at St. Pius X High School was noted as "indifferent" and it was suggested that offering scholarships to St. Pius students might show good will. It was also suggested that scholarships might be offered to graduates from St. Vincent Academy in Albuquerque.[260] In addition to attracting local students, a focus had to be placed on attracting more boarding students to fill the empty dormitory rooms. It was further noted that the Constitution and Bylaws should be reviewed and rewritten as necessary.

In the meantime, the University announced that it was offering several degree programs for interested students:

—Bachelor of Arts,
—Bachelors of Science in Business Administration, Teacher Education, Corrections, Criminology, and Medical Technology,
—Associate of Arts in Nursing, Business, Police Science, and Environmental Health.[261]

The day after the gloomy report was issued, the University announced that it was discontinuing its entire interscholastic athletic program, a mere two years after its much-acclaimed entrance into the ranks of the NCAA. With income of $1.28 million and expenditure of $1.6 million, much of it tied up in scholarships for 50 student-athletes, everyone reluctantly conceded that the program was simply not sustainable. Athletic Director Rudy Cordova said that the teams would meet their remaining commitments, but he anticipated that several student-athletes would transfer to other schools.[262] Despite the gloom, UofA crowned Lonnie Weidman as the 1968 Homecoming Queen.

1968 Homecoming Queen Lonnie Weidman.
(CSWR/UofA photo archives)

In an interview before a game with the New Mexico State Aggies, Dons basketball coach Ernie Smith, who had been coaching the team since 1962, said,[263]

> Sure, you know we have a morale problem. Discontinuing the program was a big disappointment to me and the team. We are playing for ourselves now and not for the University of Albuquerque .... At least 15 schools have offered scholarships to our kids, so we are just playing to satisfy ourselves now, and I am sure we won't have a morale problem in Las Cruces.[263]

Smith subsequently left UofA to take a coaching position in Oregon.[264]

This was the first real financial crisis that the University had faced, although, unfortunately, it would not be the last. The annual report for 1968 noted that operational costs had risen about seven percent in each of the past ten years. The report further noted that in 1964 the annual operating costs were $595,601, and in 1968, a mere four years later, they had tripled to $1.8 million. In the report Sister Marilyn said that, in the absence of federal or state assistance, the University would have to have help from private sources if it were to survive.[265]

Faculty salaries were a large component of operating costs, since, in an effort to maintain the desired student-teacher ratio, the number of faculty members had jumped from 27 in 1964 to 60 in 1968. In this context, Sister Marilyn's report noted that the several Sisters on the faculty received no compensation. In addition, the accrued debt from the ambitious building program also challenged the school's fiscal soundness: the new $1.2 million student center was not paying for itself, and the new dormitories, built in anticipation of substantially increased enrollment, were only about 60 percent occupied due to students selecting other housing options.

Even the music and drama departments, which had been a stalwart for the University throughout, were running in the red. Despite this, they were still offering "a series of excellent programs during the year."[266]

Both Kleinhenz and Comptroller Frank Burke noted that several steps to staunch the bleeding had already been taken. Room and board fees had been raised by $100 to $540 a semester; tuition had been raised in each of the past three years and now totaled $475 per semester; four academic departments—architecture, engineering, library science, and journalism—had been dropped from the curriculum; and some administrative and custodial personnel had been laid off.

Some additional financial assistance had been requested from the Sisters but, as Kleinhenz noted, "As a religious order, they are questioning how long they can continue increasing funds to meet the rising costs."[267]

In a May 1969 news conference, Sister Marilyn and Kleinhenz summarized the reasons for the school's financial struggles:[268]

—Its future had been over-estimated and under-prepared-for.
—Anticipated growth of the student body did not materialize.
—Expensive capital improvements proved to be more than the school could afford.[261]

An incoming freshman, Gloria McKinzie from Belen, asked the "people of New Mexico" to rise up and help the University:

The adult community for the past few years has become more and more concerned with our [the younger generation's] intellectual and spiritual growth. If you are truly concerned, let us work together to keep the University of Albuquerque from dying .... Surely Albuquerque can have two great universities.... You are the only ones that can keep the University of Albuquerque alive.[269]

Financial issues were not the only concern in early 1969. Inadequate campus security had also been brought to the administration's attention. Despite the fact that two security guards were on the campus all night, thefts were occurring. In addition, parking regulations, always a problem at any university, were being indiscriminately ignored, and there had been threats of bodily injury to some students. Vandalism in the dorms had also been reported.[270] These problems would persist, off and on, until the school closed.

On the positive side, a report of the accreditation visit by the North Central Association of Colleges and Secondary Schools noted that the school had an "alert, capable, and devoted faculty, clear educational goals, and well-planned, attractive facilities." However, they also reported that there was "limited laboratory space, a critical shortage of library space, significant financial deterioration (in the last ten years), and the very real possibility of overextending."[271]

The University had had some success in placing its graduates, although there was concern that more of them were taking positions outside of New Mexico. The Placement Office, under the direction of Pat Neutzling, helped students prepare résumés and obtain letters of recommendation.[272] In November 1968 the Placement Office put an ad in the *Albuquerque Tribune* which said:

> The University of Albuquerque has over 200 seniors who will be receiving B.A. and B.S. degrees in June 1969. Shouldn't you be interviewing these young men and women before they are recruited by out-of-state firms? Contact our Placement Office.[273]

Two additional bright spots in an otherwise grim 1969 were when Cheung Lung Yip, a freshman from Hong Kong, was awarded the Chemical Rubber Company's freshmen achievement award for his outstanding scholastic achievements and when shortstop Vic Ambrose was named to the NCAA All-American college baseball team.[274]

In the spring of 1968, the Student Body had reorganized itself. The Student Council which had been responsible for campus student activities and enterprises was replaced with a Student Senate which "legislates in all areas regarding student affairs and acts as a liaison between the student body and the faculty and administration."[275] As the financial and administrative roller coaster continued over the next several years, the Student Senate would play an important role.

In its application for reaccreditation in the Spring of 1969, the school noted that its mission was essentially unchanged from that noted a decade earlier—to "train the intellect which will aid the student in attaining the truth and in appreciating intellectually the fundamental principles of morality and beauty." The application noted three important changes in the last five years: [276]

> —Recognition of the University's corporate membership in the community at large as illustrated by the Nursing and Law Enforcement programs.
> —Recognition of the need to modify teaching methodology so

that students may learn as much, perhaps more, without placing upon them and their parents cost burdens because of inefficiency.
—Development of an open and free community wherein all are encouraged to free expression of ideas and notions pertaining to University governance.[261]

As the school moved into its fall 1969 term, there seemed to be some hope for a stable financial picture. Gifts from firms, businesses and foundations had increased; student aid programs had been reorganized; 14 faculty contracts had been terminated; the core curriculum had been reorganized; and several administrative savings had been implemented. On top of all of these savings, enrollment was expected to be five percent above the previous year's record enrollment.[277]

In August 1969, Kleinhenz and Sister Marilyn traveled to Chicago to receive the report of the site visit from the North Central Association. Six areas were noted as strengths:

—Changes in administration and organization.
—Strong faculty.
—Well-planned, attractive facilities.
—Clear educational objectives and goals with an interesting curriculum.
—Good cooperation between administration, faculty, and students.
—Interest in providing community services.

Seven areas were noted as needing improvement:

—Financial stability.
—Faculty office accommodations.
—Additional library and science facilities.
—Need to relocate classes from KAFB.
—Need to enrich student life.
—Need to improve counseling and academic programs for underachievers.
—Need to address the real threat to overextending in many directions.

As a result of the accreditation report, the school was reaccredited for only three years with the expectation that the areas needing improvement would be corrected in that period of time.[278]

In her 1969 annual report, Sister Marilyn said:

Some of the accomplishments which we call progress, however, have within them the seeds of distress and the continuation of the crisis which besets all institutions of higher education. I believe our constituents will understand this and, understanding it, they will strive during the coming year, as they have during the past year, to consolidate gains made and to take whatever steps are necessary to advance the objectives of the University of Albuquerque.[279]

Those objectives, as outlined for 1970 were:

—To raise $155,000 for student financial assistance.
—To develop student advisory committees to work with the administration.
—To adjust faculty salaries to "levels competitive within the region."
—To revise the curriculum into "more meaningful patterns of study."

The report also noted several accomplishments that had occurred during the preceding year, despite the financial woes. A two-year program in Police Science had been introduced in cooperation with the Albuquerque Police Department; a four-year degree program in Correctional Sociology had been initiated; two five-week summer sessions had been started; and 176 students had graduated, the largest graduating class to date.[280]

The school's financial problems were not just on the macroscopic level. In April 1969, the Student Senate was forced to discontinue the check-cashing service that had previously been provided to the students because $12,309 in bad checks had been received.[281]

The 1969 Robert Martinez was Student Body President. In a letter written in 1977, he reflected on the focus of the school on development of the individual:

It was never intended that the degree itself makes the person. Fundamental values acquired, basic skills developed, and the education and learning that take place at the University are preparation for going out into the world .... What the UofA has done will continue. It's part of the state and community. It's going to continue to offer education to the people. A degree is a degree; it's only as good as the individual.[282]

By the late summer of 1970, there was a glimmer of optimism within the administration. Support from businesses and individuals was helping to address the funding crisis; faculty reductions had eased the salary burden; and enrollment was expected to be up, with a freshmen class of 350 expected in September. Major gifts to the University included a donation of 38 acres of land plus $1,000 to the scholarship program by some of the original stockholders in Horizon Corporation, $4,200 from the Hilton Foundation of Beverley Hills, California, and a $10,225 grant from the National Science Foundation.[283]

The United States had been involved in Indo-China since the mid-1950s, but it was not until President Lyndon Johnson's controversial reaction to the so-called Gulf of Tonkin Incident in August 1964 that U.S. involvement in Vietnam started to ramp up significantly. The 1960s and 1970s saw significant activism and protests around the country, particularly on college campuses. In fact, political scientist Samuel Huntington characterized these decades as a time of "disorder, disagreement, or confusion when factions of people were at odds or estranged."[284]

The University of New Mexico was the locus of these activities in Albuquerque. While some UofA students and faculty crossed the river to join the protests, the level of activities on the UofA campus was minimal. In fact, there are only two mentions of concerns over the War in the minutes of the Student Senate—one is a motion to pass out a questionnaire on Moratorium Day in September 1969, a motion which failed to pass, and the other is the formation of an *ad hoc* Anti-War Information and Activities Committee in 1970 (with no further mention of the committee afterwards).[285]

Because of the favorable opportunities for veterans at the UofA, there was a significant population of Vietnam veterans at the school. This is perhaps one reason why there was only minimal protest activity on the campus.[286] In addition, the average age of a UofA student was 29, and a significant fraction of the student body was married, some with children. These factors probably made the UofA students less prone to join the activists. In general, they were much more concerned about the financial status of the University and whether or not it would stay open long enough for them to graduate.

The lack of outright protest participation does not mean that UofA students were unconcerned about national issues. For example, in October 1969, the National Vietnam Moratorium Committee announced a Vietnam Protest Day for October 15 in Albuquerque. Archbishop James Peter Davis was a key participant. The faculty was asked to approve of student participation, and the motion before the Faculty Senate passed, although there was some opposition.[287] The President's Executive Council also had a favorable discussion of the moratorium in their meeting on September 24.[288]

Classes were cancelled at the University on Moratorium Day (referred to in the *Sand Trumpet* as a "Day of Revulsion") to allow those students who wished to participate to do so.[289] A schedule for the day included an opening prayer at 10 a.m., followed by a full day of presentations and discussions, and ending with Mass at 4 p.m. and a communal supper.[290] The program that had been conducted at the campus was considered a success.[291] Virtually the entire issue of the October 15 *Sand Trumpet* was devoted to anti-war material.[292]

Also, in 1970, Student Senate President Joe Copeland wrote a letter to President Richard Nixon on behalf of the Student Senate The first part of the letter addressed the recent killing of four students and wounding of nine others when National Guard troops opened fire on a student protest at Kent State University in Kent, Ohio, on May 4, 1970. Copeland took the President to task, "The National Guard acted in a totally irresponsible manner ... as students and as Americans we feel a loss of confidence in your failure to recognize this." He continued with comments on the recent invasion of Cambodia and the resumption of bombing over North Vietnam, "We judge as bad faith your failure to consult with Congress on your intentions of expanding an undeclared war." In his conclusion, Copeland said:

> The majority of the Student Senate at the University of Albuquerque believe your recent statements and actions as President of the

United States of America are not in the best interests of the country or the world.²⁹³

Copeland read his letter to the President's Executive Council on May 6 and to the Faculty Senate on May 11, asking both groups the opportunity to sign. After some discussion, the Senate declined to write a note, saying that the members did not want to get involved in such a "political situation." That said, some of the faculty applauded the Student Senate for taking a stand on this important national issue.²⁹⁴

Student Senate President Joe Copeland (1970).
(CSWR/UofA photo archives)

In January 1970, Sister Marilyn unexpectedly announced her resignation, giving the school only one week's notice.²⁹⁵ She gave two reasons. First, she had been in poor health for some time, and the stress of managing the University through the ongoing financial crisis was taking a further toll on her well-being. In her letter of resignation, she wrote:

> The burdens of the office of president, even of a small university, are heavy, and for a small and fragile frame such as mine, they have become a greater cross then I can bear .... I do feel that I am leaving the University in strong hands and looking forward to a great future.[296]

In addition, she and three other Sisters at the school, all in their 20s and 30s, had asked for and received permission for exclaustration, a process by which they could establish their own community of prayer and social service, outside the direct control of their order (although still under the control of the local bishop).[297]

Just before she departed, Sister Marilyn reflected on the fact that many of the procedures in modern universities were tied to the past and probably deserved to be reconsidered:

> When the presidency of a college recently became vacant, the new appointee discovered an unusual fringe benefit of his office—he was allowed to graze one cow on the campus lawn .... This is one example of practices that might have made sense when they were inaugurated, but which have been outmoded by changing times and circumstances.[298]

Some of the processes which she suggested might be reconsidered included the overall credit system, especially the rigid requirements of certain numbers of credits for graduation, the overall grading system, and the admission policies for mature adults who had had significant world experience.

In view of Sister Marilyn's sudden departure and in an effort to counter concerns about the future of the University, Father Marcian Schneider, the University chaplain and president of the local chapter of the American Association of University Professors, noted:

> The resignation of Sister Marilyn as president of the University of Albuquerque does not mark a crisis of stability for the University.

The University has for several years now been following a policy of restructuring that will put full operational control of the University in the hands of a Board of Trustees who are local residents. The incidence of Sister Marilyn's weakening health forced a taking of this step earlier than anticipated.[299]

This sense that nothing had changed was disputed by some members of the Board. Trustee Fred McCaffrey suggested that Sister Marilyn's resignation speeded up the process of transition from a Catholic institution to a lay institution. He noted that a revision to the University's charter to transfer all assets from the Sisters of St. Francis to the Board was now being considered.[300]

6
From Crisis to Recovery

Following Sister Marilyn's sudden departure, the Sisters' provincial headquarters in Colorado Springs appointed Frank Kleinhenz as the interim president. However, his interim status did not last for long. On May 15, 1970, the Board of Trustees selected Kleinhenz from a field of six candidates to become the first lay president of the University.[301]

Frank Kleinhenz inauguration.
(CSWR/UofA, Box 18, yearbook collection)

At the same time as they selected Kleinhenz as president, the Board revamped itself, increasing its membership to 25, including both student and faculty representatives. Sister M. Barbara Ann Braun, OSF, remained as Chairperson of the Board until a new election could be held. Representatives of the Sisters now constituted only one-third of the Board. However, they still retained a veto power over Board decisions.[302]

In late 1969, the Fiscal Policies Committee of the Faculty Senate had provided a detailed report to the entire Senate. They summarized the situation in terms of a number of parameters. Initially, they noted the change of budget deficits from 1965 to 1969:

—1965–1966: $54,000.
—1966–1967: $121,000.
—1967–1968: $485,000.
—1968–1969: $140,000 (projected).

The singularly large deficit in 1967–1968 had been covered by a one-time payment by the Sisters from their hospital operating fund. This meant that, as of 1969, the current contribution from the Sisters totaled $665,000.

The cash position of the school was not much better. They had available funds of $291,200, known obligations of $509,700, and projected income of $215,000, leaving a cash deficit of about $35,000. One particular target for budget cuts was the total faculty salary. The report noted that the total salary outlay had grown from $528,000 during the 1968–1969 school year to $543,000 for the 1969–1970 school year.

The authors of the report recommended both a long-term and a short-term goal. In the short term, the goal was simply to survive. In the long term, they recommended realization of financial security through reliable budgeting and budgetary controls.[303]

A special fund-raising program, named the New Heritage Program and directed by Trustee Roger Lattanza and fund director John Daly, was announced in early 1970. The goal of this program was to raise $200,000 per year for the next five years. Several national and local corporations and foundations had already donated money and property in the neighborhood of $190,000.[304] However, Kleinhenz was cautious:

> Annual operating difficulties are being confronted by all private higher educational institutions and the University of Albuquerque is no exception. The greatest vigilance will have to be maintained during the coming years to protect every dollar of income through cost savings and control .... Cost consciousness and improved fund raising are the keys we need to turn to unlock new service programs and enlarge opportunities for more students to acquire an education.[305]

Under Kleinhenz's leadership, the financial picture continued to improve. The criminal justice program at the University had begun in 1967 and had proved to be very successful. In June 1970 the University created the Center for Law Enforcement, Corrections, and Social Services, directed by Professor Walter Niederberger, a sociology instructor since 1960.[306] In addition, the City announced that it was moving its Police Academy into two prefabricated buildings on the north end of the UofA campus.[307]

One of the earliest efforts by the new Law Enforcement center was a set of lectures and seminars for police officers and other law enforcement individuals on racial and cultural bias. Outside lecturers and local neighborhood representatives were invited to come to the University and share their experiences and concerns.[308]

However, on the negative side of the ledger, the National Institutes of Health had reduced its support for the two-year nursing program from $43,000 to $14,000, necessitating an urgent plea from the Albuquerque Chamber of Commerce to the state's congressional delegation to restore the program which was "helping significantly in meeting the demand for nursing professionals in New Mexico."[309] In addition, as noted by Senator Joseph Montoya, New Mexico had lost an estimated $8 million when President Nixon had vetoed the Health, Education, and Welfare Department's fiscal year appropriation.[310]

Even nature seemed to be holding a grudge against the University. New Mexico is not known as a "hotbed of earthquakes," although minor quakes occur along the Rio Grande Valley with some regularity. On Monday, January 4, 1971, one of the stronger of these "minor quakes," rated as 3.8 on the Richter scale with an epicenter near the University, caused $30,000-$40,000 worth of breakage and spillage in the chemistry laboratory in St. Francis Hall and $10,729 damage to the University Center.[311]

A movement that was present on many college campuses in the early 1970s was a decline in the "glorification of the individual." This also manifested itself on the UofA campus. For example, a student (and former heroin addict) chose to decorate the UofA chapel not with glorious, colorful art or sculpture, but with rustic, simplistic materials. The $A\Omega$ symbol for Christ used an old horseshoe for the Ω, and an actual plowshare tip was used for a Swords to Plowshares exhibit.[312]

In concert with the general rise of social responsibility as evidenced by opposition to the war, 1970 also saw the rise of environmental consciousness at UofA. Articles in the *Sand Trumpet* carried titles such as "Man the Polluter," "Redefining Garbage," and "Start your own War on Pollution."[313] As a further reflection of this environmental consciousness, a 20-year tradition, dating to the founding of the West Mesa campus, also ended in the spring of 1971. On April 2, when students returned to the whitewashed stone "J" on Volcon, they went not to freshen the whitewash but to dismantle the symbol. The tradition, which had been known as "J Day" and was usually a day without classes, became known as "un-J Day," and instructors were told that they could let students skip class.[314] In an undated *Faculty News Bulletin*, it was suggested that this effort to "obliterate the J" would be good for the environment and good publicity for the school.[315]

The symbol of St. Joseph on the Rio Grande which had piqued presidential candidate John F. Kennedy's curiosity, would no longer be there on the hillside. In a letter to the editor of the *Albuquerque Journal*, an environmentally-conscious citizen wrote, "We certainly can all be proud of the students of today who will take the time and effort to obliterate the carefree but destructive doodlings of another generation."[316]

The removal of the long-standing symbol was not without its opponents, however. A survey in 1966 had shown that most members of the student body were in favor of keeping the symbol (although a few suggested making it an "A"), and a student group, led by Dennis Yule, started a "Save the J" campaign, asking "Will Mount Rushmore be next?"[317] Another opponent of removing the icon noted, "Considering the amount of visual pollution such as power lines, billboards, and the like, the battle over the painted letters is hardly worth the effort."[318]

In an effort to expand the transparency of operation of the Board of Trustees, Ted Foss from the Faculty Senate asked Sister Barbara Ann to allow a member of the Faculty Senate and a member of the Student Senate to become voting members of the Board. President Kleinhenz endorsed the request.[319]

In August 1970, the Board adopted a budget with a deficit of about $200,000 over the projected revenue of $2.3 million. President Kleinhenz expressed the belief that most or all of the deficit would be made up during the year through the University's fund-raising campaign. Part of his optimism was based on the fact that $100,000 of existing debt had already been liquidated by outside fund-raising. He further noted that the goal of $200,000 per year had been exceeded by $40,000 in the 1969–1970 campaign.[320]

In August, Sister Barbara Ann appointed an Executive Committee of the Board, headed by Carol Kinney, to work on long-range planning for the University with University attorney Michael Keleher, son of one of the donors of the land for the West Mesa campus. Subcommittees of the Board were also set up to consider revisions to the school's bylaws, which had not been substantially changed since 1940, to develop a method for selecting new Board members, and to consider reintroduction of interscholastic athletics.[321]

A. Otto Miller.
(CSWR/UofA photo archives)

Ray Powell. (Sandia National Laboratories)

In October 1970, an election was held for president and vice-president of the Board. For the first time, a lay person, A. Otto Miller, was elected president. Miller, president of the American Builders Corporation, had been a member of the Board since 1966. Ray Powell, a vice-president at Sandia Laboratories, was elected vice-president. Powell had also been on the Board since 1966 and had been involved in planning for the University since 1963. The Sisters, who were still the owners of the University, would continue to be represented on the Board in the person of Sister M. Luella Schaefer, OSF, who would be the Board's secretary.[322] In addition, the previously approved representatives from both the Student Senate and Faculty Senate were added as voting members.[323]

October 1970 did not just see a major change to the Board. The student body, too, made some significant changes. The students submitted a petition to recall the entire Student Senate, justifying the request by saying that the current student body was, "Not in coherence with the Student Senate primarily because the Student Senate is not executing a philosophy of serving the needs of the student body." Following a successful recall, Sister Marjorie Hunt, a student, was elected as the new executive vice president of the Senate, replacing the ousted Joe Copeland.[324]

The UofA campus on Kirtland Air Force Base had expanded to nearly 1,500 students by the 1970–1971 school year, and in March 1971, Kleinhenz announced a new program in conjunction with the Air Force's Operation Bootstrap. Under this program, the University would cooperate with all of the armed forces in providing degree completion programs for service members. A spokesman for the University said:

> This plan is not limited in scope but is open to all areas of study. It is not a short-cut method of earning an inferior degree which means little when a person finishes his service obligation. It is, rather, a flexible program designed to eliminate the need for course work which duplicates the knowledge which a person may already have gained in activities outside the classroom.[325]

The financial picture continued to improve in the spring and fall of 1971. The Sisters were persuaded to forgive $750,000 in debt. Senator Clinton Anderson noted that the Office of Education had awarded $210,000 to the University for construction of a multi-purpose classroom.[326] Low-interest loans from a state-sponsored $4 million bond issue would also assist 146 UofA students with $195,950. After two weeks of a $215,000 fund drive, support for a new fine arts center had already reached $50,000.[327] Record enrollment of about 2,100 for the fall term, a 25 percent increase over 1970, meant that revenue from tuition and fees would increase as well. One of the drivers for this increased enrollment was the summer closure of the College of Artesia. Frank Deuble, UofA's Director of Admissions, said that the school had received and processed "a large number of requests for enrollment [from the closed community college] on a last-minute 'emergency basis.'"[328]

In September 1971, KZIA radio (later KDEF—94 FM) leased space on the second floor of Davis House to use as a broadcast studio, paying UofA $100 per month. This lease was renewed annually until 1975 when it was terminated because the school needed the space for "University purposes."[329]

The Faculty Senate had approved the concept of Associate Degree programs in the spring of 1970. The requirements were a minimum of

60 hours (20 of which had to be from UofA) and 30 hours in general academic areas.[330] Perhaps because of the improved financial picture, three new associate degree programs were announced—Medical Records Technologist, X-ray Technician, and Inhalation Therapist.[331] These programs, along with the nursing program, had first been proposed more than 10 years earlier, but had not been adopted.[332]

In an op-ed in the *Albuquerque Journal*, Bob Brown stated that "the UofA crisis has passed." He credited Kleinhenz's "drastic steps" for turning the financial picture around. Ironically, in light of future developments, he said:

> Probably the most important step in putting the college on a good financial basis has been the realization that two-year courses of various kinds are badly needed in this area and that there are many programs under which the school can work with the community .... There is no doubt but that the University of Albuquerque is an asset to the City. Working closely with the University of New Mexico and the Technical-Vocational Institute, it is helping to meet what appeared to be a crying need for junior college facilities in the area.[333]

Kleinhenz was quick to respond:

> We want to continue our four-year liberal arts courses ... we hope to set up the two-year courses so that they can feed right into the higher education process should the students decide to stay around.[334]

On a somewhat darker note, a September drug raid in Lourdes Hall netted $5,000 worth of cocaine, marijuana, methamphetamine, and drug paraphernalia. A 17-year-old student from Maryland was arrested for possession with intent to sell. This was the first major drug situation that the university had experienced.[335]

So, in the fall of 1971, despite the drug issue, things looked so bright that UofA opened a fifth branch campus to supplement the existing branches on Kirtland Air Force Base, at St. Pius X high school, on San Felipe Pueblo (two courses per semester offered for Pueblo residents), and in Colorado Springs. This new campus, called the

University of Albuquerque Rio Grande Center, began on the west side of the Rio Grande in Belen with daytime classes in the Belen Moose Lodge building and evening classes at Belen Junior High School. Mucio Yslas was appointed the branch director.[336] Planning for the new campus had begun in June when President Kleinhenz and other administrators met with representatives of the town of Belen, the Belen schools, and Horizon Corporation, a company that was developing land east of Belen. All of the individuals were enthusiastic about opening the branch in Belen, and Floyd Bailey from Horizon said, "If you want it, we'll help you get it off the ground."[337]

Initially, enrollment in the Belen branch was 89 students. The branch soon moved to a dedicated facility in a shopping center built by Horizon Corporation on the east side of the river, just south of the Belen bridge. Horizon also subsidized tuition for any of their employees who wished to attend.[338] The new facility included eight classrooms, as well as an administrative section and a library/reading area.[339]

Belen branch campus. (courtesy Sandy Schauer)

A teacher-support program in Valencia County was not a new idea. The University had offered a continuing-education class for teachers, taught by Valencia County Superintendent of Schools and UofA alumnus Raymond Gabaldon, in Belen in the spring of 1968. However, this was the first move toward having a dedicated facility in the South Valley.[340]

Nineteen seventy-one ended on a positive financial note. The balance sheet showed revenues of $1.28 million, expenditures of $1.09 million, and debt service of $145,000 with a projected surplus of $77,000.[341] With financial soundness seemingly in sight, 1972 brought more ideas and projects for the UofA. The Board adopted a report from a committee, chaired by former Governor John Simms, to develop a law school at the University, subject to sufficient funding.[342] An arrangement was also made with Albuquerque's Southwest College, New Mexico's largest career college, for UofA to accept Southwest credits in accounting, computer science, and business administration toward a full, four-year degree. UofA Dean of Careers and Special Programs, Kirby Krbec, said:

> In order to maintain the high standards of both institutions and provide the best education to its students, the University of Albuquerque faculty of the representative departments will continually review the selected offerings which are considered for credit transfer.[343]

In April 1972, the Board conducted a survey of the student body to determine how students felt about the importance of various aspects of services provided. Fifty-four percent said that the food service was very important, 39 percent rated the dormitory facilities as important, and 30 percent said that the level of noise in the dorms was important. They also ranked their satisfaction with some of the services. Thirty-nine percent rated the tutoring services as highly satisfying, but significant percentages rated campus services and maintenance as poor. Financial aid was rated as average, and support from the Dean of Students was considered fair to poor.[344]

May 1, 1972, saw a significant setback in the University's recovery when an arsonist used a flammable liquid to set a fire in room 241 of Lourdes Hall, a freshman men's dormitory. The fire spread to the rest of the building, resulting in a two-alarm blaze that left 84 men "homeless" and resulted in losses of about $1 million. Five of the firemen who responded to the call were injured.[345] Student Matthew Jaramillo recalled the smell of the burnt items that a priest friend who lived in the dorm had salvaged, and Debra Dionisi remembered that snakes belonging to one of her fellow students had crawled into the water pipes during the fire.[346]

The fire was apparently the work of either a serial arsonist who had caused similar fires at Eastern New Mexico University and New Mexico State or a copycat. Because of the possible serial nature of the crime, Kleinhenz and the administration worried that their insurance rates would go up or, worse, that their insurance might even be cancelled. So, to conserve finances until the insurance picture was clarified, the law school idea was tabled.[347] Eventually, the insurance company paid the University $581,000.[348]

A return visit by the accreditation panel was anticipated to occur in the spring of 1972. In preparation for the visit, the school put together an institutional profile which listed five objectives:

1. Design and offer community service programs.
2. Provide undergraduate educational opportunities for challenged groups such as the military, minorities, the poor, and senior citizens.
3. Preserve the integrity of a liberal arts curriculum.
4. Seek the best ways to continue to partake in furthering Christian heritage.
5. Establish and preserve operating economies.[349]

The reaccreditation visit occurred in May, and the team's report focused on the discrepancies that had been noted during the 1969 visit. They reported that over the last four years the school had endured several "disasters or near disasters." These included:

—Alleged malfeasance on the part of the Chief Financial Officer.
—Rapid turnover in the Office of the President.
—A major financial crisis.
—A decline in enrollment.
—Changes in the lay Board of Trustees.
—Damage from an earthquake.
—Damage from a fire.

With regard to these challenges, the examiners stated "That the

University has survived this series of blows and today is gaining strength and a sense of direction, representing, in the judgment of the examiners, a miraculous accomplishment."

The examiners noted improvement in the effectiveness of the faculty and the Board. They recognized improved ties to the Albuquerque community and were pleased at the dramatic improvement in fiscal stability and in the increased enrollment. On the other hand, they reported that, despite improvements, the faculty and administration were still weak, there was no long-range planning, there were unclear lines of authority, there were too many underprepared students, and the library was "completely inadequate."[350]

In a follow-up self-study report in December 1973, the school detailed point-by-point responses to the team's comments and laid out a new set of goals and objectives:

—Maintain programs unique to the needs of the area and its diverse cultures.
—Provide access to quality programs for individuals who have been blocked due to financial, scholastic, or cultural deprivations.
—Infuse Christian and liberal arts heritage into professional and technical programs.
—Be accountable for management and financial operation.
—Further strengthen participatory governance.[351]

The early years of the 1970s saw a significant growth in the number of grievances filed with the Faculty Senate. There were so many, in fact, that the Senate established a University Grievance Committee with procedures for handling grievances between students, between students and faculty, between faculty and administrators, between nonexempt workers and other groups, and between various levels of faculty members (e.g., instructors to department heads). After several years of discussion, the committee was approved by the Faculty Senate and the President in May 1975.[352]

A specific Faculty Grievance Committee was set up in 1977 and sent to the president for his approval to provide a forum for faculty to register concerns over job classification, benefits, working conditions, appointments and reappointments, tenure, etc.[353] One of the early issues that came before this committee was the question of faculty evaluations. Lawrence Desaulniers had registered a complaint that teacher evaluations should not be made by students. In a response, Kleinhenz noted:

> Contrary to rumors, the administration has never, nor ever intended, to use student evaluation results for faculty promotions, salary increases, or tenure ... to suppose that devious designs lurk deeply in the minds of administrators is a mean exercise and wasteful of the dignity that should bind us in our common endeavors.[354]

Despite this rather caustic denial, a mere two years later, the Faculty Senate passed and then-President Joseph Zanetti approved, a faculty evaluation program with the following parameters:

—75 percent, student evaluation.
—10 percent, self-evaluation.
—10 percent, peer evaluation.
—5 percent, administrative evaluation.[355]

Late summer and early winter of the 1971 school year provided some encouraging events. First, in August, the North Central Association accredited the school to award Bachelor's degrees for the next five years, at which time the school should expect another accreditation visit.[356] In October, the school received a $90,000 grant from the Veterans' Administration to recruit veterans to return to school. The Veteran's Administration estimated that only about 30 percent of returning veterans actually took advantage of their GI Bill benefits. The new program, called Veterans Education and Training Program (VETAP) was not just aimed at recruiting students for UofA, but was directed at finding academic or vocational opportunities, either public or private, for the returning veterans. The grant writers, UofA alumnus Chris Baca and Dean of Student Services Mucio Yslas, said that it was "designed to encourage the pursuit of education by those who would not or could not consider the possibility of educating themselves."[357]

On November 13, the long-awaited fine arts center was dedicated. Over the period of construction by local contractor Bradbury and Stamm, the cost had climbed to $750,000 from its original 1971 estimate of $473,000. However, one continuous "ray of sunshine" throughout the financial crisis had been the constant stream of drama and music productions, so the cost overrun was not criticized too strenuously.[358]

Artist's rendition of the University Center stage.
(CSWR/UofA photo archives)

November also brought good news from the Belen campus. At an open house, more than 100 people heard Horizon Project Manager Luis Bishop say that the establishment of an educational center in Belen was "one of the most important things that has happened to us." Students at the branch campus were praised as "pioneers," and the Student Senate officers were introduced.[359]

Finally, on another positive note, President Kleinhenz, a guest speaker at the annual meeting of the Community Council of Albuquerque, noted that, as the University recovered from its recent financial woes, it was recommitting itself to a greater level of community service, saying, "moral compassion is being substituted for academic detachment." He supported his position by emphasizing the programs in Police Science, Corrections, Sociology, and Nursing. He also noted the three previously announced health-related programs that would begin in the fall term—Radiology, Inhalation Therapy, and Medical Records Technology. A fourth health-related program, Dietetics, had also been added to the health-sciences curriculum.[360]

A July 1972 article by Frankie McCarty, the *Albuquerque Journal's* education columnist, was headlined "UofA: A Return to Life and Health" and summarized the remarkable recovery that President Kleinhenz and the Board of Trustees had accomplished. McCarty pointed out that the school had been on the brink of collapse in 1968, "Deeply in debt, with prayers, but not too much else, to offer to creditors, the Sisters running the school were apprehensive about the future of the school." Now, under lay and community leadership, UofA was back in business. In fact, the largest enrollment ever, 3,200, was anticipated for the fall term, and the budget no longer showed a deficit.[361]

Progress was being made on a number of fronts—facilities, philosophy, and curriculum. One of the major additions in 1973 was the new Center for Learning and Information Resources (CLAIR), previously known as the library. Director Eugene Kosky, PhD, described it as providing multi-media in an integrated manner. He said that it was "a modern facility where customers and the people in it look at information regardless of its format. We needed a change in name, and we needed to sweep away some of the concepts of a library."[362]

This "new look" at books, libraries, and information was in keeping with a national trend of "declining orientation towards words," attributed to the widespread use of digital computers to provide organization and standardization of information. To no one's surprise, this had a significant negative impact in curricula such as philosophy and theology.[363]

In April, Jill Baxter wrote a letter to President Kleinhenz providing a Christian Commitment statement that had been passed by the Faculty Senate:

> Academically, and at a minimum level of specification, both liturgical life and overriding philosophical and theological insights should permeate University life and the general academic area of the sciences and humanities which are the pursuit of any institution of higher learning.... In this atmosphere of scholarly fidelity to the Christian message as it comes to us through the

Church, we learn to appreciate, above all, that Christianity draws us to the double love of God and man concretely in existential relationships. Therefore, the appropriate Christian commitment of this University is the activity of Christians responding to the dual love in a way that gives primacy and honor to the life of the intellect.[364]

The improvement in financial health of the University had been noted at a Board meeting in July 1973 when President Kleinhenz reported that there would be a budget surplus of $500,000 at the end of Fiscal Year 1973.[365]

Although the liberal enrollment policy addressed the goals of increased community service, the Academic Affairs Committee expressed concern over the lack of preparation of the incoming freshman class, particularly those who came from the Albuquerque Public Schools (APS). The committee noted that most of the incoming students had poor grammar, probably because they had not had a grammar requirement since eighth grade. The history background provided by APS seemed almost random—some graduating seniors had had Chinese history, some had had Watusi history, and at least one had studied the history of Nebraska. They also noted that the APS requirements included only one class in the physical sciences. The committee recommended that no students be admitted with an ACT (American College Testing) test score below 15 and that remedial programs be provided.[366]

The school had attempted to address the issue of poor preparation by initiating an Upward Bound Program in 1965. This program was designed to help high school students who came from families without a collegiate background, students with disabilities, students from foster care, as well as those who might lack English proficiency. It was sponsored by the Office of Economic Opportunity, the agency principally responsible for overseeing President Lyndon Johnson's War on Poverty, and provided tutoring in math, science, composition, literature, and foreign language.[367] In 1969, the University received a grant of $134,000 to continue this program.[368] Elsie Scott, who had been hired as a tutor in chemistry and microbiology (and who had a parallel career as a professional belly dancer), recalled the program with some fondness. She remembered taking the students on bus trips in the summer and recalled one project in which the students built a solar crop dryer. They dried all sorts of fruits and vegetables, and some of the students even tried drying marijuana, much to the consternation of the project leaders. (Coincidentally, Elsie Scott's mother was an orphan at St. Anthony's until she was adopted in 1932).[369]

Elsie Scott. (courtesy Elsie Scott)

Additional two-year programs in Air Traffic Control (the first in the country), Hospitality Industries, and Allied Health were also announced. The Air Traffic Control program was a unique combination of liberal arts courses such as Philosophy, Theology, and Psychology and technical courses, leading to an Associates degree.[370] It was housed in a specialized facility in Davis Hall where various commercial and military aeronautical scenarios could be simulated and addressed by the students.[371] In 1975, the Aerospace program sent letters touting their offering to several aeronautical magazines including *Rotor and Wing, Sports Aviation, Aviation Travel, Professional Pilot,* and *Air Progress*.[372]

Brochure for air traffic control program.
(Keleher collection, file 11448)

In October 1973, the University applied for government funding under Title III of the Amended Higher Education Facilities Act of 1963, legislation which was designed to help developing colleges achieve a greater degree of financial stability and academic excellence. The UofA proposal noted, "UofA seeks to enter the mainstream of a developed educational institution able to sustain itself as it accomplishes its mission of servicing a wide variety of community and student needs"[373] The University's proposal cited the importance of accountability, effective management of money, time, and personnel, and ability to sustain the University's own energies once a "critical mass has been attained in size of enrollment and private funding." By the 1976–1977 school year, Title III funding would reach $250,000.[374]

In a news release, the University summarized its successful recovery:

> The University of Albuquerque has, over the last three years, experienced a phenomenon unique in the country among private colleges. It has, in every respect, pulled itself up and out of what can only be described as a financial disaster. In three years, UofA has paid off its debts and now operates within a balanced budget.... The University of Albuquerque has progressed a far pace in three years, especially in offering programs and instructional activities which meet local needs and assist the community in economic and cultural development. We wish to preserve the gains made and assure planned and controlled growth in the future.[375]

In order to once again look into the future, the University contracted with Ellerbe Corporation for help in both short and long-term planning. The company, together with representatives from the faculty, the student body, and the Sisters, undertook to examine several key issues. These included the relationship with the Order of St. Francis, potential sources of revenue and expenditures, student aspirations, faculty aspirations, and expectations for institutional development.[376] In light of the community college issue, it does seem surprising that only passing mention is made of "Albuquerque Public School career centers" and nothing specific is noted about the Technical-Vocational Institute which had opened in 1965.

In 1972, Carol Kinney convened a group of the Board to work

on long-term planning. The group conducted a wide-ranging set of interviews, with some of the Sisters, with financial specialists, with local civic leaders, and with local educational leaders. They also reviewed a number of papers on trends in higher education, financing, housing, and other pertinent topics. After reviewing all of this material, they developed a set of planning assumptions in five areas—finance, communities served by the school, students, faculty, and instructional programs.[377]

Carol Kinney.
(CSWR/UofA, Box 18, yearbook collection)

In the finance area, key assumptions were that student tuition would still be the major source of income, although greater income diversity was desirable. Also, new facilities programs, and services would be selected on a cost-benefit basis. The dependence on tuition and the lack of mention of any sort of endowment would, in the long run, prove to be an insurmountable challenge.

The assumptions as to the community served encompassed the entire state. The committee felt that the area would grow and develop industrially, and that the Albuquerque Standard Metropolitan Statistical Area (SMSA) would grow substantially. They also assumed that the community being served would continue to demand both public and private higher educational opportunities.

Students were assumed to come from a wide array of educational, cultural, and socio-economic backgrounds. As such, multiple housing options and substantial student services and activities would be required. It was assumed that students would be actively involved in UofA decision-making.

Faculty qualifications, teaching loads, salary, and benefits were to be comparable to other universities of similar size and purpose. Faculty appointments would be based on teaching excellence rather than research capability, and, like the students, faculty would play key roles in overall decision-making.

Instructional programs would be tailored to identified student needs and would be flexible to address changes in those needs. Regardless of the program, a high standard of quality would be maintained.

Although there was no explicit mention of the Catholic/Christian foundation of the school, a statement of Christian commitment was included with the planning documents in a letter from Lawrence Desaulniers to the Board of Trustees.

In a December 1973 report to the Board, the long-range planning committee provided a set of recommendations that established a governance model to address the specific detailed assumptions and goals previously specified:

> —The University of Albuquerque should remain an operating entity of the Sisters of St. Francis Seraph, Colorado Springs, Colorado.
> —The Board of Trustees should be strengthened by replacing inactive members with lay personnel committed to active personal participation.
> —A special Governance Task Force Committee of the Board of Trustees should be created and instructed to formulate alternative plans of governance that could be implemented within the next 5-to-10-year period.
> —The role of the Board of Trustees, as stated in their policies and procedures, is policy-making. Every effort should be made to

insure this remains their role and they not get involved in the day-to-day administration of the University.

—The role of the President should be clarified and clearly identified as (a) Academic Leadership, (b) Institutional Development, (c) Administrative and Financial Coordination, (d) National, State, and Area-wide Image Development, (e) Community and Interinstitutional liaison.

—Administrative restructuring should relieve the President of direct administrative responsibilities in the above areas and permit him to function at a conceptualizing and coordinating level.[378]

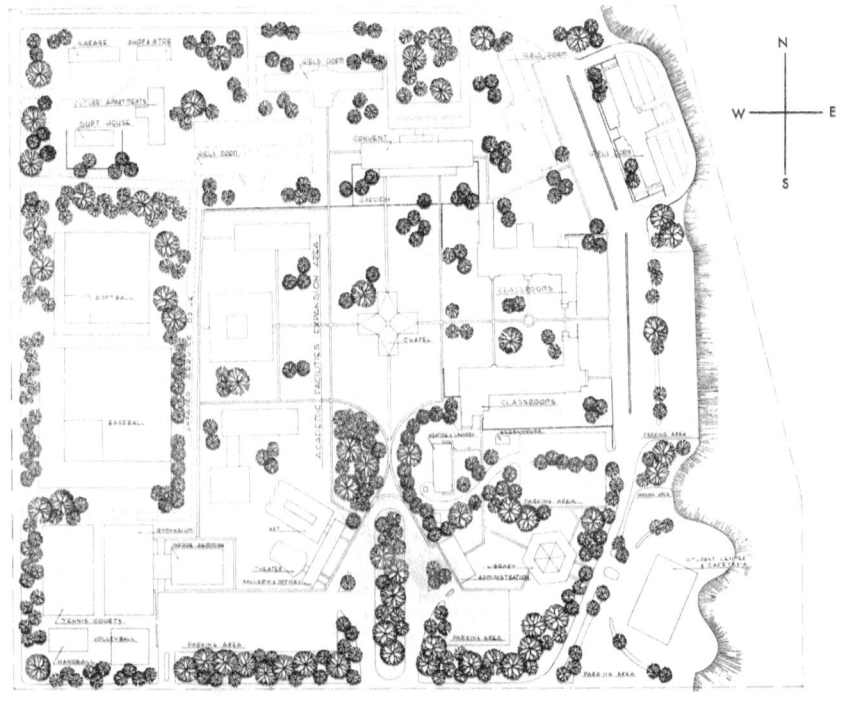

Campus of the Future

Conceptual drawing of the Campus of the Future.
(CSWR/UofA photo archives)

In 1972, the University of Albuquerque Foundation, a separate non-profit corporation, was formed "to support the University." The concept had been floated with the Board of Trustees in the form of a proposed Land Bank in September 1971. The purpose of the new entity would be to "prepare for the future growth of the University."[379] According to Article II of the corporation's Articles of Incorporation,

> The general purpose of the corporation shall be to acquire land to be used by the University of Albuquerque. In the furtherance of its general purpose, the Corporation may engage in any and all lawful activities ... including, but not limited to, acquiring land which will accommodate expansion of the campus of the University of Albuquerque and acquiring land which can be exchanged for land adjacent to the present campus of the University of Albuquerque.[380]

The Foundation's principal assets were three parcels of land—a property in Rio Grande Estates in Socorro, three lots in the Volcano Cliffs area, and 40 acres north of the campus. The last of these three was acquired in a land trade with Horizon Corporation.[381]

On June 6, 1973, after bidding farewell to the largest graduating class to date, 396 students, just three weeks before, Frank Kleinhenz, a president who had been popular with students, faculty, and staff alike, announced that he was resigning effective August 1 to accept one of "several unusual opportunities which have been presented to me."[382] By mid-fall, he had joined Starline Corporation as an executive vice president. He did not cut all ties with UofA, however, agreeing to remain on the Board and on the Board's executive committee.[383]

On August 3, Ray Powell, chairman of the Board since Otto Miller's death on February 10, announced the selection of Joseph Zanetti, Executive Assistant for Public Affairs at Sandia Laboratories, as the new president. In an editorial comment, the *Albuquerque Journal* characterized this as the "Right Choice."[384]

Joseph Zanetti.
(Sandia National Laboratories)

Zanetti had earned a Bachelor's degree from St. Mary's College in California and had done post-graduate work at the University of California at Berkeley and at San Francisco State University. He was a member of the Board of the Albuquerque Public Schools, President of the Albuquerque Chamber of Commerce, and Chairman of the Board of the Middle Rio Grande Council of Governments.

As Kleinhenz left and Zanetti arrived, New Mexico politicians praised the University as it welcomed the new president. Senator Pete Domenici, a former student, said:

> God has been good to the former College of St. Joseph on the Rio Grande.... The University still sits there on its bluff, almost like the keystone in the arch of West Mesa development.... It fills a unique place in our city's educational operation. I can also assure you that it leaves a distinctive mark on its students.[385]

Domenici may or may not have intended this to be a reference to "the city on the hill" in Jesus's Sermon on the Mount, but it is an apt metaphor for both the good times and the bad times that the University experienced.[386] In the best of times, the school served as a beacon for students seeking an alternative Catholic-Christian-oriented educational experience. In the more challenging times, the "school on the bluff" was, perhaps, indicative of an institution teetering on the edge of crisis.

Domenici's senatorial colleague, Joseph Montoya, echoed the theme:

> By taking a practical viewpoint toward education beyond the secondary level, the University of Albuquerque has helped students open the doors to employment as well as to give the students a broad educational background. The University of Albuquerque is a school of higher learning that all of us in New Mexico can be proud of.[387]

Representative Manuel Lujan was perhaps the most effusive and targeted in his kudos:

> The reputation of the University of Albuquerque is widespread and well known as one of the finer "small school" educational institutions in the country.... Many, many Albuquerqeans and New Mexicans have given greatly of their time and resources to make the school better. This is usually found in larger schools which have large numbers of alumni more proud of the football teams than the more important functions of a school of higher learning. The University of Albuquerque has been able to achieve this success without a huge athletic program.[388]

At his formal induction as president, Zanetti said that the University is "growing and at a fairly significant rate." He attributed the growth to the school's decision "not to be simply a four-year liberal arts college, but also to identify with the needs of the community. We have become an educational hybrid."[389]

Although the Zanetti appointment seemed very much in line with the School's movement toward greater community involvement, many in the student body were not pleased with the selection. Some students had publicly supported Mucio Yslas, the Assistant to the President for Student Services. They pointed out that Yslas was endorsed by the League of United Latin-American Citizens (LULAC), that he was bilingual, had a multi-cultural background, and had been with the University since 1967. They also noted that Zanetti's educational background was minimal and that he had not completed any graduate studies. In addition, they accused the Board of "Corporate Nepotism," citing the Sandia relationship between Powell and Zanetti.[390]

Mucio Yslas.
(CSWR/UofA photo archives)

Racial sensitivities were just below the surface, and the selection of Zanetti over Yslas brought them out in force. In a letter from Student Senate President Ray Padilla to President Zanetti, Padilla blasted the administration:

> You have most blatantly demonstrated a total lack of concern for the personnel attempting to improve the social and economic status of minorities through education. The surreptitious methods employed by the administration have caused concern throughout the university personnel and the student body.[391]

Ray John de Aragon, a humanities student who had come to UofA after two years at New Mexico Highlands University, wrote a pointed editorial in the February 1974 *Sand Trumpet*:[392]

> It turns out that an undereducated, under qualified, and unwanted

individual was forced upon the students, faculty, and administration against their wishes and without giving them much choice in the matter.... He [Yslas] was only selected as a finalist by the Board of Trustees to placate future reaction against them ... Rudy Cordova, PhD, was selected as vice-president in another effort to placate minority students by asking them to take second best.[391]

These diatribes were countered by an open letter to the student body by self-described "black student" George H. Anderson who complained that the rights and responsibilities of speaking for the college community had been hijacked by a small group of elected students whom he characterized as "racial bigots and small-time hoods."[393] In a letter to the editor of the *Sand Trumpet*, Yvonne Johnson also pushed back on Aragon's assertions:

> Mr. Aragon's personal perspective is often allowed to bias his evaluation of the University, and his limited awareness of the current needs of Academe results in a report that is closer to personal opinion than it is to informed facts.[394]

Student Carlos Wayne Downell wrote a letter sometime later that urged the minority students to stop fighting amongst themselves and unify their vitriol against "the Man:"

> What do Chicanos think? That their rejection of Blacks will gain them the Man's acceptance? Do Indians still believe that they must assimilate Anglo values up to and including their racism? Call it Tomism [sic], Applism, or Tio Taco or whatever. It's ridiculous and sad that the Man can split us up among ourselves and use us against each other.[395]

In a further attempt to work through the race issue, a student newspaper entitled *Black Focus* was initiated in the spring of 1975. According to the editorial page, this newspaper was "born to close the communication gap between Black students, Black Professionals, and University personnel on campus."[396]

One of the more successful programs at the University had been its long-standing Center for Law Enforcement, Corrections, and Social

Services. In its report for the end of the 1973–1974 school year, the staff of the Center noted the plans to form an Indian Justice Institute for the 1974–1975 school year and made the following request:

> The Center for Law Enforcement, Corrections, and Social Services is a recognized asset to the criminal justice community both locally and statewide. During the last few months, it has achieved prominence nationally.... It, therefore, deserves an increased commitment from the University that it may strengthen its programs of criminal justice education, research, and continue to serve community needs.[397]

The Board took the staff's request under advisement.

In a November report, registrar Rick Legoza reported encouraging news concerning enrollment and credit-hours. Enrollment was up seven percent to 3,400 and credit-hours were holding steady at 20,346. There had been a 32 percent rise in credit hours at evening and extension courses which Legoza attributed to "a much larger number of students taking full-time loads because of the larger number of degrees offered and the options available in the evening and extension division."[398]

Legoza also noted that 62 percent of the enrolled students were from Bernalillo County, 14 percent from other New Mexico counties, 17 percent from out of state, and one percent from foreign countries. The overall school profile showed that 67 percent of the students were studying at the main campus with the remainder at the branch campuses. Thirty percent of the students were in the Business Administration program, 11 percent were in Nursing, and 10 per cent in Criminal Justice, with the remaining 49 percent in one of the other departments.[399] This clearly reflects the major shift from the founding focus of the school on teaching future educators. Sixty percent of the students were men, 53 percent of the students were married, and 43 percent were minority. The average age of a student was 29.

In the spring of 1974, the faculty took another look at the Christian Commitment Statement and agreed upon the descriptive preamble:

> The University of Albuquerque is a diversified liberal arts institution of higher learning founded by the Roman Catholic Order of the Sisters of St. Francis Seraph of Colorado Springs,

Colorado. The University's programs are permeated with the values and ideals of ecumenical Christianity, humanism, and directed at fostering in the student a deeper appreciation of this Judeo-Christian tradition.[400]

Financial concerns did not escape the vision of the school's new leadership. A cautionary note about financing private educational institutions was provided by Ralph Pfeiffer, PhD, the president of the Data Processing Division of IBM, during a presentation at the second annual meeting of the New Mexico Independent College Association. Pfeiffer noted:

> Inflation has affected education in private, four-year, accredited colleges to the extent that the number of institutions running deficits has increased from one-half to 60 percent .... Here in New Mexico, fund-raising has increased tenfold from $5,500 in 1969 to $50,000 in the current year—a remarkable performance.... We need independent higher education in this country. We need that structure, organization, and output provided by private institutions.[401]

7
Community College Issues

Albuquerque Public Schools opened the Technical-Vocational Institute (T-VI) in 1965. There were 150 students enrolled in one of the vocational classes which included Automotive Repair, Carpentry, Electronics, and Machine Trades. At the same time, the University of Albuquerque (called St. Joseph on the Rio Grande for another year) was experiencing a period of significant growth and development. T-VI was small and had very different objectives and programs, so it did not appear to be a concern for the University.[402]

However, several developments between 1965 and 1970 substantially changed the relationship between UofA and T-VI. One of these was a national shift in post-secondary educational philosophy. For example, one study found that, while 70 percent of high school graduates wanted to go on to higher education, only 40 percent of their older siblings had had the same inclination. In addition, a study sponsored by the Carnegie Commission on Higher Education recommended that at least 230 community colleges should be built across the country. This proposal was designed to provide an intermediate choice for high school graduates between going to four-year colleges or not furthering their education. In fact, the authors of the study "took a dim view" of expanding the number of universities, saying, "There are enough four-year colleges now for Ph.Ds."[403] Locally, Tom Popejoy, outgoing president of UNM had argued for the need for a junior college in Albuquerque in 1967.

In 1969, the Mid-Rio Grande Council of Governments requested that William R. McConnell, PhD, Executive Secretary of the State Board of Educational Finance (BEF), undertake a study of the need for a community/junior college in the mid-Rio Grande Valley. This study was reported out a year later with a recommendation to establish a community college in conjunction with T-VI.[404]

Also in 1969, the Albuquerque Chamber of Commerce passed a resolution that asked the Albuquerque Public School (APS) administration to take action to create a community college within the boundaries of the APS district. Recognizing that starting a community college from scratch would be both time-consuming and costly, the authors of the resolution proposed a substantially faster and less costly alternative—simply expand the curriculum of T-VI to include a broader range of academic courses leading to a two-year academic degree.[405]

UofA Board member Reverend Harry Summers expressed some concern in a letter to UofA President Laurence C. Smith:

> The Chamber of Commerce idea now promoted by President Davis of UNM will be a super costly venture ... taxpayers can be forthrightly told about this.... In a day of the decline of the basic moral standards in our nation, we need to shore up our Christian-Hebraic foundations and not surrender to a neutral secularism.[406]

In a June 1969 letter to Albuquerque City Commission Chairman Pete Domenici (a future US senator and a former student at St. Joseph on the Rio Grande), Arthur Brown, Chairman of the University of Albuquerque Committee of the West Side Association, proposed the following:

> Eliminate the religious affiliation of the University to permit greater public support.
> Immediately open the former UofA campus as a two-year community college while allowing existing UofA students to complete their four-year degree programs.[407]

Brown noted that:

> I am convinced that it would be in the public interest to have UofA operated as a public or state college and university, with special emphasis on the development of a community junior college.... Its nearness to [the $13 million technical-vocational high school of being built by the Bureau of Indian Affairs in Paradise Hills]

would be an important aid in the rapid development of new technical training programs so desperately needed in the central New Mexico area if we are to meet the needs of our young people and bring needed industry into the region.[408]

Brown further asserted (correctly as it would later become clear) that the Sisters of St. Francis were more concerned about their health and hospital missions and that the debt service for running UofA (estimated by Brown to be $360,000 per year) was interfering with the Sisters' priorities.[409]

Even the UofA Board of Trustees was considering options. In a meeting in May 1969, in light of the projected $361,000 deficit, board member D. W. Falls suggested studying the possibility of turning UofA into either a community college or an extension of UNM.[410]

Community colleges, technical-vocational institutions, and branch colleges from the University of New Mexico, New Mexico State, and Eastern New Mexico University were springing up across the state. As these successful two-year institutions grew, pressure grew on APS, situated in the state's largest city, to provide similar opportunities for students within the greater Albuquerque area. Even though Albuquerque did have two four-year colleges and both of these institutions offered Associate degree programs, a groundswell of opinion arose that suggested that Albuquerque and the immediate areas of Bernalillo, Sandoval, and Valencia counties should have their own dedicated community college. Frank Kleinhenz disputed the need for a new junior college, saying that the cooperation and coordination of the several institutions of higher learning provided valuable services with only minimal needs for new tax funding.

The discussion about an Albuquerque community college continued into the 1970s. Strong divisions emerged on the two major approaches—expansion of T-VI into a community college and use of UofA as the facility to house the proposed institution. Some individuals worried that T-VI would lose its critical vocational focus and become "elitist." In addition, the legal issue of use of public funding for UofA, a private university, was raised. President Joseph Zanetti suggested that a dual-funding process could be established. The University would continue its four-year programs, and a new two-year community college would share the UofA facilities but be financially separate from the University. This was considered but not carried forward. Many, including some of the Sisters, felt that including a community college would sound the death knell for the University.

As discussions progressed, the Board and the administration came to the conclusion that the best outcome for all concerned was to have the State purchase the University. In an open letter to members of the Legislature in January of 1973, President Smith and Board Chairman Killorin listed their rationale:

> —The University of Albuquerque currently serves the academic function of a community college for the Albuquerque area with 25 Associate degree programs.
> —Tuition is high at the UofA because there is no state assistance—costs are $55 per credit-hour at UofA versus $13 per credit-hour at a community college.
> —Based on experience elsewhere, competition between UofA and a community college would reduce enrollment at UofA by 50 percent within three years.
> —Albuquerque would "build one and lose one." Why do that?
> —The University of Albuquerque programs are presently successful.
> —It would be more advantageous to transfer a functioning entity to the State rather than a non-functioning entity.
> —Eight million dollars (the proposed cost to the State for purchasing UofA) would be a bargain price, representing only about 70 percent of the school's appraised value.[411]

The open letter concluded:

> After a year of study and discussions, and particularly after consideration of the operational alternatives we would face, we feel that the two proposals before the Legislature—(1) expand the program with T-VI to include an academic division and (2) the legislation to purchase the UofA campus—are clearly in the best interest of our institution, our students and staff, the Albuquerque community, and the State.

In 1975, Sister M. Eileen Van Ackeren, OSF, Provincial Coordinator for the Sisters of St. Francis, wrote a letter to James Killorin, President of the Board of Trustees, detailing the Sisters' thoughts and concerns about the future of the University. In the letter, Sister Eileen noted the many changes in philosophy, faculty, and curriculum which had occurred since the institution was founded. Summarizing the current situation, she said:

> As a religious community, we still believe firmly in the benefits of Catholic and Christian education, but we also realize that we, as a community, can no longer finance the University .... All of us are aware of the problems and disappointments we have experienced during the past two years. The Sisters, as well as the Board, have to accept responsibility for the failures of the past two years, and, regretfully, we do so.

Looking to the future, she provided three alternatives:

1. The continuation of the University of Albuquerque as presently functioning with emphasis on the Christian commitment and with a curriculum combining liberal arts, teacher training, business administration, and other four-year courses of study that are deemed feasible to meet the vocational needs of the city of Albuquerque and the nearby areas.
2. The continuation of the four-year degree-granting institution with emphasis on a Christian commitment, even if a two-year, state-supported college is established.
3. The sale of the University of Albuquerque at a reasonable price if the pressures become too great for a state-supported, two-year college.

Sister Eileen Van Ackeren, OSF.
(CSWR/UofA photo archives)

James Killorin.
(CSWR/UofA, Box 18, yearbook collection)

She noted that the Sisters' preference would be the first alternative, although she acknowledged the issues, including the constitutional prohibition relative to state funding of private entities. As to alternative 2, she observed that that was probably "out of the question" due to funding concerns.

With regard to alternative 3, she said:

> We thoroughly agree that, if the State intends to go through with a two-year college, then the University of Albuquerque would be "dead," and then the best we could do would be to offer the institution for sale at a reasonable price to the state.[412]

To no one's surprise, faculty concerns continued throughout the discussions about the change in UofA. What would happen to those faculty members who were no longer needed? What about promotions? What about tenure?

In the spring of 1976, the University Academic Policies Committee suggested an experimental consortium between UofA and T-VI for an Associates of Applied Sciences. The proposal apparently did not get traction, since it is not mentioned in any minutes or letters after March 1976.[413]

In January, UofA attorney Michael Keleher and Board Chair James Killorin met with Alex Mercure and Joel Jones of UNM to discuss the community college issue. This meeting was partially in response to a UNM request to the legislature for a $5 million appropriation to staff a branch junior college on UNM's south campus. Everyone agreed that the current delivery of programs in Bernalillo County should be expanded because there were unmet post-secondary needs in the area. However, Killorin pointed out that, at present, about 70 percent of UofA's "deliveries" were of a "community college nature" and that UofA could not continue to exist if UNM or some other entity "with public funding" were to provide those programs.[414]

Joe Zanetti summed it up as follows:

> The crucial problem we face now was brought on by the decision of the University of New Mexico faculty to raise admission standards. This triggered other events which resulted in UNM's decision to establish a general college which would provide a

program of academic remediation and preparation to get ill-prepared students back into the mainstream of the university. This duplicates the program that the UofA offers and does it on a much cheaper basis.[415]

Inevitably, the uncertainties in the future of UofA were felt by the student body. In February 1977, President Smith tried to address student concerns over the junior college proposals that were being floated. He said that the University was "academically healthy" and that the financial issues were being addressed. He said that one possibility would be to retain part of the school as a liberal arts college if the facility were sold or leased to the state as a junior college. He also reassured the students that, regardless of the ultimate decision, nothing would happen before 1978, so seniors and juniors "need not worry."[416]

In February, the T-VI Board expressed concerns over the community college proposal. T-VI Board member Ted Martinez said that, since students would come from all over the state, it was not fair that Bernalillo County tax payers should foot the entire bill. Dave Smoker, T-VI director of pupil personnel services, noted that 67 percent of UNM students fail to graduate, even with an Associates degree, and that the cost of such a degree at UofA was very high. "That's part of the need," he said.[417]

In early February, a 10-member task force headed by Robert Huff, PhD, Executive Secretary of the Board of Educational Finance (BEF), was appointed by Governor Jerry Apodaca to develop a formal plan "for the delivery of community college educational opportunities in the Albuquerque area."[418] Both UofA Board Chair James Killorin and University President Laurence C. Smith were on the task force.[419]

The task force identified seven alternatives:

1. Creation of an independent community college on a new site with no affiliation with T-VI, UNM, or UofA.
2. Creation of an independent community college on the UofA campus with no affiliation with either UNM or T-VI
3. Expansion of the T-VI curriculum to make it an independent community college at both the UofA campus and the T-VI campuses. There would be no affiliation with UNM.

4. Expansion of UNM's lower division curriculum and services into a general college with no affiliation with either UofA or T-VI.
5. Creation of a branch college of UNM at the UofA campus with no affiliation to T-VI.
6. Creation of a branch campus of UNM at its south campus with no affiliation with either UofA or T-VI.
7. Creation of a community college through a consortium of UofA, UNM, and T-VI.[420]

The governor was in favor of a slightly modified version of alternative 3 in which UNM would have some curriculum oversight. He directed BEF to work with the new task force. The basic concept was to have T-VI provide the vocational arm of the new institution, with UofA providing the liberal arts component. Under this construct, the state would buy the UofA campus, and UNM would oversee the new school, which would operate under the auspices of the Branch Community College Act. This would provide both local tax levy support as well as the possibility of direct state appropriations.[421] The governor noted, "UofA has a long history of contributions to the State and Albuquerque. I am gratified that the institution is eager to participate with the State in solving this problem."[422]

UofA President Smith and Board Chair Killorin expressed a willingness to accept whatever recommendation came out of the task force, although Smith noted that any option that developed a community college independent of UofA would "put us out of business within three years ... because we can't compete with the public sector."[423]

T-VI Vice-President Louis Saavadra expressed concerns over ceding oversight of T-VI operations to UNM and/or the State. The Albuquerque Chamber of Commerce endorsed the version three proposal with members representing both UNM and T-VI opposing the proposal.[424] UofA President Smith remarked that turning the UofA into a community college would be "an interesting educational experience."[425]

A June 1977 survey of UofA students, faculty, administration, and staff revealed that only 52 percent of the students and 49 percent of the faculty, staff, and administration favored remaining a private institution, while the remainder preferred some form of public control. Also in June, the UofA Board seemed resigned to the inevitability of the absorption of the University into a proposed area community college. This feeling of inevitability was amplified by Smith's estimate that UofA would have to raise between $5 million and $8.7 million to continue as a private institution.[426]

In addition to the governor's task force, a subcommittee of the Albuquerque Chamber of Commerce had put together a group to study the community college issue. The group was chaired by former UofA president Joseph Zanetti. In October 1977, the committee presented what was characterized as a compromise proposal that attempted to take into account the concerns of all interested parties. Under this proposal, a community college organized under the T-VI statute would be phased in over five years. The new entity would purchase and use the existing UofA campus. Two-year programs at both T-VI and UofA would be continued, and four-year students at UofA would be "grandfathered in." A new Board of Directors would replace the current the UofA Board of Trustees and the T-VI board (which was also the APS Board of Education). There would be no oversight by or formal ties to UNM. Laurence Smith and James Killorin approved on behalf of UofA, but both UNM and the T-VI Board (with the single exception of Board President Lawrence German) opposed the proposal.[427]

In a letter to Governor Apodaca, Killorin said that both the Board and the Sisters agreed that the campus could be sold to the State for an amount not to exceed $8 million.[428]

The community college issue came to a head in 1978 when the State Legislature passed, and the Governor signed, House Bill 4, the Independent Community College Act. This provided for T-VI to expand its programs to become an independent community college, subject to the approval of the residents of the APS district. It also designated $4 million to purchase the UofA campus and $2 million for renovations.[429]

The issue was to go before Albuquerque voters in a special election on September 12, 1978. The resolution on the ballot read:

> It is proposed to expand the program of the Albuquerque Technical and Vocational Institute, composed of the Albuquerque Public School District, to include two years of college-level education, the Technical and Vocational Institute district thereby to become the Albuquerque Independent Community College district.

Shall a property tax be levied, not to exceed $4 per $1,000 of net taxable value for the support of the independent community college which will be in lieu of the levy for the operations of the Technical and Vocational Institute?[430]

In a pre-election brochure, T-VI Governing Board Chairman Lawrence German laid out the case for supporting the resolution, noting that the cost basis assured purchase of the UofA property. German and the others in favor of the resolution maintained that approval would not raise taxes, but would simply reapprove the tax rate already in place.

The election was an overwhelming defeat for the resolution with only one of the APS precincts (Corrales) voting in favor. Some members of the T-VI Governing Board, including Maureen Luna and Ted Martinez, who had opposed the resolution, said, "No one wanted to mess with the success of T-VI."[431] In the aftermath of the election, UofA Board president James Killorin said that the University which had been "in limbo because of the community college issue" was now "alive and well.... We intend to be as strong in the future as we have [been] in the past."[432]

For the time being, the issue of a community college in Albuquerque and the involvement of UofA became moot. However, the concerns that had surfaced during the 1970s remained—loss of financial support from the Sisters of St. Francis, increasing faculty costs, and ongoing maintenance and upkeep costs for an aging physical plant. In fact, Tim Keleher, attorney for the Sisters, later reported that as soon as the referendum had been defeated, the Sisters directed him to find a buyer for the school.[433]

The University of Albuquerque would struggle on, entering the 1980s with a new president, Laurence C. Smith, PhD, who was determined to bring the University back to health.

In 1986, the year that UofA closed for good, Albuquerque finally got its community college when the Legislature authorized T-VI to grant Associate degrees. It would be renamed Central New Mexico Community College in 2006 to better reflect the new mission.

8
Multiple Administrations

As the community college issue percolated in the background, life went on at the University. In March 1974, a dispute arose over Student Senate funds. Student Senate President Rudy Chavez said that $35,000 of student funds from 1973 were unaccounted for and that the records for that year could not be located. In addition, Chavez and others continued to voice their disappointment about the treatment of Mucio Yslas, whom they viewed as being passed over for the president's job when Zanetti was selected.[434]

The Student Senate financial issue came to a head when Chavez refused to disclose how $24,000 of 1974 student funds had been spent. The issue simmered for another month with letters passing back and forth between attorneys and the Board's establishment of an *ad hoc* committee to look into the issue. In early May, the committee announced that the monies in question had been satisfactorily accounted for. Chavez agreed but noted that he was considering a lawsuit because of accusations toward him of misappropriation of funds.[435]

In early 1974, some members of the Board attended a retreat with the Sisters at their motherhouse in Colorado Springs. One of the issues discussed was the school's Christian Commitment Statement. At a meeting of the Board's Executive Committee on March 27, Lawrence Desaulniers, former chair of the Faculty Senate and a member of the school's Christian Commitment committee tasked with reviewing the statement, reported that everyone at the retreat, including the Sisters, agreed that the word "Catholic" in the statement should be replaced with the word "Christian." Desaulniers noted, "We do not proselytize, but our programs are permeated with the values and ideals of ecumenical Christian humanism."[436]

The addition of the phrase "ecumenical Christian humanism," coupled with removal of the word "Catholic" shows a drift in the direction of religious humanism that would become much more evident as the school was forced to grapple with curriculum changes that focused on improving the financial situation at the school.

In March 1974, the Board was also told that the FY74 budget would be about $4.2 million but that the school might be back in the red with a deficit of between $200,000 and $300,000. The problem was a projected revenue shortfall of about 1.8 percent and expenses about nine percent above projected revenue.[437]

One of the big problems for the University, and everyone else in the country, was inflation. Inflation had begun to inch upward during the Nixon Administration, climbing above five percent during the early 1970s. Exacerbated by the 1973 Arab oil embargo and the 1979 Iranian Revolution, inflation rocketed to nearly 15 percent during the Ford and Carter administrations. This, combined with an effort to keep costs and fees down for the students, led to some very challenging times at UofA. In fact, inflation had caused operational costs to rise by between 25 and 30 percent.

In order to address the budget imbalance, the administration planned a 15 percent increase in tuition. This meant that a student taking 15 credit hours would pay $1,350 per term, which Academic Dean Andrew Imrik said was still below the average of $1,380 to $4,500 for other private institutions, some of which were "heavily endowed."[438]

Chief Financial Officer Gil Cordova gave a less-than-rosy report to the Faculty Senate in their February meeting:

> —A university the size of UofA should rely on tuition and fees for no more than 80 percent of its revenue, ideally 60 percent. UofA relied on tuition and fees for almost 90 percent.
> —The projected end-of-year deficit for FY74 would be about $150,000.
> —Monies were available from both national and local sources, but "we are just not getting it."
> —The school was making a staff reduction of about 30 individuals, 20 of whom would be by attrition, leaving about 10 layoffs.
> —There would have to be some cuts or consolidations in "non-productive" academic areas.

—President Zanetti was "away from the University most of the time" trying to raise money.[439]

Upon his return, Zanetti confirmed to the Board that tuition, which had not been raised for two years, accounted for about 90 percent of the school's revenue, about 15 percent above the national average and that, while enrollment was up to about 2,900, many of the students were not full-time.[440] Student Senate President Rudy Chavez said that, while he recognized the need for more revenue, he worried that an increase in tuition would, in the end, cause a drop in enrollment. Despite Chavez's concerns, the Board voted to raise tuition from $39 to $45 per semester-hour.[441]

Also in February, the school published guidelines for scholarships and financial aid. Under these new guidelines, students receiving financial aid had to meet four criteria:

—A minimum GPA of 3.2.
—A minimum ACT score of 25.
—Demonstrated financial need.
—Maintaining a full academic load on a degree-status trajectory.

Assuming that the student met these criteria, the minimum suggested awards were:

—Freshman: $200 per semester.
—Sophomores: $250 per semester.
—Juniors: $350 per semester.
—Seniors: $400 per semester.
—In all cases, the total award could range up to a full-tuition scholarship.[442]

By November, Board Chairman Ray Powell said that the deficit would be about $350,000, which he said would be made up from bond revenues from the Sisters. He noted that, despite the tuition hike, enrollment was up 4.2 percent.[443]

While money woes continued to be front-burner issues for administrators, the University's academic programs flourished. An $85,000 follow-on grant from the National Institutes of Health (NIH) supplemented a previous $55,000 grant for the school's biology department. The purpose of these funds was to "stimulate minority interest in obtaining graduate degrees in the natural and behavioral sciences through their involvement in research projects." In this case, two particular projects were supported. The first, led by Dr. Charles Pfeiffer, was to study the effects of colchicine, a plant-based drug that had been used to treat gout since the first century AD, on kidney function. The second, under the direction of Professor Elise Schoenfeld, was to "evaluate the microecology of water supplies and soil drainage in parts of Albuquerque and New Mexico where intestinal upsets have been recorded."[444] In addition to these scientific accomplishments, the long-standing work of the music, art, and drama departments continued with concerts, plays, and exhibitions offered both on campus and in the community.

In 1974, Zanetti appointed Miguel Encinias to be the coordinator of the Multi-Cultural Enrichment Program (MEP). This new initiative was designed to help in developing bilingual and multi-cultural programs throughout the University.[445] The program was an extension of an interim program that began in the 1960s as a multi-cultural seminar held between the winter and spring terms. The seminar held in 1970 was entitled "The Southwest—Prejudice, Progress, Potential."[446] The program would eventually grow into a significant endeavor with a teacher-training component to "train elementary and secondary school teachers in bilingual and bi-cultural education."[447] In 1977, Encinias would characterize the purpose of the program, now renamed the Multicultural Education Program:

> In the United States, the dominant culture is, of course, the Anglo culture. Our job in the MEP is to create an atmosphere that supports Hispanic and Native American cultures. We are, in effect, a microcosm of the University. Without the strong cultural support and atmosphere we provide, the program would be essentially meaningless.[448]

In January 1974, Zanetti announced his plans to bring the operating budget back into the black. He started out by saying that the rumors that the school was in "a desperate situation" were simply not true. However, he did propose several "belt-tightening" moves. Initially, he appointed

Gil Cordova, on loan from the Energy Research and Development Administration (ERDA) and currently the UofA business manager, as University Provost. In that role, Cordova would be responsible for the day-to-day administrative and academic functions of the school, freeing the president to focus on "institutional development and fund raising."[449]

Gil Cordova.
(Sandia National Laboratories)

Second, three dedicated administrative positions—Coordinator of Federal Programs, Director of Community Relations, and Director of Alumni Affairs—would be eliminated with their responsibilities being assumed by other administrators. In addition, the responsibilities of the Administrative Vice President were being absorbed into other departments. None of the individuals holding the eliminated positions would be fired, although Mucio Yslas, the unsuccessful presidential candidate with strong support from the school's Chicano students in 1973, was one of the individuals affected. Third, travel and supply expenditures were severely reduced.

The estimated budget savings, in total, were $225,000. Zanetti summed up his proposals by saying:

We are not cutting back programs but, like every other educational institution and every other business, we must live within our means. There are two ways to do this—cut back and develop new revenue. We are determined to have at least a break-even year by cutting expenses and by freeing the president to do resource and institutional development work.[450]

In a later memoir, Michael Keleher recalled that Zanetti had had little administrative experience and had failed to prepare a budget. His business manager, John Merritt, was outspoken about this issue and was terminated. Merritt subsequently moved to UNM, where he was successful.[451]

In March, the Board was told that the operating deficit would be around $284,000. Given a $129,000 surplus from the previous year, this would put the University $155,000 in the red.[452] Provost Cordova said that because of inflation (estimated at six percent), debt service of $139,000, and required matching funds for a federal grant of $49,000, the University would need $420,000 more for 1975. Cordova repeated that 94 percent of the school's revenue came from tuition, room, board, books, and fees, and Zanetti reported that he expected $190,000 in increased federal funds in 1975–1976.

On April 21, 1974, Zanetti announced his resignation as president of the University.[453] To dispel rumors, he stated that he had not been asked to resign and that the financial deficit "certainly did not cause his decision." In fact, he said that the financial situation is "looking brighter every day," and that his new position as Director of Area Development for Public Service Company of New Mexico (PNM) presented "a career opportunity in an emerging field in a dynamic company." He characterized his time at UofA as "in many ways richly rewarding" and agreed to say on as a member of the Board.[454] Provost Gil Cordova was designated as acting president and the Board established a presidential search committee chaired by James Killorin.[455]

In a marathon board meeting on May 19, the Board elected Killorin as Chairman to replace Ray Powell who was retiring. They also approved another tuition increase, raising the cost per credit-hour to $48. Cordova said that this increase would raise $165,000, based on an estimated 55,000 credit-hours. Cordova also reported that the financial picture was improving in that income was now exceeding expenditures. He said that the deficit would be about $225,000 instead of $284,000 and that a short-term loan of about $100,000 would keep the school afloat until tuition was paid in the fall.

Student body president Erma Brunswick objected strongly to the tuition hike, noting that statements had been made in March that promised no tuition increase and that this represented a 25 percent increase in the tuition during the 1973–1974 school year. She said that students "see no improvement in the quality of education from the last tuition increase and that many will transfer to the University of New Mexico because of the increase."[456]

A faculty salary increase of 7.1 percent was also announced at the May meeting, as was a "low-key" community fund drive targeted at raising between $500,000 and $1 million. These new funds would be designed to "improve services," not to "save the University."[457]

In the early summer, Board president Killorin wrote a letter to the Sisters asking for their input on the future of the school. Sister Eileen responded in early July. In her letter, she made several points. First, she noted that the Sisters desired that the University continue its present direction of offering four-year degree programs and two-year programs to meet vocational needs. However, she also pointed out that the Order could no longer afford to finance the school as it had in the past. She went on to say that the Sisters "were satisfied with the administration of Frank Kleinhenz" but were aware of the "problems and disappointments" over the past two years.[458]

Killorin said that the Sisters' reply to his query was what the trustees needed in order to plan for the future. He said that the Sisters had loaned the school $400,000 during the winter of 1974–1975, but that the school appeared to be getting its financial house in order to match revenue with expenses and pay back its various debt obligations. One small effort in the fund-raising direction was the institution of the first alumni newsletter, *Signum*, in January 1975. It was hoped that regular communication with alumni might help bring in more dollars.

In July 1974, the UofA branch in Belen appeared to be on its last legs. Although there were 150 students at the branch, the main administration was concerned that they could not maintain the accreditation of the branch to the standards of the North Central accrediting association. In addition, the lease on the property in the Rio Communities shopping center had only nine months left, and it was unclear where the branch would hold its classes. The Belen Public Schools had expressed a willingness to hold classes in one of their schools, but the decision had not been finalized. Unable to solve these problems satisfactorily, the Belen branch was forced to close in 1975.[459] Meanwhile, evening and extension classes at the other branches seemed to be moving along more comfortably.[460] In fact, instructors at other extension colleges on Kirtland Air Force Base consistently remarked about the success of the UofA "campus."[461]

There was some unrest in the student body during the summer and fall of 1975. A group of African-American students alleged that federal monies for multi-cultural programs had been diverted to Spanish-English bilingual programs with no support for the black students' needs. James Lewis, a black curriculum specialist at UofA, said, "We're sitting on top of TNT at the University of Albuquerque." He said that the black students wanted a whole program of courses lasting a year or 18 months, but UofA had limited it to two courses. The UofA Native American coordinator, Carlotta Concha, asked the Board to look into "allegations and discrepancies" related to alleged misuse of funds and discrimination against both blacks and Native Americans.[462] Black program coordinator Steve Tillet and counselor Joe Hill alleged discrimination in hiring practices and even suggested that the Board might be using "budget woes" as an excuse to eliminate certain positions.[463] Later on, Theresa Carson, an African-American undergraduate, would recall that the school "wasn't as diverse as she would have liked." She noted that she was often the only black student in her classes. However, she did point out that that was not unusual for the time.[464]

The issue of African-American representation on faculty and staff had been discussed by the President's Executive Council a year earlier. President Zanetti had acknowledged the problem, but pointed out that because of the number of tenured professors and the financial constraints on the faculty salary budget, there was very little opportunity to make room for new professors.[465]

The administration also noted that the school's affirmative action programs had been in place for several years. The program was designed for sequential implementation with the Native American portion already started and development of the black program being started by James Lewis. Cordova also pointed out that the original grant amount had been substantially reduced, thus causing a delay in total implementation of the program.[466]

Despite these assurances, Steve Tillet said that nothing had been resolved, and that Bob Jones, legal advisor to the Albuquerque chapter of the National Association for the Advancement of Colored People (NAACP), was evaluating the school's affirmative action program.[467] Tillet also wrote a letter to the school administration asking why no action had been taken and asserting that the school's program did not meet federal guidelines.[468]

The student body was not just concerned about the black studies program. Members from the off-campus sites, led by Rafael Padilla, challenged the recent student body presidential election which had elected Michael Topp. The protestors said that the election procedures did not follow the requirements of the Student Senate Constitution in that the duration of the election was too short and that only on-campus students were allowed to vote, thus disenfranchising a large segment of the student body.[469] The students solicited an opinion from school attorney Michael Keleher, who supported their position.[470] The Board agreed and rescheduled the presidential election.[471]

In a September meeting, the Board adopted an "austere" budget of $5.3 million, hoping to "erase" the $131,000 deficit from the previous year. This budget raised tuition to $48 per credit-hour, but assumed no growth in enrollment. However, Cordova noted that the school had a "rather healthy cash flow position," since projected enrollment was up five percent and projected credit-hours were up six percent. He also said that only about seven percent of the budget was "not fixed" and the only real opportunity for additional savings was in "controllable expenditures" like travel, supplies, and equipment. He said that 92 applications for the vacant presidency had been received.[472]

In its December meeting, the administration reported that the school would end the calendar year with a balanced budget and a cash balance of about $200,000. Their only major debt was the $400,000 owed to the Sisters. Despite the improvement, the Board voted to initiate the fund-raising program and invited input from Ward Dreshman, a professional fund-raising company. Dreshman suggested an initial goal of $2 million.[473]

In light of the improved financial situation, Cordova made an inquiry to APS about the possibility of purchasing the James Monroe

Middle School, which had been for sale since 1974, as a potential Northeast Heights branch location. However, the deal was not pursued beyond the talking stage because of ensuing financial issues.[474] Heights extension and evening classes continued to be held at the St. Pius X campus at Louisiana and Indian School.

On May 20, 1976, 55-year-old Laurence C. Smith, PhD, was selected as the fifth president of the University of Albuquerque.[475] His salary was $35,000 plus a $2,500 expense account.[476] Smith's previous job was as president of Westmar College, a private four-year liberal arts college in Le Mars, Iowa. Smith had an impressive resume with a Master's and Doctorate from the University of Nebraska. He had served as Academic Dean at William Woods College in Fulton, Missouri, and as Associate Professor of Philosophy at Texas Christian University in Fort Worth, Texas. He had also published more than 100 works of poetry and light verse. Perhaps the most important consideration in the selection of Smith, however, was his demonstrated fund-raising track record.[477]

In his statement to the Board, Smith said, "Probably my major accomplishment has been establishing and maintaining a good system of budget control and a basis for planning that has permitted program change, even with scarce finances."[478]

Even with a balanced budget, Smith faced an uphill challenge. The school still had major debt and, with no endowment, was forced to deal with finances on a day-to-day, cash-flow basis. Over 90 percent of the revenue still came from tuition and fees, and the uncertainties over the past years weighed heavily on the minds of prospective donors. In a July meeting of the Board of Trustees, it was noted that the enrollment figures could be misleading in terms of tuition because many of the students were part-time. The real metric was credit-hours, not head count.[479]

However, there was a general sense that the worst was now behind them. In a July op-ed entitled "A Model of Frugality" the *Albuquerque Journal* editors said:

> Continued improvement in the fiscal well-being of the University of Albuquerque, which only a few years ago was faced with the prospects of bankruptcy and closure, demonstrates what can be achieved, even in an inflationary era, through concerted

planning.... The University's dramatic turnabout was not achieved without pain, but it was much less painful than the end-of-the-road alternative. The pay-as-you-go approach was initiated during the administration of former President Frank Kleinhenz. Substantial numbers of faculty members, some with long tenure, were terminated, and a wide range of fringe-type academic programs was stripped from the curriculum, a successful intercollegiate athletic program was scrapped, without deemphasis of a well-rounded program of physical education. Meticulous attention was directed to preserving the high quality of surviving academic disciplines.[480]

Laurence C. Smith, PhD.
(Westmar Alumni and Friends Association newsletter, Vol. 7, No. 2, May 2005)

The unique and successful aerospace curriculum, directed by Dan Reece, was substantially enhanced in the fall of 1976 with the addition of several new courses. These included aviation physiology, aviation law, airport planning and design, and a private pilot ground school. The program also had new courses in hot-air ballooning and soaring.[481]

Another highly successful program was the Adult Education Program led by Martha Young, PhD. Started in 1973, the program had grown from an enrollment of 23 to an enrollment of 457. Aimed at students 25 years of age or older, the program offered a Bachelor's degree on a time-shortened basis. Sixty-eight percent of the students were seeking a degree in business administration. The program recognized that adult education "must be integrated with other pursuits of living—a family, career, leisure time, and civic activities." Therefore, programs were offered in the evenings at a location closer to the students' work locations.[482]

A demographic survey in the Fall of 1976 showed 1,358 full-time students and 1,776 part-time students with an average age of 29.5. Forty-one percent were classified as minority (29 percent Spanish-surnamed, 6 percent Native American, 5 percent African American, and 1 percent Asian). Seventy-five percent of the students were on financial aid, and 80 percent of the male students were veterans.[483]

1976 Advertisement from the *Albuquerque Journal*.
(*Albuquerque Journal*, 7/7/76, p. 2)

Unfortunately, the financial picture "clouded over" in November and December 1976. In November, a cash flow statement was released to the faculty. It noted:

—The year had started with a cumulative deficit of $181,000
—Tuition revenue was down by $82,000 from the initial projections.
—Projected revenues were $464,000, projected expenditures were $675,000, leaving a shortfall of $212,000.

The financial analyst recommended that the Board authorize a short-term loan of $100,000 to cover the expected pre-registration shortfall in December. The analyst also projected an end-of-fiscal-year deficit between $100,000 and $250,000.[484]

Smith reported that the previously reported finances were not accurate and that the books had been "out-of-balance" for several months.[485] He also said that the projected surplus would not be reached and the University would "just break even." Costs for administration had increased 12 percent; general operating costs had increased 22 percent; costs for the physical plant had increased 26 percent; and instructional costs had increased 17 percent. These costs were significantly above the current inflation rate of 6.5 percent. As an example of the problem, he pointed out that salaries were running $13,000 more than projected.[486]

Smith further pointed out that "fund raising is a duty of boards of private institutions," and he said that he expected them to participate and "make donations themselves." His report outlined the roller-coaster history of the school's finances for the last decade:

—Beginning in 1966, there were three successive years of financial difficulty that left the University with a cumulative debt of $800,000.
—In 1970, strict financial controls were instituted, and the Sisters forgave $750,000 of the debt.
—By the end of the 72–73 school years, the school had accumulated substantial cash reserves.
—By the end of calendar year 1973, the operating deficit was $400,000.[487]

In January 1977, the University released a self-assessment report as a part of the application for reaccreditation by the North Central Association of Colleges and Secondary Schools. In the conclusion of the report, the authors attempted to itemize the struggles of the University over the past few years:

—There seemed to be no clear, consistent vision for the University—some saw it as a liberal arts college with the vocational and special programs as ancillary, while others saw it as a community service institution that should respond to the needs of the community, even at the expense of reduction in the liberal arts.
—There did not seem to be clear logic as to why donors should contribute money.
—There seemed to be no clear reason for assigning priorities in resource allocation and setting up criteria for the selection, retention, and promotion of faculty.
—Because of the apparent lack of direction, factions had developed within the student body, the faculty, and the administration.
—The rapid turnover of presidents had left the faculty unsettled and suspicious of the administration.
—The student body was older (mean age in 1976 was between 27 and 35), relatively inflexible in their attitudes, did not look up to faculty in general, and seemed to project an extreme pragmatic attitude and lack of interest in liberal learning in the traditional sense.[488]

In order to understand the struggles and prioritize solutions, a detailed mission statement was provided:

The University of Albuquerque is a medium-sized, independent, and nonsectarian urban college with a Christian heritage, whose primary orientation is toward excellence in undergraduate teaching. The University itself intends to be a model of Christian humanism and the competencies it endeavors to foster in its students.... The University is constituted essentially to serve the people of New Mexico, but particularly those who are educationally and economically disadvantaged, those whose educational needs are unmet, and those with a strong cross-cultural or career-vocational orientation.... The University offers a program which preserves, fosters, and transmits the Judeo-Christian heritage mirrored in the traditional liberal arts refined for the human conditions and needs of the day. The liberal arts serve as majors, and are also the foundation and buttress of all programs. The University provides alternative and non-traditional programs to meet the ever-changing educational needs of the people. The University intends that all of its programs foster a high level of excellence in humanistic intellectual growth and in fundamental and specialized competencies.[489]

The report ended on a somewhat optimistic note,

President Smith has come to the University of Albuquerque with eight years of highly successful presidential experience, particularly in the areas of finances, the Board, faculty, and fund-raising. He has entered upon his tenure with full and warm acceptance from faculty, students, and administration.... This level of acceptance is due both to the comprehensive and open selection procedure and to the high degree of knowledge, competence, and leadership which he has brought to the University. These very qualities are seen as the most direct and appropriate response to the principal difficulties that have, and continue to, beset the University.[490]

In February 1977, Smith reported that the deficit would be $402,000 by the end of June. This was a combination of a $203,000 operating deficit for 1977 and a carry-over deficit of almost $200,000 from past years. He said that the school would have to borrow $40,000 to meet the April payroll and an additional $279,000 to meet the payroll for May. He reiterated his insistence that the Board "must launch a program to raise another $100,000 to erase the current year's deficit."[491]

Between February and May, the Board struggled to work out a budget for the 1977–1978 school year. Smith and the Board agreed on several underlying assumptions:

—Semester hours were expected to decline five percent to about 50,000.

—General inflation would be about six percent, although inflation in utility costs could be as high as 20 percent.
—The faculty was expecting a cost-of-living wage increase of six percent to match inflation.
—The assumption of gift income of $150,000 was evaluated as "high."

Four choices for dealing with this situation were suggested

1. Raise tuition by more than $3.00 per semester-hour.
2. Increase the fund-raising goal.
3. Review staff and programs to balance the budget with a tuition increase of only $3.00 per semester hour.
4. Review staff and program costs to balance the budget without any tuition increase.[492]

Each of the choices had downsides, However, by May, when the Board approved a $4.2 million budget for the 1977–1978 school year, the projected 1977 deficit had shrunk from $375,000 to $107,000, and Smith proposed some significant budget-cutting measures to bring the budget into balance. These included:

—Putting wage and salary increases in abeyance for the time being.
—Reducing some faculty and staff.
—Adjusting some curriculum, in particular,
- The number of section/classes of some subjects such as Math 100, Theology, and Adult Education would be reduced.
- The frequency of course offerings would be reduced for classes such as U.S. Government, Math 301, and Education 320.
- Classes with insufficient enrollment, for example German and French, would be discontinued.
- Some very expensive courses such as General Physics and Quantitative Analysis would be eliminated.[493]

Some members of the faculty objected to what they saw as inconsistent elimination and reduction of classes and of eliminating or reducing classes based on the income they generated. In response, President Smith said, "Some things should be kept, regardless of cost. A university is a combination of departments that make money and those that do not. Cost accounting is only part of the decision."[494] He also noted that the chair of the accreditation team had observed that "the number of small courses [at UofA] is a luxury that not even Harvard could afford."[495]

The financial situation at the school may have improved slightly, but there were still significant impacts. For example, the library reported, "The financial problems of the University have been reflected in the level of service offered by the library during the year ... fulfilling many of 1976–1977 objectives has been impossible."[496]

In April, in an effort to help the less-than-rosy financial picture and to increase the Native American outreach, the Faculty Senate approved a proposal to initiate a consortium with the Southwest Indian Polytechnic Institute (SIPI). Under the agreement SIPI students would be able to obtain an Associates of Applied Science degree through UofA in one of six disciplines: Civil Engineering, Electronics Technology, Drafting Technology, Food Service Technology, Graphic Arts Technology, or Optical Technology. SIPI students would have to meet some basic core UofA requirements but could go on to obtain a higher degree if desired.[497]

In May 1977, another survey was taken of the students, faculty, and staff to help decide on future options. The student survey noted that the median age was 27, with 42 percent female and 58 percent male. Forty-seven percent of the students were married; forty-five percent were employed full-time; and 24 percent were employed part-time. Fifty-eight percent were Anglo, 29 percent were Mexican-American, and five percent were "American Indian." Eighty-six percent were from New Mexico with 77 percent from Albuquerque. Eighty-nine percent were pursuing a degree, 55 percent during the day and 45 percent in evening classes. Sixty-nine percent were on some form of financial aid.

When asked why they chose UofA, 29 percent said they came because of the size of the school; 16 percent noted the program flexibility; and 15 percent appreciated the unique programs. The most popular courses noted were Business Administration (26 percent), Criminology (14 percent), and Nursing/Health Sciences (eight percent).

When faculty and staff were asked why they chose UofA, 14 percent noted the types of programs; 11 percent noted the Christian orientation; but, in what must have been a bit disturbing to the administration, 12 percent said that they chose UofA because they couldn't find a job elsewhere.[498]

While there were many similarities with the 1973 survey, the mean age of the student body was slightly lower, the percentage of married students had decreased from 53 percent to 47 percent, and the percentage of minority students had increased by almost 10 percent, from 34 percent to 43 percent. This minority statistic carried with it an increasing challenge for financial stability.

The survey also examined the sense of the student body and the staff as to remaining private or becoming a public institution. Fifty-two percent of the students preferred that the school remain private, but the faculty and administration was evenly split with 44 percent favoring remaining private and 42 percent favoring the public option. Seventy-four percent of the students were against turning the University into a community college, and 64 percent said that they would leave the school if that were to happen. These statistics supported the earlier estimates that the conversion of UofA into a community college would eventually kill the University.

The North Central accreditation organization revisited the school in the spring of 1977, the five-year interval having been dictated by the issues which had arisen in 1972. They reported that there were several improvements, most notably in the faculty and administrative commitment to the school. They noted the new president and saw dramatic improvements in the library and the science research program. They also noted that faculty salaries were low and that there needed to be improvements in academic leadership, recruiting, and the liberal arts curriculum.[499]

Smith, the Board, and the Sisters had all endorsed the idea of turning the University into a public institution. However, Smith realized that there continued to be a strong possibility that the University would remain private. In June 1977, he wrote a thought paper entitled "A Plan to Remain Private." In that piece he noted, "A decision to maintain and develop UofA as a private institution is essentially a financial one .... The academic mission of the University has been set and there is great satisfaction with it."

In order to reach financial stability, Smith identified three requirements:

> —The school would need to develop a sustaining fund that relieved the budget pressure on tuition and federal grants. In this regard, he noted that no private liberal arts colleges had ever successfully funded themselves out of tuition and fees alone.
> —The school would need a program of debt reduction. The current long-term debt was about $3 million, necessitating annual payments of $320,000.
> —The school would need a funding program to provide for the transfer of the campus to an independent Board of Trustees to relieve the Sisters of their responsibility for the institution.[500]

In a letter to the Sisters, representatives of the Faculty Senate strongly encouraged a sale to the Board. The Senate

> ...recognizes their [the Sisters'] concern that the school is no longer the Catholic school that it once was and, therefore, not related to their mission.... However, it is still, as it has been all these years, intrinsically Catholic.... In fact, the Christian values on which the school was founded are so deeply ingrained that a change of ownership would not erase them.[501]

The financial problem was exacerbated by a drop in the total credit-hours taken by UofA students. In the absence of an endowment or a significant donor program, the principal source of revenue for the school remained tuition. In September 1977, Academic Dean J. Peter Carey announced that the school had experienced a seven percent decrease in total credit hours, due mostly to an 89 percent decrease in the enrollment in the off-campus air traffic control program.[502]

In addition to the reduction in enrollment, there was a major issue with respect to registration for the fall semester. The registrar and several other key people in the registrar's office had resigned. In fact, the most experienced individual left in the office was a person with just six months of clerical experience. This resulted in a very challenging registration process. Smith reported that a new Registrar with considerable experience had been hired and would start on October 1. Smith felt confident that the new person would be able to straighten out the problems that had occurred during the fall and that registration for the spring term would proceed smoothly.[503]

A strong vote of support and confidence came from the community of veterans who were students at the University. Vietnam veteran Dan Kenney, speaking on behalf of the military fraternity, Chi Gamma Iota, a campus fixture since 1967, said that Albuquerque needed to have a four-year private institution as an alternative to the University of New Mexico. He said that the business community and civic groups should support the University. He also criticized the Archbishop saying, "The Archbishop should become more involved, even though he is very busy. He could put out just one letter and get some help." Kenney's criticism extended to the entire local Catholic community, "I think it is a crying shame the Catholic church can't drum up support among its own people, perhaps through separate collections, bake sales, and other fund-raising activities."[504]

Kenney's assertion that local Catholic authorities should subsidize the University, was later demonstrated as moot in an op-ed in 1986. *Albuquerque Journal* writer Mary Engel noted that only 14 of the nation's 235 Catholic colleges received financial assistance from their local archdiocese and that, in most cases, this support was minimal.[505]

University Public Relations Director Sarah Hogg noted that the University, though once "Catholic-oriented, now considered itself to be a "Christian," rather than a Catholic, university. She also said that over 5,000 letters had been sent out to private donors.[506]

9
Out of the Frying Pan and into the Fire (again)

With the community college issue apparently settled and a new president on board, UofA tried to paint a rosy picture of the situation. The University posted a number of advertisements in local papers touting its courses. The ads started with the slogan "We're looking ahead. Are you?"

Advertisement from the *Albuquerque Journal*.
(*Albuquerque Journal*, 10/8/78, p. 18)

They then noted "in the past few weeks, many people have asked us 'What is the future of the University of Albuquerque'" Their response was

—The University will continue as a private university. The UofA will maintain its sensitivity to the educational needs of the community by offering:
- A traditional day academic program.
- A unique evening degree-granting program.
- Classes at sites convenient for Albuquerque residents.
- A time-shortened degree program for adults over 25.
- Educational alternatives you won't find at other schools.[507]

However, problems lurked beneath the veneer of health, prosperity, and plans for a bright future.

The school's financial woes were illustrated in President Smith's report to the Board at its April 1978 meeting:

As a matter of actual operation, we were able to "get by" with only borrowing $75,000 from the Sisters of St. Francis and $30,000 internally. We were able to postpone payments to Saga Foods, Inc. in the amount of $25,452, to the IRS in the amount of $19,798, and to the Employment Security Commission in the amount of $2,000 .... While we have operated on our budget very closely, no reduction in the prior year fund balance deficit has been made.... The projected deficit for the current year of $16,702 has to be added to the fund balance deficit of $369,000 to give a potential total for our projected cash flow shortage.[508]

The Provincial Council of the Sisters of St. Francis had begun to withdraw from active management of the school as early as 1966, and they had long tired of the chronic roller-coaster financial situation and emotional burden of administrative issues that seemed to plague the school. It was clear to the Board, Laurence Smith, and much of the administration that the Sisters were more and more anxious to divest themselves of the school. In October 1978, Sister Eileen told

President Smith that the Sisters "had become exhausted after two years of mounting financial pressure" and intended to close the school in December 1979.[509] This was followed by a news release from the motherhouse which outlined their problem:

> The Sisters are no longer in a position to support the financial requirements of the University and, just as importantly, we find ourselves almost totally separated from our religious mission as it relates to the University.... The Board of Trustees was able to improve the financial situation by adding academic programs that were more income-producing. This resulted in changing the direction of the college from liberal arts to a high percent of offerings that were career-oriented classes. However, these changes in our academic offerings, to ease our financial problems, were accomplished at the cost of departing further and further from our religious mission of providing education in a Catholic environment.

The press release went on to state:

> In addition to this widening breach between our academic programs and our religious mission, there is still another factor which influences our decisions.... Our interests have been redirected more to the care of the aged, both in ambulatory and skilled facilities, and elementary education rather than higher education.[510]

The Sisters position was clarified by their attorney, Tim Keleher, in a letter to the school's attorney Mike Keleher (Tim Keleher's cousin) in September 1978:

> The Sisters are looking into an expansion of St. Francis Gardens ... also an application for a housing project for the elderly ... some problems in Nebraska. What I am trying to say is that the UofA is one of many institutions that require some deep study, but the Sisters must look at the overall picture and not just one segment.[511]

Mike Keleher wrote a letter to Sister Eileen voicing strong protest that the decision to close the school in 1979 had been made without any involvement of the Board. He concluded the letter by saying, "I hope the decision is not a final one."[512]

The Faculty Senate had become extremely frustrated with the Sisters approach to divestiture and their apparent unwillingness to involve key players such as the faculty in these momentous decisions. In late October, Julius "Jack" Cranston, Chair of the Faculty Senate, wrote a scathing letter to Sister Eileen:

> Sister Eileen—I find it incredible—absolutely incomprehensible—that you would deliberately and unnecessarily destroy something of great value. This school is surely something of great value, something precious.... The school, as a private Christian college, has a uniquely important value to this community and to society in general.... I am trying to understand why you have decided to extinguish this college.... If the University were facing bankruptcy or some equivalent financial disaster, then I could understand ... but the University of Albuquerque is not facing imminent financial crisis.... Since the defeat of the community college referendum, there has been a mood of cautious optimism among the faculty and staff ... we believe that we can establish a financial stability which will complement and support our continuing academic successes.... However, we need some time and we need your cooperation.[513]

In November, in another letter from Killorin to Sister Van Ackeren, the Board formally transferred to the Sisters their request to be considered as a future owner of the school.[514]

In December 1978, the fact came to light that the Sisters had solicited offers to sell the school and had received proposals from the Government of Iran, the Archdiocese of Santa Fe, and an unidentified party willing to pay $13 million and retrain the current employees. The Sisters considered that none of these were desirable or feasible.[515] The Sisters were also negotiating with Parks College in Denver to purchase the University.

Jim Killorin said that the Board was in agreement of the need to "relieve the Sisters of their financial responsibility," although they did not yet know exactly how that was to be accomplished. One approach under serious consideration was the sale of two parcels of land—the so-called south campus, which was no longer used, and the sale of the 40-acre parcel of land just north of the campus. With regard to the Sisters' discussions on sale to another entity, the Board noted in a December 28 letter that, of all the solutions presently under consideration, the Parks College alternative appeared the most favorable.[516]

Parks College, Inc. was a private, Denver-based organization with branch colleges in seven states, including one in Albuquerque. These colleges offered business administration degrees as well as courses of study in environmental and health sciences. Initially, Joe Lee, President of Parks, had said that it was highly questionable that Parks would buy the UofA because they would not need a facility the size of the University. However, as negotiations proceeded, his opinion would evolve.[517]

Joe Lee. (www.legacy.com)

In his letter, Killorin noted that the Board favored the Parks alternative, subject to three assurances:

—That the faculty, staff, and employees be given one-year

termination notices.

—That the purchaser ensures that students currently enrolled, especially those making "suitable academic progress," be allowed to complete their degrees.

—That the Sisters assure the students by January 9, 1979, that current programs would continue at least through the spring of 1980.[518]

Killorin further stated:

While the purchase proposal projects continuation of all programs for at least one year after change of ownership, we need assurance that programs will not be interrupted during the negotiation and transition period.

To provide a further alternative should the negotiations with Parks College fall through, the Board reminded the Sisters of its own proposal to take ownership of the University.[519] The Faculty Senate weighed in in October 1978, urging the Sisters to consider the Board's offer and asking for their careful consideration of the sale of the school:

We understand and deeply sympathize with your desire to divest yourselves of financial responsibility for the school. However, we urge you to do so in such a way that the good work begun and carried on here by you for so many years can continue.[520]

The Faculty Senate also requested to be a part of the discussions on the disposition of the school:

The crucial importance of current negotiations on the future of the University of Albuquerque is of such vital concern to the faculty that a representative of the Faculty should be present at any and all future negotiations dealing with the disposition of the University.[521]

Tim Keleher, the attorney for the Sisters, negotiated with the various parties through the end of 1978. He characterized the discussions as those between "a willing buyer and a willing seller." He noted that no dollar amount had been established. One of the issues affecting the price was potential enrollment for the spring 1979 semester. If enrollment exceeded 3,000, the dollar amount offered would increase; if below 3,000, it would decrease.[522]

In early March, Killorin asked for a meeting with the Sisters to discuss the status of the negotiations. Faculty spokesman Warren Lee said that the Board should, "take responsibility and whatever action to see that no future harm comes to the UofA. We are asking the Board to notify the Sisters that the Board itself is the legal owner of the college."[523]

Although Lee was wrong about the legal ownership, the concerns of the faculty were clearly expressed. In fact, both the Board and a consortium of the faculty, staff, and administration had provided separate offers to purchase the school. The faculty proposal included:

—Assumption of an existing debt of approximately $3.5 million.
—Retention by the Sisters of ownership of the south campus (valued at approximately $1 million).
—Retention by the purchasers of the 40-acre north campus for future growth.
—Installment payments by the purchasers to the Sisters over a ten-year period.
—Being a part of the purchasing community would be a condition of employment.[524]

It was estimated that the Sisters would receive about $7.5 million under the faculty proposal. The proposal by the Board was very similar except that it contained a lease-back arrangement for the property, and the Sisters would realize about $6.8 million plus the cost of debt service.[525]

Killorin also expressed a desire for the Sisters to seriously consider the offer of both the Board and Archbishop Robert Sanchez, on behalf of the Archdiocese of Santa Fe, to take over management of the school. However, Sanchez made it clear that he would not purchase the school with the purpose of having it continue as a University.[526]

Robert F. Sanchez, Tenth Archbishop of Santa Fe.
(collection of the Archdiocese of Santa Fe)

President Smith reported that the Sisters had taken positive steps toward divestiture and that the future of the school was now in the hands of the faculty and the staff.[527] There was significant pushback by the students and faculty requesting that the Sisters reconsider their decision and expressing a strong preference for the Board to take over the school rather than for Parks to assume responsibility.[528]

Board chair Killorin also weighed in. In a letter to both Sister Eileen and the Sisters' Provincial Council he requested that "in the spirit of working together" the Board be involved in any divesture/continuation decisions. He also pointed out that all but two members of the Faculty Senate preferred the alternative of having the Board purchase the school.

In addition, the Faculty Senate had expressed a willingness to defer 10 percent of their salary to support the Board's purchase proposal.[529]

Although the Board had recommended to the Sisters that Laurence Smith be retained as president after any sale, Smith had seen the writing on the wall and had begun to look for alternative employment opportunities as early as October 1978.[530]

In a flurry of correspondence between the Board and the Sisters in January and early February 1979, several concerns were expressed. Cranston said that the failure of the Sisters to confirm in writing their assurances to keep the school open was hurting spring enrollment.[531] Sister Eileen responded that Cranston's concern simply reflected a "missed communication," but she noted that:

> You, as well as others, must realize that divestiture of a facility such as the University of Albuquerque cannot be accomplished in a short period of time, nor without pain and heartbreak for anyone deeply concerned.[532]

Cranston pushed back again in an early February letter, and the Faculty Senate sent a telegram to Sister Eileen "urgently requesting that you do not, repeat do not, ask for the resignation of Dr. Smith."[533]

In an early February 1979 interview with the *Albuquerque Journal*, Smith noted:

> Our students are extremely frustrated. We felt the failure of the Sisters to give assurances hurt registration for the last semester. We had projected our enrollment would be down 10 percent but it is down 20 percent.[534]

He continued that the Sisters "had not discussed their decision to sell the school with either the President or the Board of Trustees prior to announcing it publicly." He further observed that the Sisters had not even considered the Board's own proposal to take over the school. Smith said that the school had been prepared to start 1979 with a balanced budget, but because of the publicly-discussed uncertainties, enrollment would be down and faculty, employees, and staff were seeking other opportunities.

Tim Keleher was incensed by Smith's public statements and proposed to his clients that Smith should step down:

> If Dr. Smith is not happy with the UofA, he should resign instead of accepting a paycheck and eating our bread. Dr. Smith will offer, as far as I am concerned, his resignation, or I will recommend that he be terminated.[535]

Smith fired back, "I was hired by the Board of Trustees, and I would assume that if resignation was required, it would come from the Board." The faculty also fired back saying that Keleher was autocratic:

> Are we to assume that Keleher is suggesting that when one believes that matters are being handled incorrectly or unjustly, that one should resign, quit, or give up? Then certainly all the staff and students should resign because they too are unhappy, again not with the UofA, but with the handling of their fate.[536]

In a memo from Bob Wirth to Homer Milford, Wirth cautioned, "Beware of Tim Keleher!"[537]

Michael Keleher also pushed back on Tim Keleher's request in a letter in February 1979. He rebutted Tim Keleher's recommendation that Smith resign or be fired. He also laid out the legal complexities associated with ownership of the school. In addition, he said that since the Sisters were actively seeking buyers for the school, that there were potential conflict of interest problems with some Sisters being on the Board of Trustees, since their loyalties were obviously conflicted.[538]

In March 1979, the Sisters formally rejected the Board of Trustees' offer because it was "financially unsound and could not guarantee either satisfactory transfer of ownership or long-range continuation of the school."[539]

The tension between the Sisters and the University administration continued to fester. At a tense meeting with students and faculty on February 3, 1980, Tim Keleher assured the audience that the University would remain open "next week, next month, next year, and the following year, either operated by the Sisters of St. Francis or a prospective buyer." However, Smith pointed out that the assurances of being open until at least May of 1980 requested by Killorin in the December letter had not been explicitly provided by the Sisters, and he saw "no way to resolve that particular issue at this time."[540]

The Sisters had rejected both the offer by the Board and the offer by the faculty, but at the February 8 Board meeting, they attempted to pour some oil on the troubled waters.[541] Despite their reassurances, the meeting was very contentious. Concern was raised over the credibility of the Sisters. The media was accused of misrepresenting the school's condition. President Smith pointed out that because of the uncertainty as to the future of the University and the associated media reports, several key administrators and administrative assistants had resigned, leaving a significant gap in the school's ability to operate efficiently. In addition, recruiting was suffering.

Michael Keleher noted a further concern about solving the perennial financial woes:

> There have been a series of crisis periods at the University from 1968 to the present time. First, the University dropped the athletic program, then Sister Marilyn resigned, then Frank Kleinhenz, Joe Zanetti, and Gil Cordova. And when Dr. Smith was here just six months, the community college issue came up and then the sale. In the light of problems such as these, you cannot go out and seriously collect money.[542]

Sister Eileen, announced that the University would stay open at least through the spring of 1980, although she made no commitment beyond that date, and that the Sisters were not asking for Laurence Smith's resignation.[543] This announcement was clearly a relief, but both Smith and the Board said that they still needed resolution on the question of the sale of the school and the Board's offer if the Parks College effort fell through. Smith argued that the school would have a deficit of $234,000 in 1979, $170,000 of which was due to the fact that the Sisters' assurances had been too late in coming.

Sister Eileen pushed back, noting that she felt that her December letter had been clear on all the assurances. She further added, "We've been credible all these years, so why not now?" She further assured the Board that they would "divest themselves of UofA ownership in an honorable way."[544]

As the negotiations proceeded, Tim Keleher said that one of the sticking points was the need to raise about $7 million to cover indebtedness to individuals and institutions who had financed various campus projects. He estimated that, with interest included, any prospective purchaser would have to raise as much as $9 million.

On March 1, the Sisters announced that they were in tentative agreement with Parks College for the sale of UofA. Tim Keleher, speaking on behalf of both the Sisters and Parks, told representatives of the students and faculty that the deal was contingent on the Sisters obtaining a $2 million loan. He also noted that an offer from the Archdiocese of Santa Fe had not been competitive with the Parks offer.[545]

Acting on behalf of the Board, Jim Killorin, using the UofA bylaws, said that the Board had the right to call a special meeting to discuss the impending purchase. He said, "We are not part of the negotiations; we feel that we should be a part of the negotiations. The faculty and students are our constituents, and they rely on us to protect their interests."[546]

Shortly after the news of the impending sale was public, students approached the State Legislature with concerns over transferring credits to other institutions and retention of records should the University close. Judith Pratt, a Democrat representative from Bernalillo, sponsored House Bill 541 which required that post-secondary schools that closed or were closing had to make provisions for students who had not yet completed their courses of study and that required that all student records from such institutions be made available in perpetuity. It passed both houses and was signed by Governor Bruce King.[547]

In anticipation of an impending set of purchase offers, President Smith provided a list of questions and answers that he felt the Board would need to provide to any purchaser. Important among these were the prospect of declining enrollment because of the circulating rumors of the impending closure of the school (recall that income from room, board, books, and tuition was over 90 percent of day-to-day revenue), cash flow problems, and a probable deficit of about $500,000 by the end of the fiscal year.[548]

As the potential for sale of the University and probable dissolution of the University Corporation proceeded, Michael Keleher provided some options, based on the non-profit, educational nature of the Foundation, for the future of the University of Albuquerque Foundation, should the school close:

—The Foundation could donate its assets to a suitable charity;
—It could transfer its assets to the Sisters; or
—It could merge with some other non-profit educational entity.[549]

Eventually, the holdings of the Foundation, which had essentially been dormant since its founding, were transferred to the University.[550]

Another exchange of letters between Michael Keleher on behalf of the school and Tim Keleher on behalf of the Sisters occurred in mid-March. According to Tim Keleher, the Sisters felt that a fair price for the University would be $12 million, based on a current appraisal. Michael Keleher countered that the Board would pay $5.3 million in the form of cash and land transfers.[551]

The Student Senate strongly objected to sale of the University to Parks. In a letter from Juanita Martinez, President of the Senate, to the Board of Trustees, she said:

> We find programs and course offerings by Parks College Corporation to be unsatisfactory and academically repugnant.... We hereby request that the Board in no way, publicly or privately, negotiate with Parks College, Inc. of Denver, Colorado.[552]

On March 15, President Smith gave a formal report to the Board in advance of their scheduled March 16 meeting. He included in his report information on enrollment, admissions, and cash flow. He concluded by saying:

> I hope you will resist the temptation to look at it and say, "There is no hope." We have a choice of three decisions: either the Board gets the University, Parks gets the University, or the Sisters get the University and close it. Only if we have not agreed on one of those three options by the end of our meeting tomorrow will I accept the reality that "there is no hope."[553]

In the first half of the all-day March 16 meeting, the Board presented another proposal to take over management of the University. In this proposal, the Sisters would keep the south campus and take ownership of the 40-acre parcel. The Board would assume all indebtedness and no money would directly change hands.[554] The Sisters decided to meet behind closed doors to evaluate the offer. Coming out of the meeting, Sister Eileen formally rejected the Board's proposal, saying:

> After hours of careful consideration, the proposal made this morning by the Board of Trustees of the University of Albuquerque has been rejected. The Sisters of St. Francis of Colorado Springs will continue to operate the UofA in its present form.[555]

She continued:

> In line with the suggestion by the present Board that the Board of Trustees be restructured, the resignation of the present Board of Trustees will be accepted .... I and all my council wish to express with appreciation the many years of dedicated service and unselfish devotion that the Board of Trustees has given to the University of Albuquerque.[556]

Killorin said that the Sisters gave no reason for their rejection, but he opined that finances were the basis for their decision. He said that the Board had offered the nuns 40 acres of land north of the campus plus eight acres and two dormitories south of the campus, a package estimated at $2.8 million with an outstanding $750,000 mortgage.

After the Sisters had withdrawn from the meeting, the Board discussed three options for dealing with the Sisters position:

> —Quietly accept the Sister's request for the Board to resign.
> —Stonewall the request, and let the Sisters take some action, perhaps a demand that the Board resign, possibly followed by District Court action.
> —The Board could request the District Court appoint a Board with possible action by the Attorney General.

After some discussion, option one was adopted.

At the same time that the Sisters rejected the offer by the Board, they also dropped the Parks proposal to purchase the college. However, they did negotiate a contract with Parks to manage the school on their behalf with the possibility of an eventual sale to Parks in the future. This contract was contingent on obtaining $2 million in financing to keep the school open through May 1980. Joe Lee said that if the $2 million could be obtained, he felt that the University's situation could be "turned around" within a year.[557]

Lee also reassured students that there would be very few changes and that there would be only a minimal presence of Parks personnel. He said that the rumor that Parks intended to turn the school into a business or vocational trade school was completely false. Lee, the Sisters, and the Board stipulated that the school would continue to be operated as a private, non-profit, four-year, Catholic, liberal arts institution.[558]

Despite his reassurances, Lee did offer a note of caution for faculty members. The faculty had been given no guarantee of tenure if the school was opened past May 1980. Warren Lee, a professor of history, said, "The faculty has little stake in the future of this place." Although Parks saw a "brighter future," they cautioned that the school must be "run as a business." Both the faculty and the student body expressed some skepticism.[559] In fact, when Leonard DeLayo, lawyer for the faculty and students, expressed concern about the potential treatment of faculty relative to contracts and tenure, Tim Keleher responded that Delayo was "an idiot."[560]

On March 31, Laurence Smith tendered his resignation. He agreed to remain through the spring semester as an advisor to the new administration with the title of "President Emeritus." After the end of the spring semester, he would leave with one year's severance pay. Clifford Smith, manager of the Parks College Albuquerque branch and an ordained Lutheran minister with two Master's degrees, was named acting president.[561] As he accepted the position, Smith made it clear that he was an employee of the UofA, not Parks.[562]

Reverend Clifford Smith.
(CSWR/UofA, Box 18, yearbook collection)

April finally brought some good news to the beleaguered campus. The First National Bank in Albuquerque agreed to a three-year amortization loan for $2 million with withdrawals being taken as needed. In return for the loan, the Sisters took out a third mortgage on the main and south campuses and signed a letter of guarantee to pay back the note if the UofA was unable to do so. Tim Keleher noted that the bank was making the loan "purely as a community contribution because, from a banking standpoint, it stinks!"[563]

Students protesting negotiations with Parks. (*Albuquerque Journal*, 3/23/79, p. 1)

In April, a new Board of Trustees was named. While the previous board had consisted of local lay individuals, the new Board included seven nuns from the Sisters of St. Francis, two lay advisors from Colorado Springs, Joe Lee, and representatives from the faculty, student body, and administration. The only local Albuquerque member was attorney John Kirk. Along with naming the new board, Clifford Smith was named permanent president.[564]

In order to address the estimated 1979 $600,000 operating deficit (an increase of $366,000 over his predecessor's earlier estimate), Smith imposed a 24 percent increase in tuition (from $53 to $75 per credit hour) and a 15 percent increase in room and board for dormitory residents (from $820 to $940 per year).[565]

Smith also wrote a letter to local business and community leaders asking for their help and support. He said that, despite adverse publicity, UofA is "alive and functioning. It is a viable institution, and we intend to keep it viable." However, he went on to note, "There is an essential relationship between community support, successful recruiting, and a viable, dynamic university. We need your support and cooperation if we are to succeed."[566]

In May, the Sisters and the new Board decided not to take out the loan with First National. In its place they opened a $2 million line of credit with Shared Management Services, Inc. of Colorado Springs. Because this avoided the need for remortgaging property, this was considered by the Board to be "more in our interest."[567]

One of the overriding factors in the Sisters' decision not to sell was a finding that they could not legally transfer ownership of the non-profit college to a for-profit entity. They could only relinquish control to an autonomous non-profit entity such as the Board of Trustees or the Archdiocese of Santa Fe.

With much of the negotiating fading in the rear-view mirror, the school held its fortieth commencement on May 12 at the Albuquerque Convention Center. Four hundred six degrees were conferred, including a special award to State Representative Judith Pratt for her sponsorship of House Bill 541. Jack Graham, president of Albuquerque Federal Savings and Loan was the commencement speaker.[568]

By June, the school had obtained the requisite funding, and recruiting efforts for the fall semester of the 1979–1980 school year were progressing well. As a result, the new Board of Trustees "permanently rescinded" the May 1980 closing date.[569]

On Tuesday, June 5, President Clifford Smith met with faculty and staff and announced the following:

—UofA would continue as a four-year, liberal arts, Catholic university.
—There would be "very few changes" in UofA programs during the 1979–1980 school year.
—The possibility of a sale of the school sometime in the future remained.
—Because of the flurry of publicity about finances and administrative changes during the past few months, the accreditation institution,

the North Central Association of Colleges and Secondary Schools, would be on site during the next week "to see how things are going."

—The faculty termination clause which would have terminated faculty contracts in May 1980 had been lifted, and tenure for faculty had been reinstated.

—The 1979 budget would include raises for staff. However, faculty raises would be held in abeyance, pending projected increases in enrollment.

—The Sisters and the Board had signed a management agreement with the school.

—A contract had been signed with Management, Inc. of Denver, Colorado, to manage the school until November 1, 1979. At that time the contract "might be reviewed." Joe Lee, owner of Parks College Management, Inc. was also the owner of Management, Inc.

—A faculty member, biology professor Homer Milford, and a student, Ricardo Campos, were added to the Board.[570]

So, in the late spring of 1979, the UofA had weathered another storm. The community college issue had lasted for more than a decade, but the crisis of ownership and management had gone on for only about six months. Despite the shorter duration, the emotional intensity was significantly greater. Now, however, the financial situation was much improved: a new management team led by Clifford Smith was in place; Joe Lee said that he did not intend to purchase the University and had resigned from the Board; the one-year termination clause for faculty had been lifted; the May 1980 closure was rescinded; and enrollment for the fall semester was progressing well.[571]

Despite what seemed like a rosier picture, the Executive Committee of the Faculty Senate felt obligated to warn the student body about the potential impact of the administrative uncertainties that were still swirling around the University. Prior to registration for the Fall 1979 semester, they published a memo which stated, "Our best advice is to make maximum use of current course offerings, and get in as many hours as possible within your own time limitations."[572] To partially offset the doom and gloom, students were informed that a new copy machine had been purchased (two cents per page) and typewriters were also available.[573]

In a somewhat lame ending to the statement, they added,, "When you come to register, bring a friend." In a particularly prescient statement, the accreditation team from NCA said, that "few, if any, actually know who is running the University" and that the school was "in a state of turmoil and not in control of itself."[574]

10
A Civil War on the West Mesa

Things seemed to be back on a smoother course with Clifford Smith at the helm and debts being settled. The Sisters agreed to purchase the 40-acre parcel of UofA land just north of the campus and had agreed to provide $215,000 over the next three years, assuming that the school could provide matching funds.[575] Throughout the fall and winter of 1979–1980, the Board was occupied in discussions of the governance and ownership time table as they worked toward the conversion of the University from private to public ownership.[576]

In March 1980, during their accreditation visit, the North Central Association had asked that the Colorado-centric Board be replaced by a board with more local representation. This was accomplished in March with the addition of nine local members: Patricia Boyle, William Eglington, Robin Kinsella, Gena McKee, Don Morgan, Sabino Olivas, Sosimo Padilla, Robert Singer, and Jack Wesenberg.[577] The accreditation was renewed later that spring.[578]

Sister Eileen Van Ackeren had agreed that the ultimate goal was to transfer ownership of and financial responsibility for the University "in a year or maybe two" to the reconstituted Board of Trustees, led by local real estate investment manager Don Morgan, a *cum laude* graduate of UofA.[579]

Despite the rosier picture, there was still concern, particularly among the ever-restless student body. They vociferously opposed the tuition increase from $78 to $95 per credit hour (with corresponding raises in room and board rates) voted by the Board, noting that this was in sharp contrast to the current University of New Mexico rate of $28 per credit hour.[580] Business manager Alan Weiser said that, even though the University appeared to be headed for a balanced budget of $6.9 million for the 1979–1980 school year, there were still obligations and a $1.7 million debt. In addition, inflation running at 14.5 percent was hitting operating costs hard.[581]

Academic Dean Jack Cranston noted that enrollment, which had been declining from 3,123 in 1976, was down seven percent to about 2,100, largely due to the uncertainties of the past several years. Despite the decline, the University graduated 524 individuals, the largest cohort on record, on May 15, 1980. One hundred nineteen of the graduates were from the nursing program.[582]

The importance of the nursing program, illustrated by the percentage of graduates from that program, plus the ongoing community demand for more nurses, led to a major push for a four-year, BS Nursing program to be instituted. The Faculty Senate passed a proposal for this program to begin in the fall of 1980. That start date was missed, but the request was passed along to the Board in November 1980.[583]

The general level of ennui relative to higher education across the country was reflected in a presentation by Brother Cyprian Luke Roney to the students and faculty of the College of Santa Fe in September 1980:

> There is a pervasive gloom setting over higher education which is a reflection of the changing mood in America today—a shift away from our traditional optimism to doubts about ourselves and our institutions. Already the 1980s are being labelled the "Aching 80s" because of declining enrollments, inflation, rising energy costs, litigiousness, alleged lack of national leadership, world interdependence, terrorism, environmental damage, and so on and so on.[584]

Another shock to the system occurred on September 30, 1980, when President Clifford Smith was abruptly fired by the Board. The alleged issues, as expressed by Board President Don Morgan and faculty representative Warren Lee, had nothing to do with any sort of scandal, but simply reflected a loss of confidence in Smith's performance and a "conflict between Smith and the Board's financial committee about future financial plans for the UofA." Warren Lee said that "he should have stepped down earlier."[585] In response to the firing, Smith said, "As far as I know, I have not received any directives telling me that I had somehow gone against Board policy. To my knowledge, I have never had any clashes with the Board."[586]

Academic Dean Cranston was named acting president and a search committee was established to fill the position. Cranston noted that the dismissal of Smith should have no negative impact on the University, "Hopefully, we'll go right along with no problems at all. We're exactly where we were before, except for the change at the top administrator's position. Our goals remain the same."

Julius "Jack" Cranston.
(CSWR/UofA, Box 18, yearbook collection)

In particular, he said that the Sisters continued to press for relief from the financial strain of supporting the University. The agreement to transfer ownership to the new board remained in place, subject to the University's ability to operate "in the black."

In November, some respite from the seemingly endless financial woes seemed to be on the horizon. The state legislature was expected to pass a tuition assistance bill that would permit state aid to students in private universities, something that had been sought after for several years. Unfortunately, the bill was killed in the Legislative Finance Committee.[587] In addition, private donors had contributed almost half of the $215,000 that the UofA had to raise to match the outlay by the Sisters. Another significant contribution toward this goal was made by Continental Airlines.[588]

In the fall of 1980, the administration was considering imposing a merit pay system on the faculty. As one might expect, the faculty pushed back on this concept. Professor Lawrence Desaulniers and the Faculty Advisory Committee said:

> Although the Faculty Advisory Committee, and presumably the faculty generally, agree with the basic assumption that meritorious performance deserves recognition and reward, it is the opinion of the Faculty Advisory Committee that a full-fledged merit pay system is, at present, an inappropriate mechanism for achieving this goal.[589]

Not only had finances begun to improve, but the once-powerful Dons basketball program had been revived by Coach Leon Palmisano after a 12-year shutdown. All 15 of the new players were walk-ons. The first game for the new team was against New Mexico Tech in the Ernie Smith gym on November 22, 1980. The Dons lost 50-36 but Coach Palmisano was not disappointed, "We are in an embryo stage. We need to be patient and build a good program."[590]

The transfer of ownership from the Sisters to the Board also showed progress on January 9, 1981, when Archbishop Robert Sanchez told the Sisters that, in contrast to his earlier concerns about archdiocesan ownership of a college, he approved the transfer. His approval contained a provision for a long-term lease of the campus by the Board at no direct cost to the University. The provisions of the lease, drafted by the Sisters' attorney, Tim Keleher:

> Provide for a 20-year term with successive renewal periods of 15 years as long as the University continues to operate as a Christian

institution of higher learning and continues to meet certain other conditions.[591]

The lease would cost the University $10 per year.

Of course, the Archbishop noted that the arrangements, when finalized, would have to be approved by the Vatican's Sacred Congregation for Religious and Secular Institutions in Rome.

In May 1981, the school hired Diana Steigler, a development consultant, to help with the general financial situation. One of the first things that Steigler did was to solicit help from the faculty in identifying potential donors. In a letter, she asked each faculty member to provide her with names of three individuals who might be willing to donate to the school.[592]

In light of the increased sense of stability, the School announced the formation of the Bridge International School in August 1981. This new initiative was designed to provide intensive English language preparation and cultural adaptation for students from Latin America, Mainland China, and the Middle East.[593]

The issue of faculty salaries was raised as the Fall 1981 term began. The Faculty Affairs Committee of the Faculty Senate noted that there was a significant disparity between salaries at UofA and comparable institutions and that salaries at UofA were 35 percent below those at UNM. They further said that salary increases over the past ten years had not made up for inflation and that they were consistently below increases in the cost of living.[594]

By the late summer of 1981, the presidential search had focused on 42-year-old Frank Welch, PhD. Welch had been president of Lincoln Memorial University, a private liberal arts university in Harrogate, Tennessee, for the past eight years. A sociologist by training, he had a Bachelor's degree in Higher Education and a Master's degree in Family Relations, both from Florida State University. In addition, he had done follow-on studies at Harvard. According to local Tennessee newspapers, Welch had "rescued" the Tennessee school from the brink of bankruptcy.

The Presidential Search Committee selected Welch despite strong opposition from the Faculty Senate. In a July note from the Senate to the Search Committee, the faculty registered concern over both Welch and another candidate, a Dr. Weisenberg. Both men were rated 93 percent unacceptable by the faculty with the comment, "In our opinion, this institution would not survive the presidency of either Dr. Welch or Dr. Weisenburg"[595]

Faculty concerns notwithstanding, Welch took over the reins of UofA on September 15, 1981.[596] He characterized himself as a "doer and a shaker," saying, "If I can't move it or I can't shake it, I'll replace it."[597] He went on to say:

> We need to create the attitude on the part of the local community that the University of Albuquerque is the community college for Albuquerque. Right now, we're a four-year community college. Perhaps later we'll be a community college that offers graduate degrees as well.... What that means to me is, if there's a need in the community, we want to fill that need. If a corporation needs a place to hold an annual meeting, we want them to use us. If a community organization needs judges for an essay contest, we want to provide them. We want people to ask us to do that.[598]

This statement represents the strongest movement away from the Christian humanist philosophy toward the religious humanist philosophy. With this emphasis, the school had moved significantly away from its original Catholic roots.

Frank Welch, PhD.
(courtesy Lincoln Memorial University)

Welch noted that he hoped to raise the enrollment to 3,000 by the fall of 1983. With a burst of self-confidence, he proclaimed:

> I am probably the first person to be president here who is trained to be a college president. My profession is a professional college president. None of the obstacles facing the UofA is insurmountable. We have great strengths. Generally, the curriculum is excellent. Most small liberal arts schools have been reluctant to recognize the changing needs of higher education. Undergraduates today are not going to buy a "pure" liberal arts education. But this school has gone about the business of offering very marketable programs. All of these things are extremely positive.

Characterizing UofA as a David to UNM's Goliath, he went on:

> We're an alternative to a large, state-controlled institution. Anything operated by the state has to have a huge bureaucracy. A big institution must fit the needs of a majority of students. Students have to fit into the majority pattern. Students with special needs get lost. We already have many minority students, many mature adults, and many alternatives to lock-step-type programs here.... We're located in a city with ten percent population increase each year, and the West Mesa is where it's all going to happen. We're, physically, a place where growth is going to take place. The potential for us is here if we maintain our academic integrity. The finances will come along.

Needless to say, much of this did not sit particularly well with the "large, state-controlled institution" across the river.

In February 1981, Acting Academic Dean Andrew Imrik had requested the formation of an Academic Structure and Delivery Committee from the Faculty Senate to "find more efficient and economical structures and operations in the academic area without loss of quality of services to the students or a change in our overall objectives." The committee, headed by Professor Eleanor Noble, reported its findings to the Faculty Senate on September 18, 1981. The report, which arrived just after Welch had assumed the presidency, provided 44 recommendations, each with a rationale and implementation suggestions. It seems clear from these recommendations that enrollment, which, of course, was still the primary source of funding for the University, was on the minds of the committee. In addition to recommendations for increasing enrollment, there were others that addressed involvement of the Board of Trustees, improvements in the advising structure, faculty load recommendations, and suggestions for evaluation of experimental programs.

With regard to specific degree programs, the committee recommended dropping several Associate degree programs, including Spanish, Fire Technology, and Theater. The rationale given was that the enrollment in these two-year programs was below the "number necessary for quality and vitality." There was also the suggestion that some programs be merged. A probationary period of two years was suggested for programs that did not meet the enrollment standards.[599]

The Faculty Senate was also asked to consider the reintroduction of interscholastic athletics. In a letter to the Board, Faculty Senate President Eleanor Noble raised concerns over this proposal, particularly over financing. Her letter listed four priorities for the Department of Health, Physical Education, and Recreation. In order these priorities were:

—Physical education for all students.
—Intramural sports.
—Extramural sports for more competitive athletes.
—Varsity athletics for elite athletes.

Some programs, including Adult Education and the four-year Nursing program, were endorsed, and it was suggested that the Business and Criminal Justice programs be evaluated as potential graduate programs. An important bottom line in the report was that there was a need for an "organized, comprehensive fund-raising plan."

In an October board meeting, a six percent faculty pay raise was approved, and in November, Welch submitted a report which laid out a plan for sweeping changes to be implemented in the Fall 1982 term. According to Welch, the 23-page document had had "some" faculty input:

—Eleven full-time faculty positions would be eliminated, and the remaining faculty would be required to increase their teaching load from 12 to 15 hours per semester.

—Faculty raises of either six percent in direct salary or seven percent in fringe benefits would be instituted.

—The number of classes offered would be reduced from 318 to 268.

—The length of each term would be reduced from eight weeks to seven weeks.

—Prospective students with significant and pertinent life experiences could be awarded up to 30 credit-hours for these experiences.

—Academic departments would be reorganized into seven colleges, each with its own associate dean. Welch would appoint the associate deans, and he would, for the time being, retain the role of overall Academic Dean.

In the conclusion of the report, Welch noted that:

While there are limits to the flexibility which I can accept, many components which I have included in these recommendations do have great opportunity for modification. You have already contributed much to the shaping of these proposals. I am asking you for further input.[600]

He gave the Senate just a month to reply, requesting their input by mid-December.

Predictably, the radical restructuring met with opposition from both faculty and students. Not only were details of the program such as the tuition increase and teacher layoffs of concern, but the fact that they were "imposed from above" by Welch and the Board was disparaged. In a response dated December 1, the Faculty Senate noted that the "changes advocated by the report are so sweeping in concept as to change the very nature of the school ... to survive at any price is to cease to survive" They also pointed out that the reduction in the length of each term would seriously diminish the educational quality: "No department, no course can be so truncated without serious reduction of subject matter, to say nothing of short-changing students who pay a substantial tuition"[601]

The issue of subdividing the university into colleges, each with an associate dean, was also criticized:

> Having arbitrarily called itself a university, the school is now divided into "colleges" headed by "associate deans" without real power of decision.... Two of these "colleges" cannot even offer degrees.... The purpose would seem to be "management efficiency.".... When are we going to get down to being simply a good small college? The faculty should make no decisions until it has had time to think.[599]

The Faculty Affairs Committee of the Faculty Senate registered some concern with the idea of solving the financial problems by limiting faculty salaries while, at the same time, increasing the teaching load:

> When an academic institution is struggling to survive, the easiest way to decrease expenses is to limit faculty salaries and increase faculty workloads.... It may preserve an institution but not an institution worth preserving.[602]

They also argued for a 24-hour annual teaching load, all "overload" assignments to be reimbursed at the contract rate, and a cost-of-living increase:

> The current University of Albuquerque faculty salaries are shockingly below the averages for colleges of the same size and type.... To ask for a 25 percent increase in workload without offering a 25 percent increase in salary plus a 10 percent cost-of-living increase is unthinkable.[603]

Although Welch asserted that he would continue to work with the faculty, he pointed out:

> If the issues at this institution are financial stability and academic integrity, I intend to assume the power to make those changes and retain that power and bring this institution to financial stability and academic integrity.... I have come into an institution that has run in the red for so long, it's not even funny. What it has is a

reputation, buildings, and debts, and the hope that in future we can get better.[604]

The relationship between Welch and the Faculty continued to deteriorate. On December 18, 1981, long-time professor and chair of the Academic Affairs Committee, Joan Gibson, tendered her resignation saying, "I find my attitude toward and philosophy of faculty governance, academic integrity, and fundamental human relations to be entirely incompatible with those of the new administration."[605]

At its annual meeting in mid-January, the Board elected John Robert, an Albuquerque consulting civil engineer, as chairman.[606] After the meeting, Welch reported that the Board had adopted a statement of institutional purpose that recognized the liberal arts foundation of the University, but stressed that the new emphasis would be on career fields. He also reported that the school had not had to borrow any money for the last six months and that the short-term debt was down by another $100,000 to $215,000. Only ten days later, he reported that this debt, too, had been liquidated.[607]

John Robert.
(CSWR/UofA photo archives)

In a Faculty Senate meeting on February 26, with Welch present, Professor Eugene Brown rose to speak:

> I suppose if it is possible for a state to have a totalitarian regime, it is possible for a college to have a totalitarian administration. I would suggest, Dr. Welch, that you are everything here: you are the president, academic dean, comptroller, personnel director, publicity director.... You have created on this campus an atmosphere of fear, suspicion, and terror. Now you take my name to your council of deans, say bad things about me, place your council under a gag rule, and send one of your quislings to tell me I am not wanted at the school.... You cannot buy my soul; I will not burn incense before your statue.[608]

By April 1982, the complaints had become a torrent.[609] In a series of letters between Eleanor Noble, chair of the Faculty Senate and John Robert, chair of the Board of Trustees, Noble had repeatedly requested a meeting between the faculty and the Board. On March 29, Noble wrote:

> The theme running through all those connected with the concerns is destruction of due process. There are strong feelings on campus that the academic integrity and institutional stability of UofA are seriously threatened.[610]

Roberts responded by simply saying "you have not followed the procedures outlined in the Faculty Handbook."[611] Professor Parajon took it one step further, writing to State Senator Budagher[612] and to the Sisters.[613] His missive said:

> I make my plea hoping that the Sisters can stop the arrogance of this man who is converting this place into a battlefield. Power has blinded him to such an extent that he is calloused and has no compassion, concern, or respect for faculty, staff, or students.

On October 31, the Board and the Sisters signed the first agreement for the ownership transfer. The conditions that were stipulated were:

—Approval by Rome of the transfer as a conditional gift from the Catholic Church to the community.

—Payment of all long-term debt to which the Sisters were obligated.

—Operation of the school as a Christian, liberal arts college, including courses in theology and Christian philosophy.

—Limitations on the Board's right to encumber campus land and buildings as collateral for future loans.

—The right of the Archbishop of Santa Fe to appoint a director of campus ministry.

It was further stipulated that if any of these provisions were violated, ownership would revert to the Sisters.[614]

By mid-December, after nearly three weeks of intense negotiations, Welch held a news conference to report that he had obtained faculty concurrence with most of his requested changes. He agreed to step down as Academic Dean, but reserved the right to appoint the seven deans of the various colleges. A large part of the revised settlement were provisions for up to a full-year of salary for laid-off faculty, along with offers to assist in finding them alternative employment, either at UofA or elsewhere. However, he did say that there would be no faculty pay checks for July through August, since the contracts expired in June and new ones didn't start until September.[615]

When asked about the financial condition of the University, Welch said, "The financial status of the University is weak. It is a situation that cannot be corrected within a very short period of time." He went on to explain that the short-term debt had already been substantially reduced, from $530,000 to $315,000, and that additional savings were being realized by staff reductions.[616]

In another attempt to generate support from alumni, a program entitled Partners in Progress, chaired by Gena McKee, was initiated. The alumni were asked to contribute $74,500 to meet an end-of-year goal of $214,500 to match a donation by the Sisters.[617]

Despite Welch's assurances that he and the faculty were now in step with each other, the problems with the faculty did not go away for long. As an indication of the divide forming between faculty and administration, the faculty grievance procedure was amended to add, "If the President is the person who gave rise to the grievance, the grievance committee shall submit its report to the Board of Trustees." This arose because of a grievance that had been filed against President Welch.[618]

In January 1982, Welch reversed course on his decision to step down as Academic Dean, simply saying, "I have changed my mind." When further accused of "contempt toward students, staff, faculty, and the university's past," he shot back:

> That's about the most asinine thing I have ever heard. I have been nothing but sensitive to people. I've been very concerned about the decisions I've had to make. They (the faculty) want me to feel guilty about what I've done and I feel no guilt. I've made decisions that are for the overall good of the institution.[619]

Following several faculty resignations, Faculty Senate President Eleanor Noble wrote a letter to the entire faculty:

> It is evident that the faculty is divided if not fragmented.... Differences of opinion have been so great that they are threatening faculty governance.... Indeed, it is possible that all elected and appointed Faculty Senate officers will resign before the Spring Semester.[620]

As a follow-up to the letter, a questionnaire was sent out to the faculty. The results were reported out in mid-January. Twenty-seven percent of the faculty did not respond, raising some concerns that there was a rather high level of apathy among the group. Of those that did respond, most were generally supportive of the Faculty Senate and its governance model. Eleanor Noble ended the report by saying, "I recognize, of course, that, as Chairman of the Senate, I do not have the confidence of all of you, but let's take a breath, put on our positive hats, and try together."[621]

Throughout the heated discussions between Welch and the faculty, the Board of Trustees and nearly half of the professors, including Academic Vice President Nancy Martinez, supported Welch's changes.[622] However, some, including some of the Sisters, registered concern. Former UofA president Sister Viatora said, "Why most members of the Board should support Dr. Welch in his management by intimidation is unfathomable.... What an injustice!"[623]

Other members of the Order were more supportive of the Board's position, although there was a thinly veiled request that Robert step up and solve the problems:

> We have recently received many letters which cause us great concern regarding the University of Albuquerque.... We thank you and the local Board members for your concern and efforts in alleviating the tense situation within the University.[624]

Meanwhile, the Faculty Senate forwarded its January letter to the North Central Association with copies to the American Association of University Professors.[625]

For several years the faculty had been attempting to obtain collective bargaining rights for its union, the United University Professors of New Mexico. In September 1977, the National Labor Relations Board had certified the union as a legitimate bargaining agent, but the school appealed based on a recent Supreme Court ruling, *National Labor Relations Board vs Yeshiva University*. This decision labeled most tenure-track faculty as "managerial" and the program one of "shared governance." This ruling excluded the faculty from the right to collective bargaining under the National Labor Relations Act of 1935.[626]

In an impassioned presentation to the Faculty Senate in April 1980, President Smith had addressed the issue of unionization, noting the divisiveness that the problem had caused between the faculty and administration:

> I am very much concerned with the adversarial relationship that we have and with the tension that is created among us as faculty, students, and administration.... I come to ask that we somehow arrive as adults at a position from which we can communicate with one another and do so as a university was designed to do so.... I believe that the [Yeshiva University] decision says that we are not eligible to have a union.... I am asking you to let the attorneys do whatever attorneys do ... and let us give up our participation for the sake of the university, for the sake of what we have known about its ongoing life, about its competency, its quality.... I ask that we, in essence, go about our jobs.[627]

In July 1980, based on the appeal filed by the school's attorneys, the National Labor Relations Board reversed its earlier decision, finding that under the UofA's "shared governance" model, the faculty were, in fact, managers since they had substantial control over both academics and academic personnel. Based on this finding, the University notified the union that it would ignore the existence of the United University Professors.[628] Union president and long-time faculty activist Warren Lee said that the faculty would appeal the new decision and would "continue to represent the interests of the faculty in every possible way."[629]

In a vote of confidence in Welch's management of the University, the faculty and staff were clearly split: 47 percent were supportive while 53 percent voted "no confidence."[630] The files contain numerous letters of support for Welch to the Board of Trustees.[631] However, all of the letters of support are dated on May 10, 1982; virtually all of them are from administrative staff, including individuals working directly for Welch; and the wording on the letters is almost identical. Whether these letters reflect real support or something else is unclear.

Faculty contracts for the 1982–1983 school year were due to be signed and submitted by April 6, 1982, but in February, the Faculty Senate voted to delay the submission pending legal advice. Professor Joan Gibson said that revisions to previous contract language had been rushed through with little time for discussion. In particular, she noted that classroom time had been increased from 12 to 15 hours per week, and there were revisions to faculty evaluation procedures. Faculty member Gene Brown even accused President Welch of "compiling a hit list" of teachers who would not be receiving raises because they had voiced opposition to the president's methods and policies while others would be receiving raise packages of 25 percent to 30 percent, including salary and fringe benefits. Several of the academic deans confirmed Brown's allegations.[632]

In the faculty meeting on February 26, 1982, Welch replied, "I can make no further modification to the contract. The longer we wait, the more detrimental it is to the institution. The Board offers the contract and the faculty can accept or reject it."[633]

Speaking directly to Welch, Brown said:

You have created here a climate of suspicion, fear, and terror. You are everything here, Dr. Welch. You are head of everything from top to bottom. A college is supposed to be a democratic process. It is everything but that here.

Speaking to the faculty, Brown said:

I've heard some of you say you are tired of strife, that you want peace. But if you want peace, it is bought at a price. Peace is not the absence of something, but the presence of honor and justice and charity.

As the deadline for signing and submitting contracts drew closer, Welch said that 32 of the 75 faculty members still had not complied. The Board sided with Welch, and the faculty members obtained legal counsel and threatened a court injunction to delay the contract submittal date.[634] On April 7, District Court Judge Gerald Cole denied the injunction, but said that the faculty members could continue to sue the University for breach of contract, even if they had signed and submitted the disputed versions.[635]

In a letter to the faculty, Eleanor Noble, the chairperson of the Faculty Senate Executive Committee said, "President Welch has offered a contract which appears to offer a great deal but which really offers little, and which appears to take away little but really takes away a great deal."[636]

In a formal statement, the Faculty Senate voiced what it characterized as "University-wide concerns" with President Welch's actions. They alleged:

1. Possible violations of the University of Albuquerque regulations on academic freedom and tenure.
2. Possible violations of provisions of the Faculty Handbook.
3. Possible violations of academic freedom.
4. Possible violations of employment agreements.
5. Problems with internal university management.
6. Questionable use of financial aid monies.
7. Community relations.
8. Intimidation.

The statement concluded:

> The overall situation is now one in which most, if not all, protection of due process for faculty and staff has been subverted, and in which academic integrity, as well as institutional stability, are threatened.[637]

The dissident teachers did indeed file a suit which requested the court rule that:

> —The Faculty Handbook and regulations on academic freedom and academic tenure should continue to govern employment relationships at the school.
> —Welch's actions had made the employment relationship with the faculty unclear and uncertain and had subjected the faculty to undefined and illusory employment conditions and terms.
> —Welch's actions were in violation of the current contract.
> —The UofA should be enjoined from altering or abolishing the published salary scale and also be enjoined from altering the tenure status of faculty members.
> —Welch should be prohibited from excluding the Faculty Handbook and regulations from next year's contract.[638]

A hearing on the lawsuit was docketed for 1983.

During the contract negotiations, in the spring of 1982, the faculty received an unsolicited letter from the Southern Association, another accreditation group, that said that while at Lincoln Memorial University, Welch

> ...did a very poor job of public relations in effecting necessary but difficult changes and, at worst, irrevocably damaged himself as an institutional leader in the eyes of a significant portion of the university community.[639]

In addition to protesting the contract and filing a lawsuit, the faculty wrote a four-page letter with substantial supporting documentation to the American Association of University Professors (AAUP), alleging that Welch had violated existing regulations, agreements, the standards of the profession, and any decent ethical standards.[640]

Not surprisingly, Welch dismissed the claims:

> What is the AAUP? It has no power whatsoever. In today's job market the AAUP has little clout. We're not responsible to them. So, they censure us—so what? I can replace any faculty member at the UofA anytime I want. This investigation is not a crucial issue. It doesn't bother me in the least.[641]

When told of Welch's disparaging comments, University of New Mexico Faculty Senate President Richard Williams said that Welch "better damn well listen to the AAUP because they are the most respected association of faculty nationwide. It is irresponsible for an administrator to say he will ignore AAUP."[642]

Once again, the UofA Board stood behind Welch. Board Chairman John Robert said:

> The Board is aware of the issues that have been brought before them through direct correspondence and through the media. The Board has duly considered all the claims and counter-claims. The Board asserts its categorical support for the programmatic changes, improvements, and modifications which President Welch will implement on the UofA campus.[643]

Robert also noted that the Board saw no threat to accreditation based on the president's actions.

The daily newsletter, called *Today at UofA* (a replacement for *Newslines*) steered completely clear of the administrative controversies that were roiling in the background. A typical edition included job openings, pets for sale (cats, roosters, etc.), cartoons, and humorous contests such as "Real Men," "Real Women," "Best Necktie," and "Prettiest Dress." The June 29, 1982 edition also offered the services of a typist for term papers, although no cost-per-page was given.[644]

In their final meeting of the 1981–1982 school year, the Faculty Senate voted "no confidence" in Welch by a margin of 57 to 47.[645] In response, Welch remarked, "If changes are made which are viewed as tyrannical, arbitrary, or counter to tradition, all I can say is the institution is more important than any individual."[646] A note in the *Sister Lode* stated that when Welch was introduced at the 1981–1982 commencement ceremony, "Not one person clapped."[647] On the other hand, some of the administrative personnel were fervent supporters of President Welch. One said, "Welch has done more in his first three months than past presidents have done in an entire year."[648]

It seemed obvious from the relatively close margin in the no-confidence vote that the faculty was not unified. In addition to the close vote, there were also closely contested elections for Faculty Senate president and vice-president, as well as a debate over who was eligible to vote in these elections.

John Trever political cartoon.
(courtesy John Trever)

Disagreements between faculty and administration were not unique to UofA. The University of New Mexico had similar issues dating back to the presidency of David S. Hill in the 1920s and continuing, with a few periods of respite, through the administration of Gerald May in the late 1980s.[649]

In another interesting, but controversial, turn of events, President

Welch, Board Chair John Robert, and some alumni had proposed that the University hire Coach Norm Ellenberger to revive the UofA basketball program. Ellenberger had been fired from UNM in December 1979, after allegations of forging athlete's transcripts, doctoring grades, recruiting violations, and payments to athletes. In fact, the NCAA had slammed UNM with 57 violations. Ellenberger was later tried and acquitted in federal court but was convicted in state court on 21 counts of filing false travel vouchers and fraud.[650] Ellenberger expressed interest in discussing the job with President Welch.

Alumnus Guy Riordan, an Ellenberger supporter, opined:

Once the alumni graduate from the University of Albuquerque, they go their separate ways and there are no ties back to the University. We felt that this [hiring Ellenberger] could reestablish identity in the community and show the University is a viable institution academically as well as sportswise.[651]

In their May meeting, the trustees voted not to revive the basketball program which had been stopped in 1969. This also solved what would almost certainly have been a publicity nightmare for the University.[652]

By late June, Welch reported that he was "99.9 percent sure" that there would be no deficit during the upcoming school year, and he claimed that a majority of the faculty now supported him. He also noted that the faculty would receive large raises in the coming year because "he wanted to have a well-paid faculty."[653]

Only two weeks after Welch's statement of support by the faculty, all but one of the instructors in the highly successful nursing program resigned, citing restrictions in academic freedom, a reduction in staff, and a change of leadership within the program. Tenured nursing professor Margaret Schaefer, RN, a member of the program since 1968, said, "With the conditions at the University as they are, I don't believe that we can continue to provide excellence in education."[654]

One of the principal concerns of Schaefer and her colleagues was that program director Jo Vander Meer, RN, had been asked to step down as director, although she could remain on staff as an instructor. Vander Meer attributed her demotion to her report to the New Mexico Board of Nursing of the Welch-instituted changes to the program. She noted that this report was mandated by the nursing program's accreditation requirements. One of her colleagues, Lydia Ward, RN, said, "She was demoted because she opposed Welch and did not follow his mandates." Welch countered the nurses' allegations by saying that Vander Meer's demotion was "a simple administrative decision. I was looking for someone who could upgrade the program."

In a presentation to students and faculty as the 1982–1983 school year began, Welch claimed that the "earth-shaking changes" and the crisis of the past year were over. He said that the school had made a good beginning toward building quality, financial stability, academic integrity, and a sense of community. He also offered that the controversies had had a positive effect. He said, "My name is now a household word."[655]

Welch's speech was not well received. Several faculty members boycotted the event entirely; about 20 individuals got up and left the auditorium during his presentation; at least one professor stood up in the front row and turned his back on Welch who was speaking from the podium; and Student Senate president Neil Candelaria announced a petition that called for Welch's resignation. Candelaria said that the petition would be sent to the Board, to the papal nuncio in Washington, DC, to Archbishop Sanchez, and to the Sisters of St. Francis in Colorado Springs.[656] The student body as a whole increased the level of protest, accusing Welch of "behaving like an old-fashioned dictator in a banana republic and not like the president of a respected university."[657]

Despite the internal picture of dissent and protest, Welch put on a much more positive view in a presentation to the West Side Council of the Albuquerque Chamber of Commerce in early October. He said that the faculty had been reorganized to remove teachers who had no students; the short-term debt of almost $600,000 had been eliminated; faculty compensation had been improved; and for the first time in 64 years, the school had a balanced budget.[658] He noted that the University had shifted from an emphasis on liberal arts to "the real world." He also asserted that "the majority of the people who are here today are pleased with the changes." His bottom line was, "the University of Albuquerque has decided to survive."[659]

Another shock occurred on November 27, 1982, when the Vatican's Sacred Congregation for Religious and Secular Institutions informed Sister Stephanie McReynolds, OSF, the Vicar Provincial of the Order, that it would not approve the transfer of the university to the lay board. In a purported "unrelated move," the Board had taken itself out of the ownership equation on December 4, saying that they would support the Sisters as they explored other alternatives, including soliciting other religious orders who might be able and/or willing to take over operation of the school.[660]

At the end of December, the Board had finally had enough of the dissent that had gone on ever since Frank Welch had assumed the presidency. They started an investigation into the various issues that were at the root of the problems. Gena McKee said that the proximate cause for the investigation was the firing of two professors who had been "outspoken critics of Welch." Faculty Senate Chairman John Lucas said, "I hope that this can be a positive step in resolving the internal difficulties of the UofA. However, on the basis of past experience, any optimism on this score must be quite guarded."[661] Welch's November 18 arrest in Corrales for drunk driving probably didn't help any arguments on his behalf.[662]

At the January 10, 1983 board meeting, Welch tendered his resignation, saying that his only reason for doing so was that he did not believe that a Protestant, such as himself, could run a Catholic institution. In announcing his resignation, he said that he felt very positive about the institution's future. He specifically cited a $500,000 increase in the school's net worth, the first such surplus in a decade and final payment of the loan for the Fine Arts Building.[663] As had happened so many times in the last few years, the Board put together yet another presidential search committee.[664]

In what some characterized as "an attempt to reach beyond the grave and punish those who opposed him," Welch issued termination contracts to four faculty members—Jack Cranston, former acting president, Yvonne Jehensen, head of the Honors program, John Lucas, head of the Faculty Senate, and a professor in the medical assistance program. Welch characterized the termination contract rationale as "lack of growth and declining enrollment in the adult education program." Cranston noted, "Of course it has declining enrollment, he shut it down!"[665]

Just a month later, the Board confirmed the appointment of 54-year-old Norbertine priest, Father Alfred McBride, O. Praem, from the St. Norbert Abbey in De Pere, Wisconsin, as the acting president. McBride held degrees from St. Norbert College, Catholic University, and International Credential Formation in Belgium. He also had done post-doctoral work at Oxford University. The abbot of McBride's order, Right Reverend Benjamin T. Makin, praised the appointment:

> In appointing Father McBride as acting president, you are choosing a man of wide experience, great depth of perception—a deeply religious man. He is a rare, irreplaceable man, capable of turning a multitude of talents toward the good of others.[666]

Sister Stephanie McReynolds, OSF, speaking on behalf of the Sisters, also endorsed the McBride appointment:

> It is a blessing and an honor to have Father McBride, who is nationally and internationally known and respected in the field of Catholic education, become the president of the UofA. The Sisters and the Archdiocese will continue negotiations with other Catholic orders who have expressed an interest in assuming ownership of the school. The Norbertines have indicated an interest in the school but have made no commitment.[667]

McBride described his approach to the new challenge by saying he would be, "a listener, a slow decider, and a good delegator.... I have no magic answers. I believe in the stimulus of questioning and the gift of wonder."[668]

On April 22, 1983, on the occasion of his fiftieth day at the helm of the University, McBride shared his thought on the status and future of the school:

> —UofA would continue to be a Catholic school and would operate in a liberal arts tradition.
> —The University would stop its open admissions policy.
> —The values of Catholic identity, enrollment stability, and academic quality would determine the school's future.
> —Hispanic enrollment should be expanded from 32 percent to 50 percent.
> —The University must "retrench" creatively. "We are doing many things poorly. We should do well what we are equipped to do."
> —The school should return to 16-week semesters, and all faculty

should be on a tenure track.

—The University must become financially self-reliant—tuition is too low; annual giving is too low. Fund drives at poor inner-city Catholic high schools would put us to shame.[669]

In his first press conference, McBride laid out his goals for "providing a good education for our students:"

1. Teaching them how to study.
2. Opening them to a knowledge of civilization—past and present with an eye to the future.
3. Offering them a religious and moral awareness.
4. Preparing them for their life careers.
5. Assisting them in their dreams of self-realization and self-fulfillment.[670]

Father Alfred McBride, O. Praem.
(CSWR/UofA, photo archives)

11
Peace and Progress

In March 1983, the UofA faculty and staff presented Father McBride with a peace pipe. Receiving the gift, he said, "I think we have to have a new beginning, an era of good feelings." McBride, never seen without his own pipe in hand, brought a national and international reputation as a religious educator to the troubled campus. He was enthusiastically welcomed by the faculty, the student body, and the community as a whole. He said that he hoped to bring stability and continuity to the campus. "It would be very foolish of me to make any major decisions for a long while. I have to think of the long-range results."[671]

McBride said that developing an endowment for the University would be critical to assuring its future financial health.[672] The idea of an endowment had first been floated in 1972, but the day-to-day financial challenges had consistently overridden the idea.[673] McBride also expressed some dreams for the university—dreams of increased enrollment, dreams of an endowment to support scholarships and lift the burden of day-to-day financial concerns, dreams of a student body who could make a four- or five-year commitment, and dreams of a high-tech center. However, he cautioned that...

> We have to be careful not to turn out "hackers." I never think about "high-tech" without thinking "high-touch." If we forget that, we're just producing technicians. We have to turn out human beings.[674]

McBride's "long while" for thinking about the future ended just two months later when he announced some of the changes that he intended to put into place, starting with the upcoming fall term but extending over the next several years. He planned to:

—Emphasize the school's Catholic mission by requiring courses in Catholic doctrine and by building a church on campus.
—Ending the school's long-standing free admission policy over a five-year period by specifying minimum ACT and SAT scores.
—Raising tuition gradually by as much as $1,000, noting that the UofA's tuition was the eleventh lowest of 12 similar schools.
—Stressing liberal arts rather than a technical-vocational curriculum.
—Actively recruiting high school graduates rather than non-traditional adult students.
—Raising the Hispanic enrollment from 32 percent to 50 percent and establishing a National Center for Hispanic Culture and Studies.
—Capping enrollment for full-time day students at 2,000.[675]

In response to questions about reductions in the popular vocational programs, McBride said:

We must do more than prepare people to earn a living. The most marketable skill of all is how to live, not just how to make a living, but how to live grandly and gloriously. If you sit before your Apple computer and you haven't had the literature and religious and history and philosophy courses, you won't have the imagination to use it.

In answering a question about the near-constant financial challenges, McBride quoted Matthew 6:33, "Seek ye first the Kingdom of God, the rest will be given unto you." He said, "I ask the community, 'seek ye first to create a quality education.' Then you will attract what you need to make it possible." These statements show the clear intent of Father McBride to rein in the drift toward religious humanism and restore the Christian humanistic philosophy with a strong Catholic foundation.

In order to assist him in meeting his goals, Father McBride hired Sister Jo-Ann Flora, SND, to replace Nancy Martinez as Academic Dean. Sister Jo-Ann, a member of the Sisters of Notre Dame, came to UofA from Trinity College in Washington, DC, where she had chaired the Linguistics Department. Martinez returned to her former position as Associate Dean of General Studies.[676]

During the summer of 1983, the Faculty Senate was renamed the Faculty Forum, although there did not appear to be changes in the *modus operandi*. However, in subsequent years the constitution of the Faculty Forum was modified to change its role from a legislative body to one that focused on studying policies and making recommendations to the various organizational units.[677] In addition, McBride suggested, and the Board approved, removing the faculty and student representatives from the Board.[678]

Pre-registration for the fall term of the 1983–1984 school year began in August with an expected enrollment of 1,500, including 500 freshmen. Incoming students would be offered a new Associates degree path in computer science using the school's new Prime 552 computer. This state-of-the-art machine had a whopping two megabytes of solid-state memory and 158 megabytes on a disc drive.[679]

Sister Jo-Ann Flora, SND.
(CSWR/UofA, Box 18, yearbook collection)

In September, seven months after his appointment as acting president, Father Alfred was confirmed as permanent president by the Board of Trustees. In an editorial in the *Alumni News*, Father Alfred reaffirmed his "requirements" for the University to succeed in no uncertain terms:

—We must become a great Catholic university. When a church school sells its soul for money, it deserves to close.
—We must demand quality.
—We must do a few things well, instead of many things badly. Universities that try to be all things to all people deserve to fail.
—We must attract money and stop grubbing for it. In higher education, the secret of success is to offer a good product that is worthy of support.
—We must stand up for family and faith. A university should illuminate and sustain what is perennially good in faith, family, and flag.

By September, the "race" to find a new owner following the Vatican's rejection of transfer to the Board, a lay organization, was essentially down to one candidate—the Archdiocese of Santa Fe. Two religious orders—the Norbertines from Wisconsin and the Christian Brothers who operated the College of Santa Fe, the only other Catholic college in the state, had both considered the proposition and decided not to go forward. The Archbishop's office had no direct comment, saying only that the archdiocese was "one of many options."[680]

During the fall of 1983, a different problem surfaced. Roberta Humphreys, a former UofA records clerk who had recently resigned, reported that in July she had discovered nine student transcripts that appeared to have been altered to improve grades, speed up graduation, list courses that were never taken, and, in one case, create a completely fictional identity. She said that she had reported the issue to McBride and attorney Randall Glover in August, but that nothing appeared to be happening, and she was concerned that the administration was covering up the issue. In fact, for a time she referred to the situation as "Recordsgate."[681]

McBride and Glover denied that there was any sort of cover-up, saying, "We are investigating. The administration has taken steps, but we go very slowly because we wouldn't want to harm the reputation of anyone. We have no proof." At McBride's request, the Albuquerque Police Department was brought into the case in mid-October. Deputy District Attorney Steve Slusher noted that altering a transcript would constitute forgery, a third-degree felony, punishable by up to three years in prison.[682]

The police department concluded its investigation in December, identifying two current and one former student as the culprits. However, McBride elected not to press charges:

> We have identified those who were involved. We have corrected their transcripts to the right ones. They have been notified to that effect and admonished, and we're going to let it go at that. We will not issue any uncorrected transcripts.[683]

In addition to "Recordsgate," there were unsubstantiated rumors that under the previous administration there had been drug and even prostitution activities in some of the dormitories.[684]

During the fall of 1983, the Archdiocese became concerned that St. Pius X high school was unable to accept some qualified students because of size limitations at its Northeast Heights campus. One alternative under considerations was opening a new Catholic high school in space at UofA that was currently leased to a private company. McBride liked this idea for both financial and religious reasons, but the Archbishop said that some parents might not be enthusiastic about mixing high school and college students on the same campus.[685]

Despite his misgivings, Archbishop Sanchez decided to go ahead with the new school. At a press conference in February, he announced that St. Joseph on the Rio Grande High School would open in Madonna Hall on the UofA campus in August 1984 with an enrollment of 125. Davis Hall, the eventual home of the new school, would be renovated and converted from married student housing into classrooms. Sister Rose Therese Wich, principal of St. Mary's School in Albuquerque, would be the new principal.

The community college idea, which had been rejected by voters in 1978 and which *Albuquerque Journal* education writer Susan Landon characterized as "a ghost that haunts Albuquerque," also resurfaced in October 1983. This time the specter rose in the form of one of several recommendations in a report to the City Council from the Educational Task Force of the Goals for Albuquerque Committee. Although the report said that the two-year Associates and certificate programs at the UofA and UNM should continue "for now," it asserted that a community college should be established in Albuquerque "which would have as its purpose the offering of certificates and Associates degrees for a variety of careers and for lifelong learning and enrichment." Once again, despite McBride's intention to eliminate the two-year programs, the threat of substantial enrollment challenges in the near-term was surfacing.[686]

In January 1984, McBride took one of his major steps in returning the University to its liberal arts roots by announcing the phasing out of the two-year programs. The phase-out plans included dropping the very popular two-year nursing program, although the four-year nursing degree program would be retained. In that regard, he introduced Mary Jane Farrell, RN, PhD, who would take over the four-year program from Betty Gayle Boyle, RN, appointed by Frank Welch during the 1982 nursing controversy, who agreed to return to a teaching position.[687]

In March 1984, Gena McKee was elected as the new Board chair, replacing John Robert who had died suddenly on January 16. McKee was a UofA graduate in the Honors Program and a four-year member of the Board. In addition, Carol Kinney, a Board Member from 1971 to 1979, and Judge Tom Mescall, a district court judge and UofA alumnus, joined the Board. Mescall remarked, "I think that UofA is entering into a golden age of success under Father McBride."[688]

On Monday, April 9, 1984, the long-awaited transfer of ownership from the Sisters of St. Francis to the Archdiocese of Santa Fe became final. Vatican approval had been obtained in February, but finalizing details had postponed the final transfer. Father McBride noted that at the time of the transfer, the University had assets totaling about $25 million, no short-term debt, and long-term debt of about $2 million.

Sister Stephanie McReynolds, OSF, Provincial President of the Sisters of St. Francis said:

> We believe that in transferring the UofA to the Archdiocese that our mission of serving the Church in the Southwest will continue. Like most religious communities today we have fewer religious women to carry out all of the responsibilities demanded of our

present apostolic commitments. And, in addition, we cannot overlook the financial contributions we have made to the UofA in the past which we can no longer continue. The UofA has weathered financial problems in the past, necessitating a number of bail-out loans from the Sisters.[689]

Sister Stephanie McReynolds, OSF.
(CSWR/UofA, Box 18, yearbook collection)

Father McBride said that fund-raising was progressing well and that he believed that the school would not prove to be a financial burden to the Archdiocese.

In the summer and fall of 1984 and into the new year, things seemed to be moving along smoothly—two previously vacant dorms were being reopened, the college and city had begun joint work on a 17-acre soccer and football complex, and fund-raising was exceeding expectations.[690] Father McBride noted:

> Since I took office in March 1983, fund-raising has tripled. Largely because of this, in the fall I will start to see my dream—

that the UofA become known as a traditional four-year liberal arts university—take shape.[691]

The president also reversed his decision to phase out the popular two-year health programs—Nursing, Respiratory Therapy, and Radiography:

Being the only Catholic college in the area offering health courses, we decided to keep them. The school has such a long tradition of health care. I think a religious school should be in the field of mercy.[692]

However, he noted that these programs cost more to provide than the tuition supported, so, "Now that we've decided to keep it, I've got to go out and find money for it."

Esther Shir, then known as Kris Warmoth, was the reference librarian at the school. She recalled that the library was badly in need of maintenance and that whenever it rained, the staff had to run around the building placing buckets to catch the drips from the ceiling (She also recalled that Father Thomas Hogan, the chaplain at the school, had a pet lamb that followed him around the campus, wearing a diaper to minimize problems! Naturally, the lamb was named Agnus Dei (Lamb of God), but everyone just called her Agnes).[693]

So, as the spring term moved along, the pipe-smoking Father Alfred could afford a bit of a smile. The specter of a community college had lost some of its immediacy, the transfer of ownership issue had finally been resolved, the financial picture appeared to be brightening, and the discord that had plagued the school for the last several years was fading into the past. In addition, the Legislature had passed the Student Choice Act which provided for state aid to students in private universities.[694] In the fall of 1984, a yearbook, *La Herencia*, was planned for the first time in 13 years.[695]

Fund-raising proceeded apace during the spring and summer of 1984. McBride announced a $5,000 challenge by local retailer David Cooper, owner of Cooper's Western Wear. Cooper said that he would donate $5,000 a year for the next three years if the college could find 24 people who would match his donation. By January, McBride reported that he already had 14 of the 24 identified, and Cooper said to tell the rest that "this little Jewish boy has made the challenge."[696]

In addition to direct fund-raising, recruitment was also moving in an upward direction. Director of Admissions Elsie Scott was traveling across the state and meeting with high school counselors to acquaint them with the University and its mission. In addition, she made a trip to Taiwan and came back with applications from 65 prospective students. She also hosted a "fancy dinner" for APS counselors at which Father McBride spoke glowingly about the prospects for the University, emphasizing its focus on liberal arts and critical thinking.[697]

The 1984 mission statement and set of goals and ideals were very similar to the earlier versions that reflected the point of view of the Sisters of St. Francis, although they do have somewhat different priorities. Under Father McBride's oversight, the mission had three components:

—Maintain the Catholic identity.
—Provide a liberal learning environment.
—Emphasize academic excellence.

Similarly, the goals and ideals reflected McBride's philosophy:

—Teach critical thinking.
—Transmit culture.
—Clarify religious and moral values.
—Minister to student self-realization.
—Provide a means for livelihood.[698]

These statements of mission, ideals, and perspective were both evolutionary and cyclical. In fact, Father McBride expressed a strong interest in returning the school's name to St. Joseph on the Rio Grande to reflect its rejuvenated Catholic identity.[699]

Theresa Carson, a business administration student from 1982 until 1986 has fond memories of her time at UofA during the McBride administration. She had chosen the University because it was smaller and "a bit more intimate" and because it "catered to adults and folks with families which UNM did not." The faculty and students were "kind and compassionate," particularly so since she was pregnant during part of the time, and "everyone took care of me." One of her fondest memories was taking an elective fly-fishing course which included practicing casting techniques in the gymnasium and ended with a trip to the San Juan River where she "slogged through the water in a pair of waders."[700]

12
Inevitability

Father McBride's smile did not last long. At the March 1985 Board meeting, the University was declared to be in a "state of extreme emergency." The Board predicted a $2.7 million deficit for the 1985 fiscal year. As in previous years, the cause appeared to be declining enrollment, down to 1,200 from the previous year's 1,500. McBride and McKee both agreed that enrollment was unlikely to increase until the school's reputation was re-established.[701]

Several faculty members, including long-term activist Warren Lee, were dismayed that the crisis had appeared so suddenly. McBride said that the school had hired an independent auditor and that when the audit report came back, he [McBride] was "overwhelmed by the size of the deficit." "I was truly not aware a month ago when I talked to the faculty," he insisted.

In order to deal with what he characterized as the "changed reality," McBride put together a multi-point plan:

—Expenses would be reduced by $200,000 by the end of UofA's fiscal year on August 31, although details of how this was to be accomplished were not specified.
—A balanced budget would be designed for both fiscal years 1985–1986 and 1986–1987.
—The University would aggressively pursue fund-raising and long-term financing.
—Faculty and staff would be involved in developing solutions to the financial problems.
—A "brother relationship" would be established with the College

of St. Thomas in St. Paul, Minnesota, which had expressed interest in establishing programs in the Southwest.

—Current tuition would be maintained, if possible.

—Some of the recently tightened admission standards would be relaxed, although they would stop short of open admission.

—Everyone would be encouraged to pray for divine assistance.[702]

In an anonymous letter to Gena McKee and the rest of the Board, a writer who self-described as "One Who Has Been Badly Hurt," excoriated McBride and Sister Jo-Ann Flora. The pair were characterized as "shoddy administrators," "power-mad," "vicious," "and ignoramuses." The author gave a list of 23 named individuals, plus "nurses and others," who quit or were forced to leave and said "Sister still has a long hit list." The writer concluded the diatribe with, "This pair and everyone connected with the school have been the laughing stock of the city .... If something is not done soon, these power-mad maniacs will destroy the college."[703]

The role of Sister Jo-Ann in the administration was viewed by some as the dominant force. Father McBride was characterized as a great man but a weak leader. He was accused of acquiescing to Sister Jo-Ann in most decisions, even some that went against his initial goals. This led to divisions within the administration and what some felt to be a toxic work environment for both faculty and staff.[704] One former administrator who preferred to remain anonymous characterized the administration as a "real rat hole." Another administrator recalled the dread felt whenever one was called to the second-floor offices where Sister Jo-Ann resided. This individual said that the Sister's treatment of underlings was so draconian that she acquired the nickname "Atilla the Nun."[705]

To make matters even worse, the Reagan Administration's efforts to reduce the national deficit included a budget cut of $8.7 billion from student financial aid programs. Secretary of Education William Bennett said that some college students would have to consider divestiture, "like a stereo divestiture, an automobile divestiture, or a 'three-weeks-at-the-beach' divestiture." He argued that students, like farmers and other special interest groups, would have to "take their lumps" if the huge federal deficit was to be reduced. Bennett's rather glib remarks did not sit well with UofA students like Valerie Hinshaw, a 33-year-old single mother of five, who said, "If this budget cut is passed, I can kiss my college education good-bye and my dreams, too."[706]

On March 21, the University announced the layoff of 18 staff members and McBride predicted that there would also need to be faculty reductions for the next school year. Warren Lee said that the faculty was working together to determine which programs would be retained and which would have to be dropped.[707]

The Trustees met in closed session on Tuesday, April 2, to determine whether the university would stay open or close. McBride admitted that he may have been at least partly responsible for the drop in enrollment when he moved quickly to raise standards and eliminate programs.[708]

Community leaders all spoke up in support of keeping the University open. Many also noted that UofA's fiscal challenges were no different than those of other private colleges around the country. In fact, John Maio of the Sperry Corporation and a member of the Albuquerque Economic Forum, noted that between January 1, 1980, and July 1, 1982, 26 private colleges had closed, five merged with other private colleges, and one shifted to public control.[709]

President McBride saw establishment of an endowment as a key element in keeping the UofA afloat. He suggested that a "comfortable endowment" would be $10 million in eight years, of which $2 million could be used for student scholarships.[710]

McBride also floated the idea that the school should strive to attract more out-of-state students. His vision seemed to be to create a "Little Ivy League School" with students who would be willing to pay higher tuition. One major problem, however, was a lack of dormitory space. The existing dorms were either committed to other activities or badly in need of renovation. In fact, Madonna Hall was not only in bad condition, but there were rumors that a 95-year-old nun who had died in the building still haunted it.[711] Father's idea was to house the incoming students with local families. The concept of family housing was met with some skepticism by the admissions staff and was never actually implemented.[712]

At its Tuesday meeting, the Board voted unanimously to keep the school open. In addition, McBride announced that Frank Kleinhenz, the UofA president who had dragged the school out of the red between 1970 and 1973, would be returning to the school as chancellor. He was to replace Sister Jo-Ann Flora who had resigned in protest over the relaxation of admission standards.[713]

Kleinhenz, who had left his job at Starline Printing to become Albuquerque Mayor Harry Kinney's chief administrative officer in 1974 and who was called by some "the shadow mayor of Albuquerque," took a 29 percent pay cut to come back and try to rescue the UofA one more time. When asked about this decision, he said, "I am returning to where I belong. How I got into city work, I'll never know. But I am essentially an educator." In addition to being an educator, Kleinhenz was very popular with his colleagues. Elsie Scott recalled that he was also quite a tease and always had a prank or two for the staff.[714]

Kleinhenz said that he loved a good challenge, "You look for something that really twists you up in knots for a while. And that is what I thrive on."[715] As it turned out, even Frank Kleinhenz would be stymied by this particular Gordian knot!

When new contracts were issued on April 29, 1985, 15 non-tenured faculty members were told that their contracts would not be renewed. In sharp contrast to earlier such moves under Frank Welch, Rosalie Otero, Faculty Senate President, said that the faculty accepted both the outcome and the process:

> Naturally, we wish there hadn't been any cuts because many of the people leaving are excellent teachers. It's a loss to us. But I realize that they had to be made, and I think, for the most part, they were done reasonably according to the Faculty Handbook.[716]

In June, the university began to organize the $10 million University of Albuquerque Legacy Campaign with the help of Community Counseling Services, a professional fund-raising company. William B. "Bing" Grady, president of SunWest Bank of Albuquerque, was chosen to head the effort with Archbishop Sanchez as honorary chairman.

The actual campaign began in September, but even with this new campaign underway, Kleinhenz said that it would be a year before they could determine whether or not the university could weather this latest crisis. He added that "there has to be some evidence in a very short time that the institution is viable." In this case, viability would be determined by increased enrollment and community involvement in the first phase of the Legacy Campaign.[717]

William A. "Bing" Grady.
(*Albuquerque Journal*, 6/21/85, p. 13)

In July, the school was put on probation by its accreditation provider, the North Central Association of Colleges and Secondary Schools.[718] The association listed a number of areas that needed to be corrected by the University:

—The school must achieve a balanced budget.
—The school must show progress toward eliminating all debt.
—The school must have a viable program in place to boost annual giving and build an endowment.
—Given that the school had had eight presidents in the last 15 years, it must show some stability in top administration.
—The school must achieve some stability in chief financial and academic officers. The Association noted that the latest academic vice president, Sister Jo-Ann Flora, had resigned shortly after their visit in March.
—The school must reconcile its mission statement with the types

of classes being offered and the types of students it desires to recruit.[719]

In an August reply to the North Central accreditation organization, McBride struck an upbeat tone. He said that both registration and residency hall occupancy for the fall term were up for the first time since 1975. He also pointed out that the budget was improving and that the worrisome debt service had been reduced by $1 million. The long-needed endowment drive had been started with a $10 million target to be pledged over the next three years and collected over the next seven.[720]

In what, in retrospect, seems like a desperation move to revive enrollment, the school went directly against its originally stated policy and introduced or re-introduced three new Associate degree programs. First, they revived the popular Adult Education program which had accounted for 25 percent of the school's enrollment until it was cancelled in 1982. This program, led by John Lucas, enabled students to complete most regular majors with 90 credit hours instead of 120, while meeting the general studies requirements with a series of five condensed liberal arts seminars.[721]

Second, a program in the Department of Business Administration, emphasizing sales with both two-year and four-year tracks, was designed and was touted as "the only such degree program in the West." Ed Chum, president of Professional Salespersons of America and a collaborator with UofA in the new program, noted, "Sales people are 30 million strong and only eight universities are offering degrees."[722]

Finally, in February 1986, the administration announced a new Associates program in Hospitality in conjunction with the New Mexico Hotel and Motel Association. The program, scheduled to begin less than a month later in March, would be led by Javier Cano, a seven-year veteran of Marriott Corporation.[723]

By the end of December 1985, the Legacy Campaign had raised $700,000 and Grady noted that they were probably a month ahead of schedule. Kleinhenz reminded everyone, however, that these funds were to build an endowment, not to reduce the deficit. Increased enrollment and careful management of expenses would be required to handle that problem.[724]

Also in December, the faculty undertook an organizational overhaul. They changed the name of their organization from Faculty

Forum to Faculty Assembly, "in order to better reflect the functions of the group" and revised the Faculty Handbook and the School Catalog.[725] This change put in place a less hierarchical management approach for the faculty. Chancellor Frank Kleinhenz, in an uncharacteristically caustic remark, said that he "could live with any faculty organizational model" because he was of the opinion that "faculties contribute little to policy-making because of their internal bickering, ego-tripping, etc."[726] In addition, in the Faculty Assembly minutes for December 5, Kleinhenz characterized the school's financial situation as "terrible."[727]

In February, the State Legislature further added to UofA's enrollment woes when the Senate passed a bill allowing the T-VI to grant two-year degrees. Since about 25 percent of UofA's students were enrolled in two-year programs and since T-VI's costs were about one-tenth of UofA's $130 per credit-hour, the threat was clear. McBride noted that even if the bill didn't pass this legislative session, the handwriting was on the wall. UNM also opposed the bill, noting that it would cost them about $4 million per year.[728]

Frank Kleinhenz and student protester.
(*Albuquerque Journal*, 2/12/86, p. 4)

On Tuesday, February 11, 1986, the UofA Board met together with the Finance Committee of the Archdiocese of Santa Fe. Going into the meeting, the trustees were wearing stickers that read, "Miracles do happen."[729] Unfortunately, this time the miracle did not happen. Coming out of the meeting was the announcement that all had been dreading—the hard work and prayers called for earlier had been insufficient. The school would have to close after the completion of the August 1986 summer session.[730] In a letter to the Student Body, Father McBride said, "It is with deep regret and a sense of loss that we will close the University of Albuquerque on August 15, 1986."[731]

Columnist V. B. Price, noting the issues at both UNM and UofA, said, "Albuquerque used to be a college town. Now it smells like an academic battlefield littered with politicians bloating in the sun."[732]

13
Demise and Disposition

The announcement of the closure for the University of Albuquerque was confirmed by a formal vote of the Board of Trustees on February 18, 1986.[733] However, the announcement did not mean that the doors were immediately closed and the lights turned off. There was significant work to be done. Students needed to have a way to finish their studies; faculty members needed to be helped to find new employment; a summer program had to be planned and conducted; the school's valuable real estate needed to be repurposed; and the local community parishioners who had worshipped in the school's chapel for years had to be accommodated.

At a Faculty Assembly meeting in late February, there was an extensive discussion of faculty concerns relative to closing the school. Five specific issues were raised:

—Concerns over the future of faculty members who were over 50-years-old but were not yet eligible for pensions or Social Security.
—Concerns over the projected pension amounts. Because the school's salaries had been very low, pensions would be minimal for most faculty members.
—The need for health benefits to be transferred to the Archdiocesan medical plan to prevent loss of medical coverage.
—Concerns over severance pay.
—The need for committees to help students find new schools and to help faculty members to find new jobs.[734]

A critical meeting with representatives from the Board of Trustees, the Faculty Committee for Closing the University, and the Archdiocese was held on March 5. The Board members stated that the Board would remain active until August, at which time it would "cease to exist." They also reviewed the rationale for closing the school. They cited four reasons, all financially based:

> —Insufficient revenue because of poor enrollment.
> —The lack of an endowment.
> —The longstanding debt (estimated at $250,000 for the 1985–1986 school year alone) and associated debt service.
> —Competition from other institutions who could offer similar courses for significantly less money.

The Faculty representatives raised their concerns about terminal contracts and low pensions. They noted that, because of the late notification of the decision to close the school, it was very challenging for them to find new jobs. They also raised the threat of litigation.[735] Rose Cosden, chairperson of the Faculty Affairs Committee, said:

> We've heard about the school's financial problems every year and every year the school went on. So, this closing really was a surprise.... The responsible, humane, and legal thing to do is to take care of us.[736]

Classes continued at the University through May when the last Commencement for the School was held on a gray, rainy May 16, at the Kiva Auditorium in the Albuquerque Convention Center. Hundreds of students, faculty, staff, and alumni attended the event where Archbishop Sanchez said that, while the school was closing, its spirit would live on. "I believe our spirit remains strong, and so the poet speaks to each of us today that there is indeed a tear and a smile in our eyes."[737]

The faculty and staff at UofA were saddened by the closure of the school. In August, just before the doors were closed for the last time, they held a wake for the college. Everyone wore black arm bands, they had a barbeque, and, reportedly, a lot of drinking occurred.[738] The last alumni event was an all-class reunion scheduled for May 17 and 18 at the campus.[739]

Theresa Carson, one of the graduating seniors, recalls receiving a letter that had been sent to all students that confirmed that the school was closing. That letter "really hit her." She said that graduation day was "bittersweet"–she remembers a feeling of satisfaction that she "made it through," but a bit of sadness that UofA would "no longer be a choice" for prospective students.[740]

It is a bit ironic that after years, even decades, of front-page coverage of the school's financial and administrative challenges, the announcement of its final commencement was relegated to a short, three-paragraph piece in the lower right-hand corner of page four of the *Albuquerque Journal*.[741]

The last play offered by the school's much-vaunted theater arts program seemed appropriate in light of the school's situation–Bertolt Brecht's *The Caucasian Chalk Circle*, a play about the possibilities for the future of mankind despite human shortcomings. This drama, directed by Christy Mendoza, was performed in mid-April at the University's Fine Arts Center.[742]

The last play.
(CSWR/UofA photo archives)

Of course, students who were graduating from the school that term received their diplomas or certificates on May 16. However, lower classmen were not left to fend for themselves. A solution in the form of the College of Santa Fe (CSF) was being implemented.

The College of Santa Fe was first established as St. Michael's College in Santa Fe by the Institute of the Brothers of the Christians (commonly referred to as the Christian Brothers) in 1859. Although the institution was a high school, it was referred to as a "college," following the European custom of referring to all secondary schools as colleges.[743]

The actual college of St. Michaels split from the high school in 1947 when it moved to the former Bruns Hospital property. The name was formally changed to the College of Santa Fe in 1965. Interestingly, there were very few interactions between the UofA and CSF during the early years of the college. The two Catholic institutions did compete in some athletic events, but there was very little interchange on the academic or administrative level.

The heads of the three New Mexico accredited private institutions did meet frequently in the 1970s to discuss the mounting financial crises and to work together to avert the pressures and circumstances associated with impending deficits.[744] In addition, in April 1973, Ray Powell, chair of the UofA Board of Trustees, responded to an earlier letter written by Harold Saueressig, chair of the CSF Board:

> We are much enthused with your suggestion of a joint committee to establish cooperation efforts that will be mutually beneficial.... I think our two institutions can be considerably stronger working together than going our separate ways.[745]

Little did they know then how that cooperation would manifest itself thirteen years later.

On March 4, 1986, Brother Donald Mounton, a member of the Christian Brothers and the President of the College of Santa Fe since 1981, directed his Vice President, Brother Clarence Fioke, to establish a branch of CSF on the UofA campus.[746] In a statement to the UofA Student Body, Mounton had assured students that CSF would "carry on the tradition of a Catholic, liberal-arts college in Albuquerque." He also noted that CSF planned to offer programs and courses that would lead to majors at their Albuquerque campus on a continuing basis and that

CSF would assist those students in their final year of either a Bachelors or Associates degree program to graduate with a UofA degree. In a letter intended to reassure the UofA students, Mounton and McBride said, "A page has turned. The book has not closed."[747]

Brother Donald Mounton.
(courtesy of the San Francisco New Orleans District Archives)

Brother Clarence Fioke.
(courtesy of the San Francisco New Orleans District Archives)

As the plight of UofA became more and more obvious, Mounton contacted Archbishop Sanchez and asked if CSF could help the Archdiocese when UofA finally closed its doors. Sanchez liked the idea and invited Mounton to the February meeting of the Board at which the closing was to be formally announced. The meeting, which had been publicized, was attended by several other institutional representatives, and the parking lot was "crowded by cars." Mounton was ushered in through a "hidden back door," and, at the end of the meeting, CSF was asked to "help pick up the pieces."[748]

The arrangements for former UofA students who elected to stay on at the CSF branch were clarified later in March. Only UofA juniors would be eligible to pursue UofA degrees through CSF. Associate degree students who had completed 55 of the 90 hours required for graduation would be allowed to continue and receive a UofA diploma.[749]

An April 1986 note from Brother Fioke thanked students for help in organizing for the fall 1986 semester and provided answers to a number of Frequently Asked Questions about course offerings, financial aid, availability of transcripts, etc.

CSF was to lease Lourdes Hall from the Archdiocese of Santa Fe and "teach out" any seniors and juniors that were near their final terms. Other students would be allowed to enroll in CSF and could graduate with either a UofA or a CSF diploma/certificate. CSF noted that the cost to attend that school was $125 per credit-hour, slightly less than the cost they had been paying at UofA.[750]

After some discussion, the CSF administration elected to eliminate daytime classes at the former UofA campus in favor of evening and weekend classes. Classes that were retained from the UofA curriculum included Bachelor-track programs in management, accounting, management information systems, public administration, humanities, elementary education, nursing, business, physical sciences, psychology, and sociology. Any courses that did not have enough enrollment to cover costs were eliminated.[751]

In December 1986, the *Albuquerque Journal* reported that students who had transferred to CSF from UofA were happy with the new environment. In fact, 202 of the UofA students had found a home either on the UofA main campus or at the Kirtland Air Force Base Branch which CSF continued to operate.[752] Although CSF intended to stop the nursing, respiratory therapy, and radiography programs, current students would be "taught out." Students in respiratory therapy and radiography would be transferred to Pima Medical Institute in Albuquerque with a choice of receiving either a UofA or a Pima diploma.[753] Both the University of New Mexico and T-VI also offered to accept UofA students.

Andrew Imrik, who had come to the University as a professor of business administration and economics in the fall of 1958, assumed the position of Coordinator of Business Administration at the CSF branch.[754] He remarked:

> We have a great amount of student satisfaction. If the College of Santa Fe could be accused of anything, it would be going overboard in its quest for excellence. We are pushing more for quality. UofA was in the process of going out—that's a hard time to push for quality.[755]

The first graduation for students from the new branch of the College of Santa Fe was held in May 1987.

According to both Michael Keleher and James Cooney, the revenue from the CSF students at the former UofA campus was significant enough add a few years to the life of the College of Santa Fe, which, like so many private, religiously-affiliated schools, was "hanging on by a financial thread" in the face of expanding opportunities for students to attend much less expensive public institutions. CSF was not immune to the same problems that beset UofA. They struggled with financial problems from the start; they faced community college competition in Santa Fe; and they experienced rebellious faculty. They managed to stay afloat until 2009, when they, too, closed their doors.[756]

The state unemployment department recognized the issues associated with a large group of individuals being released at one time and expedited unemployment checks for the newly-unemployed UofA faculty and staff. Several of the faculty, including librarian Kris Warmoth, were hired by the recently-opened UNM branch campus in Valencia County.[757]

CSF said that it would make every effort to provide jobs for the UofA faculty, but it made no promises, since the curriculum was clearly going to change. By December 1986, 40 of UofA's former faculty members were on staff at the CSF branch, mostly in part-time positions.[758]

Not all of the faculty was pleased with "the new normal." On May 14, 1986, 15 faculty members filed a $14.3 million lawsuit against the UofA, the Archdiocese of Santa Fe, Father Alfred McBride, and Frank Kleinhenz.[759] The allegations were breach of contract and misrepresentation. In particular, the plaintiffs alleged that, as early as 1979, the Archdiocese had secretly planned to relocate St. Pius high school to the UofA campus and that the University "intentionally or negligently led the plaintiff faculty members to stay on by taking a series of actions that gave the impression that it [UofA] would stay open." In addition to the $14.3 million, the faculty members asked for compensation for lost wages, since they had been notified of the University's closure too late to find comparable jobs.[760]

Of course, the defendants denied the allegations of secrecy and pointed out that the Faculty Handbook, an integral part of the plaintiffs' contracts, said that notice of contract non-renewal did not apply in the case of closure of the entire university.[761] In August 1986, the university offered to pay each of the plaintiffs $319.84 or pay for health insurance coverage through the end of December 1986.[762] The lawsuit was settled by mutual agreement and dismissed with prejudice on November 28.[763]

One particular faculty member deserves particular attention as the school ended its long fight for life—Andrew Imrik, PhD. When the school closed, he was the longest serving faculty member, having come to the school in 1958. And even after the school closed, Imrik stayed on to run the Business Administration program at the CSF branch college. Perhaps Sister Marilyn said it best when she awarded the James Marshall Distinguished Faculty Service Award to Imrik in 1970:

> Some have called him "the wizard of words" and others "the aristocrat of the classroom." He is indeed a man of many parts and talents, tied together with tremendous stamina and determination..... He works tirelessly to advance the University and has served in key positions within the University structure in the service of his colleagues.... He has played a major role in helping to direct the University's destiny.... It is fitting that this award should go to a man whose concern for his fellow man is so genuine, yet so unobtrusive. We express on this occasion our grateful appreciation to Dr. Imrik for choosing to be one of us.[764]

Dr. Andrew Imrik.
(CSWR/UofA photo archives)

Dr. Imrik continued to teach at the College of Santa Fe and New Mexico Highlands until 1993. He died in Albuquerque on November 4, 2006, at the age of 84.

The last faculty Assembly meeting was held on May 1, 1986. There was significant bitterness expressed by several attendees. Long-time professor Lawrence Desaulniers said, "Even if your presence (i.e., the faculty, et al.) won't save the University of Albuquerque, your absence will save the Archdiocese of Santa Fe!" Several members suggested candidates for honorary degrees at the upcoming commencement. These included Muamar Khadafy, Imelda Marcos, Baby Doc Duvalier, and Board Chair Gina McKee. Secretary Kris Warmouth closed the minutes with, "RIP dear old UofA."[765]

Father McBride did not languish without a job for long. In September 1986, Monsignor Daniel Hoye of the National Council of

Catholic Bishops assigned him to be the coordinator of the planned visit by Pope John Paul II to the United States in the fall of 1987.[766] He continued to serve the Church in a number of high-level positions, including as the Ecclesiastical Assistant for the United States, as a consultant to the Archdiocese of Boston for the implementation of the Catechism of the Catholic Church, as Professor of Homiletics and Catechetics at Pope St. John XXIII National Seminary in Weston, Massachusetts, and as Spiritual Director for the U.S. branch of the World-Wide Mission called the "Aid to the Church in Need." He died at the Norbertine Abbey in De Pere, Wisconsin, on October 23, 2003, at the age of 91.[767]

Frank Kleinhenz, the man who saved the school in the 1970s and tried to do so again, went on to serve in state and local politics. He died of a heart attack on December 18, 2002, at the age of 77 and, because of his World War II service, was buried in the National Cemetery in Santa Fe.[768]

At the time of closure, the University was running a deficit of two million dollars and had long-term debt of about six million. In addition, considerable monies had been collected from donors to the Legacy Campaign to support an endowment. Under direction from the Vatican, the Archdiocese agreed to assume responsibility for the deficit and the long-term debt.[769] They hoped to recoup part of these costs by leasing facilities at the former UofA to various organizations. In April 1986, Bing Grady wrote letters to the various individuals who had contributed to the Legacy Campaign. All of the $180,000 collected so far was in an escrow account; none had been spent. Grady offered to return it to the donors. He also offered the possibility of turning it over to the University to help to defer expenditures through the August closure date.[770]

The University Foundation had been dissolved in 1979, and its assets plus the 40-acre parcel had become a direct holding of the University.[771] These assets became a part of the Legacy Campaign in late 1983.[772] According to McBride, the Foundation's holdings in 1985 were:

—Property in Rio Grande Estates in Socorro worth $2,400.
—Five acres in Paradise Hills worth $25,000.
—One lot in Paradise Hills worth $22,000.
—Twelve acres near Double Eagle Airport worth $65,000.
—Cash of $72,750.[773]

These assets were turned over to the Archdiocese as a part of the overall debt reduction effort.

The University of Albuquerque had begun life as a summer program, so it was probably appropriate that it should end its life the same way. The last official activity of the school was its 1986 summer program. In this case, a major part of the program was the hosting of the Second Annual Southwest Theological Institute, a program that included both classes and workshops. The first of the series was a week-long seminar on Art, Symbolism, and the New Testament, led by Sister Giotta Moots, Director of the Sagrada Art School in Old Town and the person who built the devotional chapel of Our Lady of Guadalupe in Old Town.[774]

The most valuable asset of the now-defunct school was its 60-acre site on the West Mesa. Contrary to the allegations by the faculty plaintiffs in the lawsuit, the St. Pius relocation to the UofA site had not been "on the books" since 1979. Although it was true that the high school intended to vacate its site on Louisiana Boulevard in the Northeast Heights, the preferred location was actually Parenti Field near Indian School and Interstate-25.

St. Pius X high school had opened in 1956 in the basement of St. Charles Borromeo church in Southeast Albuquerque. A full campus at the intersection of Indian School and Louisiana was completed in 1959, but it was not until closure of UofA became certain in February 1986 that the decision to relocate to the UofA campus was made. In fact, several St. Pius parents complained about this choice, citing travel distances, increased expenses, and safety concerns. However, the Archbishop confirmed the decision to move with a date for occupation of the new campus to be in the fall of 1988. When the school came to the West Side it would merge with St. Joseph on the Rio Grande High School, but the combined schools would retain the St. Pius X name.[775]

St. Pius High School. (author's collection)

Modifications and renovations of the U of A campus to accommodate the high school began in earnest in April 1987. In November 1987, a new gymnasium was approved for the school. St. Pius basketball coach Bill Duffy described the old gym: "It's archaic. The bleachers don't work and the floor has more dead spots than the average cemetery."[776] The statue of St. Pius X was moved to the new campus, but the statue of St. Joseph remained in a place of honor on the quad in the center of St. Pius X High School.

Statue of St. Pius X.
(St. Pius X High School)

Statue of St. Joseph.
(CSWR/UofA Photo Collection)

Archdiocese of Santa Fe Catholic Center.
(author's collection)

In September 1986, the Archdiocese moved its offices from its Morningside location in the Northeast Heights to the second floor of the University Center Building at the former UofA. This move provided the Archdiocese with much needed space and saved money by occupying a building already owned rather than renting a facility.[777]

According to former librarian Esther Shir, the library's collection was distributed to other Franciscan missions in Africa. The Chavez collection went to the University of New Mexico where it currently resides in the Center for Southwest Research and Special Collections. The College of Santa Fe also kept some books from the collection.[778]

Beginning in the 1970s, local families had begun coming to Mass at the University of Albuquerque chapel, and in 1981 they asked the Sisters if they could be part of the campus ministry. College Chaplain Father Thomas Hogan agreed to have these folks as part of his parish, and they continued to come to Mass in the chapel dedicated to St. Cecilia in the University Center.

Services continued in the University Center while the St.

Pius renovations were completed and after the new high school was established in 1988. By 2000, the population in the vicinity of the former UofA had expanded considerably, and on November 26, 2000, a new church located about a half mile west of the campus was completed and dedicated to St. Joseph on the Rio Grande.

St. Joseph on the Rio Grande parish church.
(author's collection)

A mere two years after the University had closed, while buildings still stood, only the statue from the venerable but troubled school remained.

14
Retrospective

From 1920 to 1986 the University of Albuquerque and its direct ancestors were an integral part of the Albuquerque educational scene. For much of that time, the school was small, stable, and focused. In contrast, for the last two decades of its 66-year life, the University rode a roller coaster which not only lurched from highs to lows, but also threatened to leave the tracks at any moment.

The school started as a summer program for teaching nuns from the Poor Sisters of St. Francis Seraph of the Perpetual Adoration. The Sisters would come to the St. Anthony Orphanage in Albuquerque for what is now referred to as continuing education. In 1921, the annual summer school became the St. Francis Summer College.

The college grew in both size and popularity, eventually becoming a year-round teachers' college that admitted sisters from a number of orders as well as some lay teachers. In 1940, the school was formally chartered as the Catholic Teachers' College of New Mexico. For a time, the school was managed by the Archdiocese of Santa Fe, but it reverted to the Sisters of St. Francis in 1947.

The school moved from the orphanage to a former Congreationalist mission school on South Second Street in 1946 and was renamed St. Joseph on the Rio Grande. It remained at this location until it moved to a brand-new location on the West Mesa in 1951.

In 1966, the name was once again changed, this time to the University of Albuquerque. Not long after it became the University of Albuquerque, the roller-coaster ride began. In the next 20 years, the school would have ten presidents and would experience gut-wrenching financial cycles.

So what were the reasons that the school enjoyed success and eventually succumbed? There are two overriding issues—identity and stability—and a number of subissues. These issues and subissues are all intertwined, but they can be artificially separated for the purpose of analysis.

IDENTITY

In its earliest years the school had a singular, universally-agreed-upon purpose: it was a Catholic teachers' college. The administration and the faculty, all Franciscan priests and nuns, were in charge of a student body that consisted of Catholic nuns. The curriculum was completely aligned around the well-defined objective of producing commited, capable teachers for parochial schools. Even when the management changed from the Sisters of St. Francis to the Archdiocese of Santa Fe and back to the Sisters in the 1940s, the focus remained the same.

In the late 1930s and early 1940s, the school retained religious faculty, leadership, and mission, but opened the student body to "Catholic young men and women who intend to follow the teaching professions." In 1940, the enrollment included 100 students from religious orders and 140 lay students.[779]

As the school expanded from St. Anthony's to the campus at Our Lady of Lourdes, the curriculum broadened, and the school began to take on more of a liberal arts identity. Although teacher education remained a critical part of the school's curriculum, the course offerings broadened to cover a more typical set of college offerings—sciences, humanities, arts, etc. Despite this expansion, the Catholic foundation remained.

In 1956, perhaps in reaction to the increasing push for liberal arts and sciences, a committee tasked with examining the integration of curriculum and mission noted that the purpose of the school was:

> ...to produce the perfect Christian. The student, on graduation, should take his place in society as "priest, prophet, ruler, and maker," and he should excel in all four roles. The most perfect Christian will be produced by the most perfect education.[780]

In 1958, Father Sullivan reiterated this emphasis on the Catholic and Christian foundations for the school:

It is not expected that a teacher be a fully trained philosopher and, at the same time, have mastered his own special field of knowledge.... But the teacher is expected to accept Thomistic principles and to teach nothing in contradiction to them.[781]

As the University entered the decades of the 1960s and 1970s, it experienced a significant growth in enrollment, growing from 500 in 1960 to a peak of 3,400 in 1974. However, it also faced a series of financial challenges. As a result, it began to drift away from its original purpose. Under the guise of community service and in recognition of the challenges posed by the movement for support of a junior college in Albuquerque, the school offered technical and vocational programs and established several branches. In 1973, President Frank Kleinhenz noted:

We want to continue our four-year liberal arts courses ... we hope to set up the two-year courses so that they can feed right into the higher education process should the students decide to stay around.[782]

In 1978, the school issued another mission statement which said:

The University itself intends to be a model of the Christian humanism and the competencies it endeavors to foster in its students.... The University is constituted essentially to serve the people of New Mexico, but particularly those who are educationally and economically disadvantaged, those whose educational needs are unmet, and those with a strong cross-cultural or career-vocational orientation....The University offers a program which preserves, fosters and transmits the Judeo-Christian heritage mirrored in the traditional liberal arts refined for the human conditions and needs of the day.... The University intends that all of its programs foster a high level of excellence in humanistic intellectual growth and in fundamental and specialized competencies.[783]

Note the emphasis on Christian humanism, service to the people of New Mexico, especially those who are disadvantaged, and the focus on "humanistic intellectual growth" and "fundamental and specialized competencies." These certainly reflect the influence of Vatican II's emphasis on Christian humanism as contrasted with the pre-Vatican II philosophy of producing a perfect Christian prepared to take his place in society as "priest, prophet, ruler, and maker."

The Sisters of St. Francis were keenly aware of the shift in mission and philosophy over the years. Their mission, too, had shifted, and they also were concerned with the increased financial burden that they were being asked to bear:

> The Sisters are no longer in a position to support the financial requirements of the University and, just as importantly, we find ourselves almost totally separated from our religious mission as it relates to the University.... The Board of Trustees was able to improve the financial situation by adding academic programs that were more income-producing. This resulted in changing the direction of the college from liberal arts to a high percent of offerings that were career-oriented classes. However, these changes in our academic offerings, to ease our financial problems, were accomplished at the cost of departing further and further from our religious mission of providing education in a Catholic environment.[784]

Finally, President Alfred McBride decided that the way to solve all of the problems was to pull the school back from its movement toward religious humanism and return the school to Christian humanism and its Catholic roots by getting rid of most of the two-year vocational programs:

> We must do more than prepare people to earn a living. The most marketable skill of all is how to live, not just how to make a living, but how to live grandly and gloriously. If you sit before your Apple computer and you haven't had the literature and religious and history and philosophy courses, you won't have the imagination to use it.[785]

In an op-ed piece in the *Albuquerque Journal* following the decision to close the school in 1986, long-time educational writer Mary Engle characterized the problem as a "chameleon identity."[786] In effect, the school seemed to be trying to be all things to all people. On one extreme you had leaders such as Frank Kleinhenz and Frank Welch, driven largely by financial concerns, who focused on a more pragmatic technical-vocational approach. On the other hand you had Father Alfred McBride who tried to bring the school back to its Catholic liberal arts roots.

The 1976 statement from the pre-reaccreditation self-assessment captures the essence of the identity concern:

> There seemed to be no clear, consistent vision for the University—some saw it as a liberal arts college with the vocational and special programs as ancillary, while others saw it as a community service institution that should respond to the needs of the community, even at the expense of reduction in the liberal arts.[787]

This basic conflict in identity fed directly into the stability issues.

STABILITY

The overall question of stability has two interrelated components—finances and leadership. The school's best years were its early years as a University. From 1947, to 1967, the school had only two presidents—Sister M. Viatora Schuller, OSF, and Mother M. Basilia Kugler, OSF. Because of this continuity of leadership, there was a continuity of management. From 1967 to 1986, there were ten presidents, each with a different background and different perspective on how the school should operate.[788]

Compounding the school leadership issue was the ownership debate. With the exception of the short Archdiocesian interlude in the 1940s, the school had been owned and operated (either directly or indirectly through proxy organizations) by the Sisters of St. Francis since the 1920s. As the school moved into the 1960s, it became increasingly clear that the goals of the school and the Sisters had substantially diverged, and that the Sisters were no longer interested or able to deal with the challenges of running the school. This uncertainty colored many of the decisions that were made by the administration and the Board of Trustees and contributed to the financial uncertainties that faced the University during its last two decades.

While the frequent changes of leadership and confounding

ownership problems were internal to the school and its top level oversight, there were issues that were essentially beyond the control of the school administration. In particular, the question of the need for a community college in the Albuquerque area forced the University into a decision space over which it had little control.

Starting with Tom Popejoy's comments in 1967, there was an increasing hue and cry for a community college in Albuquerque. The State Legislature, the Governor, the Albuquerque Chamber of Commerce, and the Albuquerque Public Schools all weighed in to the discussion. The fact that the University had a substantial technical-vocational element in its curriculum (as much as 70 percent of the courses at one point), coupled with the constant financial problems that beset the school, led many to believe that an obvious solution to the question of a community college was to simply turn UofA into a community college. The overwhelming vote against this proposition in 1978 stayed the question, but the multi-year back-and-forth meant that potential students at the University were always looking over their shoulder to see if the school was about to go away.

The leadership, ownership, and community college issues all contributed to the problem of financial stability for the school. During its formative years, the school was underwritten by the Sisters of St. Francis as a part of their mission of education. However, as the school grew, the financial needs increased and, at the same time, the Sisters mission began to evolve more toward hospitals and elder care and away from schools.

Although it was commonly thought that a Catholic university received most of its funding from the Church, that perception was incorrect. In one study, only 14 of 235 Catholic colleges in the United States received support from their local diocese, and even then, the support was minimal.[789] In fact, most of the revenue (as much as 94 percent) came from tuition, room, board, and fees. Thus, the revenue stream for the University was intimately tied to enrollment and out-of-area students who lived in the dormitories.

On the other side of the ledger, expenses were only related to enrollment in the predictive sense. With an "if you build it, he will come" attitude in the 1960s, the University had guessed that enrollment would grow to 2,000 to 3,000 full-time students and had built a campus and faculty to accommodate that growth. When that growth did not occur fast enough, the mortgages associated with real estate, facilities, infrastructure, staff, and tenure did not go away. In addition, during the 1970s and early 1980s, inflation skyrocketed in the United States, meaning that costs rose even more dramatically.

Since revenue was directly related to enrollment, and since enrollment was negatively correlated with tuition increases, the University found itself in cyclic financial straits. Many universities, both public and private, have faced similar situations. Having an endowment that provides a consistent revenue stream exclusive of enrollment is one solution to this problem. Although establishing an endowment was first suggested in 1972, no action was taken until the mid-1980s when it was too late to have any positive impact on the University's financial situation.

An operating deficit was first reported in 1965, although the Sisters had underwritten costs that certainly exceeded revenue since the school had been founded. The deficit grew to $327,000 by 1969. Frank Kleinhenz managed to stem the tide of red ink by 1973 when the school had its first balanced budget, although substantial debt remained. Deficits returned after Kleinhenz left although both Gil Cordova and Frank Welch managed to drive them back to zero. However, Welch's tyrannical demeanor introduced such turmoil at the University that it actually contributed to the eventual downfall. Deficits returned (and substantial debt remained) under Father McBride, skyrocketing to over two million dollars in 1986 when the school was forced to close.

Dissension is another stability issue that dogged the University in its later years. When the student body was mostly nuns or lay Catholic school teachers, there was, unsurprisingly, very little controversy. However, liberal arts colleges are famous for their restive student bodies and faculties, and the decade of the 1970s was rife with dissension over environmental issues, social and racial issues, and the Vietnam War. Some university presidents were able to deal with these issues and with the necessary belt-tightening, without fanning the flames of discontent, but some, in particular Frank Welch, fanned rather than dampened the flames. Faculty and student protests were a near constant fixture during his regime, significantly distracting the focus of the University from its educational mission.

Despite all of the negative problems, fond memories of the school abound. During an informal and unscientific social media poll of former students and faculty conducted in the summer of 2020 there were almost no negative comments. Comments included "Some of my fondest memories," "Loved it," "The best job ever," "Great memories," and "My wife loved the school."[790]

Judith Taylor, RN, an associate professor of nursing in the late 1970s, recalled that "being a nursing instructor at the UofA was one of the best jobs I ever had." She noted that the students were "wonderful, enthusiastic, and hard-working" and that the leadership of the program, especially Jo Vander Meer, was "lovely and competent."[791]

Theresa Carson "loved all of the business-related classes and felt that she received "a high value for the money spent." She said that the course work provided a "good foundation for her later career in management."[792]

Elsie Scott, a teacher and administrator from 1975 to 1986, felt that she, personally learned "so much" and that the school "turned lives around" in such a way that "anyone could go to the school and be successful."[793]

In the end, what do we make of the "school on the bluff" metaphor used by Senator Domenici in 1973? Students seeking an alternative educational experience with a Catholic-Christian, or Christian-humanism focus certainly saw the University as a beacon or like Jesus's "City on a Hill." Despite the financial and administrative ups and downs, this beacon remained bright and steady. On the other hand, the "school on the bluff" could just as easily be described as the "School on the Brink" as it frequently teetered on the edge, lurching from crisis to crisis until it finally was forced to close.

And so the University of Albuquerque came full circle. It started in 1920 as a summer program for Catholic school teachers with a strong emphasis on religion and theology, and it ended in August 1986 with the conclusions of a summer program in theology. Despite all of its problems, the University of Albuquerque made a indelible and lasting contribution to the history and culture of the Land of Enchantment.

Presidents
of the University of Albuquerque and its Predecessors

Sister M. Mathias Boyle, OSF (superintendent), 1922–
Reverend Bernard Espelage, OFM, 1928–
Reverend Albert O'Brien, OFM, 1927–1937
Reverend Dr. Hyacinth Barnhardt, 1937–1940
Father William Bradley, 1940–1942
Father Jules N. Stoffel (acting), 1942–1944
Father William Bradley, 1944–1946
Sister Agnes de Sales, OSF, 1946
Reverend Edward T. McCarthy, 1946–1947
Reverend Robert Wilken, OFM, 1947–1949
Mother M. Basilia Kugler, OSF, 1949–1953
Sister M. Viatora Schuller, OSF, 1953–1967
Sister M. Marilyn Doiron, OSF, 1967–1970
Frank Kleinheinz, 1970–1973
Joseph Zanetti, 1974–1975
Gil Cordova (acting), 1975–1976
Laurence C. Smith, PhD, 1976–1979
Reverend Clifford Smith, 1979–1980
Julius "Jack" Cranston (acting), 1980–1981
Frank Welch, PhD, 1981–1983
Father Alfred McBride, O. Praem, 1983–1986

Notes

1. Order of St, Francis, better known as Franciscans.
2. Order of the Canons Regular of Prémontré, better known as Norbertines or Premontratensians. This order was founded in Prémontré, France, in 1120, by St. Norbert of Xanten.
3. *New Testament, New Jerusalem Bible.* New York: Doubleday and Company, 1966; *Rio Rancho Observer*, 8/24/73, p. 2.
4. The information on early New Mexico Catholicism is taken from Taylor, John M. *Catholics along the Rio Grande.* Charleston: Arcadia Press, 2011 and Chavez, Fray Angelico. "Two Hundred and Fifty Years Before Lamy," Archdiocese of Santa Fe, nd.
5. Mondragon and Stapleton. *Public Education in New Mexico.* Albuquerque: University of New Mexico Press, 2005. p. 3.
6. Quivera is thought by some to be located somewhere near the present-day location of Salina, Kansas, and Cicuye is the original name for Pecos.
7. Avant, Louis. " History of Catholic Education in New Mexico." UNM Masters Thesis. 1940; *Santa Fe New Mexican*, 8/24/49, p. 5.
8. Mondragon and Stapleton, op. cit., p. 6.
9. Avant, op. cit, p. 6.
10. Ibid.
11. Mondragon and Stapleton, op. cit., p. 7.
12. Tórrez, Robert J., "El primer y principal ramo: An Examination of the Status of Education in the Mexican Era New Mexico," unpublished manuscript, 2021.
13. Ibid.
14. Taylor, John M. *Dejad a los Niños Venir a Mi—A History of the Parish of Our Lady of Guadalupe in Peralta* (third edition). Albuquerque: LPD Press, 2005; Melzer, Richard A. *Captain*

Maxmiliano Luna—A New Mexico Rough Rider. Los Ranchos de Albuquerque: Rio Grande Books, 2019.
15. Chavez, Fray Angelico. *But Time and Chance*. Santa Fe: Sunstone Press, 1981.
16. Defouri, Reverend James. *Historical Sketch of the Catholic Church in New Mexico*. San Francisco: McCormick Brothers, 1887, p. 28.
17. Horgan, Paul. *Lamy of Santa Fe*. New York: Farrar, Straus, and Giroux, 1975.
18. The information on Aline Bonzel and the Sisters of St. Francis of Perpetual Adoration is contained in "A Brief History of the Congregation of the Sisters of Saint Francis of Perpetual Adoration," an unpublished and undated paper written by Sister M. Honora Hau, OSF, and Sister M. Rayneria Willison, OSF. The paper and supplementary information was provided by Sister Stephanie McReynolds, OSF. More information can be found in a pamphlet entitled "One Hundred Years" in the University of New Mexico's Center for Southwest Research and Special Collections, University of Albuquerque collection 507 (hereinafter denoted CSWR/UofA), Box 5, folder 8.
19. "Christian Angelology," 12/24/18, https://hazelstainer.wordpress.com/2018/12/24/christian-angelology).
20. An order of nuns, brothers, or priests is one that has papal authorization. The First Order of Franciscans are exclusively male; the Second Order are exclusively female; and the Third Order is open to either gender. The Regular designation denotes that they follow the rule of St. Francis which, simplified, states that "members of the Third Order Regular set forth to follow Jesus Christ by living in fraternal communion, professing the observance of the evangelical counsels of obedience, poverty, and chastity in public vows, and by giving themselves to innumerable expressions of apostolic activity." https://www.atonementfriars.org/wp-content/uploads; 2019/02/Rule-of-the-Third-Order-Regular-of-St.-Francis.
21. "A Brief History," op. cit.
22. OFM stands for Ordo Fratrum Minorum or Order of Friars Minor. The name literally means "order of lesser brothers," and is attributed to St. Francis himself who rejected all extravagance in an effort to more closely follow the life and teachings of Jesus Christ.
23. Much of the information on the earliest days of the school were obtained from "A Brief History of the University of Albuquerque," an

unpublished and undated paper written by Sister M. Viatora Schuller of the Sisters of St. Francis of the Perpetual Adoration, (CSWR/UofA, Box 1, folder 7). Additional information is taken from Cordova, Rudy. *The History of the University of Albuquerque as reflected in its Athletic Program—Part II—A Chronology of the Historical Events*, published privately in 1981.

24. SJ stands for Society of Jesus, the formal name for the Jesuit order.
25. New Mexico Historic Building Survey, HABS No. NM-149.
26. *Albuquerque Journal*, 8/22/49, p. 7.
27. The term "normal school" is an early name for what are now referred to as teacher-training schools.
28. *Albuquerque Journal*, 6/2/22, p. 5, 6/19/22, p. 8.
29. *Albuquerque Journal*, 6/11/25, p. 8; Keleher collection, file 13323, University of Albuquerque Self-Study Report Prepared for the North Central Association of Colleges and Secondary Schools, 12/3/76.
30. *Albuquerque Journal*, 8/3/27, p. 3, 6/3/28 p. 5; *Clovis News*, 5/29/19, p. 6; *Catholic Advance* (Wichita, Kansas), 7/11/41, p. 1.
31. *Albuquerque Journal*, 6/3/28, p. 5, 6/16/33, p. 4.
32. Barney, Robert K., *Turmoil and Triumph*. Albuquerque: San Ignacio Press, 1960. pp. 178-80.
33. Davis, William E. *Miracle on the Mesa, A History of the University of New Mexico, 1889-2003*. Albuquerque: University of New Mexico Press, 2006, p. 137, quoting Barney.
34. Simmons, Marc. *Albuquerque*. Albuquerque: University of New Mexico Press, 1982, pp. 358-361.
35. CSWR/UofA, Box 16, folder 1, *Signum*, Vol II, #4, 11/74.
36. *Albuquerque Journal*, 7/13/37, p. 10.
37. *Albuquerque Journal*, 6/21/38, p. 5.
38. Cordova, op. cit., p. 86.
39. CSWR/UofA, Box 11, folder 1, Self-Survey of St. Joseph on the Rio Grande, 6/15/54.
40. *Albuquerque Journal*, 7/6/56, p. 44.
41. Cordova, op. cit; *Albuquerque Journal*, 1/6/40, p. 4.
42. Keleher collection, file 13328, Certificate of Incorporation of the Catholic Teachers' College of New Mexico, 3/19/40.
43. Schuller, op. cit.
44. *Albuquerque Journal*, 9/2/40, p. 7.
45. CSWR/UofA, Box 1, folder 33, library reports 1940-1960.
46. Email from M. L. Keleher to John Taylor, 1/5/21.

47. Simmons, op. cit., p. 367.
48. *Albuquerque Journal*, 7/25/42, p. 8.
49. CSWR/UofA, Box 7, folder 8, faculty meeting minutes, 6/12/41.
50. CSWR/UofA, Box 7, folder 8, faculty meeting minutes, 6/6/43. In 1967, the faculty would finally gain access to direct secretarial support and a state-of-the-art IBM Selectric typewriter (CSWR/UofA, Box 8, folder 1, 11/13/68).
51. *Albuquerque Journal*, 9/20/45, p. 11.
52. Simmons, op. cit., pp. 371-372.
53. Davis, op. cit., p. 181.
54. Davis, op. cit., p. 184.
55. CSWR/UofA, Box 1, folder 35, letters from Gerken to orders, 2/13/44.
56. CSWR/UofA, Box 1, folder 37, letters from Gerken to orders, 6/25/40.
57. CSWR/UofA, Box 1, folder 20, Annual Report—1956-1957.
58. Felicita Sachs Baca was the mother of 1957 graduate Mathias "Matt" Baca.
59. *Albuquerque Journal*, 4/4/46, p. 1, 8/19/56, p. 30.
60. *Albuquerque Journal*, 4/4/46, op. cit. The former St. Anthony's Orphanage is now a Job Corps building.
61. In the summer of 2020, a lawsuit was filed in New Mexico District Court alleging physical and sexual abuse of the boys living at St. Anthony's by both clergy and nuns. The lawsuit specified abuse during the 1950s and 1960s, although there are implications that it may have occurred earlier. However, there are no assertions of involvement by the faculty or students of the college while it was still at St. Anthony's. The current administration of the Sisters of St. Francis in Colorado Springs has denied that such abuse ever happened at the orphanage (*Albuquerque Journal*, 8/20/20, at abqjournal.com; kob.com, 8/25/20).
62. CSWR/UofA, Box 1, folder 34, letter from Jennings to teachers, 8/17/38. The North Central Association of Colleges and Secondary Schools was later known as North Central Association of Colleges and Schools or simply as NCA and was dissolved in 2014 (en.wikipedia.org). The successor accreditation agency is now known as Cognia.
63. CSWR/UofA, Box 1, folder 34, correspondence between Jennings, Coniga, Bradley, Deferrari, Knode, Wilken, 1938-1950.
64. *Santa Fe New Mexican*, 1/3/46, p. 1.
65. CSWR/UofA, Box 14, *Catholic Teachers' College Bulletin*, 1946-

1947.
66. CSWR/UofA, Box 1, folder 6.
67. *Santa Fe New Mexican*, 4/22/47, p. 10.
68. CSWR/UofA, Box 8, folder 8, faculty meeting minutes, 1946-1947.
69. Ibid.
70. Schuller, op. cit.; CSWR/UofA, Box 8, folder 8, faculty meeting minutes, 1946-1947.
71. CSWR/UofA, Box 15, *C.T.C Chimes*, Vol. 1, No. 1, 10/47, p. 1.
72. Cordova, op. cit., pp. 3, 88.
73. Cordova noted that most of the players and cheerleaders had Hispanic surnames. Cordova, op. cit., p. 3.
74. CSWR/UofA, Box 15, *The Don*, Vol 2, No. 2, 11/48, p. 1.
75. *Albuquerque Journal*, 5/23/49, p. 5.
76. CSWR/UofA, Box 1, folder 10 and Box 4, folder 7, special supplement to *The Observer*, 1980, p. 6.
77. CSWR/UofA, Box 14, Catholic Teachers College of New Mexico catalog, 1949-1950.
78. Cordova, op. cit., p. 89
79. CSWR/UofA, Box 15, *The Don*, Vol. 4, No. 2, 12/20/50, p. 2.
80. stmarystarr.com; CSWR/UofA, Box 14, College of St. Joseph on the Rio Grande catalog, 1950-1951.
81. Schuller, op. cit.; the deed is filed in Bernalillo County, Book D 137, pages 633-637 (Keleher collection, files 0572 and 9023).
82. *Albuquerque Journal*, 1/15/50, p. 13; 10/14/52, p. 13.
83. Keleher collection, file 13423, letter from Sheets to Vern Hansen and Alfred Dohl, 5/12/74.
84. Keleher collection, file 00572, Keleher memoir, 5/1/91.
85. Cordova, op. cit., p. 90.
86. Michael Keleher served as the attorney for the University of Albuquerque after joining his father's (William A. Keleher's) law practice in March 1962. He eventually served as secretary to the Board of Trustees until March 16, 1979 (Keleher interview 7/2020).
87. *Albuquerque Journal*, 6/13/50, p. F1.
88. CSWR/UofA, Box 15, *The Don*, Vol 5, No. 1, 11/29/51, p. 3.
89. *Albuquerque Journal*, 7/26/52, p. 1, 8/20/52, p. 2.
90. *Albuquerque Journal*, 9/11/58, p. 29.
91. Keleher collection, file 9023, *El Luminario*, volume 5.
92. Hall, Ruth K. "Young and Dynamic College." *New Mexico*

Magazine, Vol 31, 8/63, p. 24.
93. Cordova, op. cit., p. 92.
94. Hall, Ruth K. op. cit., p 25. The statue is still in place on the quad at St. Pius X High School.
95. CSWR/UofA, Box 17, folder 1, *UofA Newslines*, 4/23/80.
96. Interview with Matt Baca, 7/25/20.
97. Ibid.
98. CSWR/UofA, Box 9, folder 10, faculty minutes 9/19/67; Cordova, op. cit. pp. 8-12; *Las Cruces Sun-News*, 2/2/51, p. 6.
99. *New Mexico Catholic Register*, 2/21/60.
100. *Albuquerque Journal*, 9/18/68, p. 17; *Albuquerque Tribune*, 3/26/71, p. 1.
101. CSWR/UofA, Box 15, *Focus*, Vol. 4, No. 1, 10/12/60.
102. CSWR/UofA, Box 9, folder 10, faculty minutes from 9/19/67, 9/24/67, 11/7/67.
103. Interview with Matt Baca, 10/9/20.
104. *Santa Fe New Mexican*, 11/27/63, p. 4.
105. CSWR/UofA, Box 15, *Focus*, Vol. 4, No. 1, 10/12/60, p. 2.
106. Elsie Scott interview, 8/16/21.
107. CSWR/UofA, Box 9, folder 10, faculty minutes 4/13/68.
108. CSWR/UofA, Box 15, *Yucca*, Vol. 2, No. 1, 10/16/57, p. 2; Cordova, op. cit., p. 96; CSWR/UofA, Box 16, item 5, *Dialogue*, Vol. 1, Fall 1976.
109. Cordova, op. cit., p. 100.
110. CSWR/UofA, Box 1, folder 14.
111. CSWR/UofA, Box 15, *Mesa Messenger*, Vol. 1, No. 3, 3/19/54, p 4.
112. *Clovis News-Journal*, 10/22/54, p. 1; *Albuquerque Journal*, 1/26/54, p. 18.
113. CSWR/UofA, Box 11, folder 1, Self-Assessment, 1954.
114. CSRW/UofA, Box 11, folder 20, 12/84 Self-Study Report, accreditation history.
115. CSWR/UofA, Box 8, folder 8, faculty meeting minutes, 12/2/55.
116. *Albuquerque Journal*, 11/14/54, p. 16.
117. *Albuquerque Journal*, 3/20/52, p. 16.
118. *Albuquerque Tribune*, 3/28/68, p. 25.
119. Cordova, op. cit., p. 22.
120. Drama, which would become one of the University's long-standing programs, was actually started as a club in the winter of 1955

(CSWR/UofA, Box 7, folder 2, minutes of faculty meeting, 1/7/55).
121. *Albuquerque Journal*, 7/6/56, p. 44.
122. CSWR/UofA, Box 7, folder 2, minutes of faculty meeting, 2/3/56.
123. Newman was canonized by Pope Francis in October 2019.
124. CSWR/UofA, Box 7, folder 2, minutes of faculty meeting, 2/3/56.
125. CSWR/UofA, Box 8, folder 8, faculty meeting minutes, 10/4/57.
126. Ibid.
127. CSWR/UofA, Box 10, folder 7, minutes of the Academic Affairs Committee.
128. CSWR/UofA, Box 7, folder 1, minutes of faculty meeting, 9/7/56.
129. CSWR/UofA, Box 15, *Yucca,* Vol. 2, No. 8, 5/26/58, p. 2.
130. CSWR/UofA, Box 5, folder 17, Annual Report of the St. Joseph library, 1955-56.
131. CSWR/UofA, Box 6, folder 1, Board of Trustees minutes, July 1, 1958.
132. CSWR/UofA, Box 15, *Focus*, Vol. 3, No. 6, 4/11/60, p. 1.
133. This is the original spelling of the city name. It is derived from the name of the home of Fernando de la Cueva on the Portuguese-Spanish border. The name comes from the Latin words *albus querques* which mean white oak.
134. Interview with Matt Baca, 7/28/20.
135. *Albuquerque Journal*, 1/12/59, p. 13.
136. CSWR/UofA, Box 8, folder 8, faculty meeting minutes, 3/6/59.
137. www.aquinasonline/com.
138. CSWR/UofA, Box 7, folder 3, minutes of the faculty meeting, 5/1/59.
139. CSWR/UofA, Box 8, folder 8, faculty meeting minutes, 4/3/59.
140. CSWR/UofA, Box 11, folder 2, self-survey 1959.
141. www.rebirthofreason.com.
142. In fact, 426 of the 505 students were Roman Catholic. Seventeen were Methodist, 15 "Protestant," and 12 Baptist. CSWR/UofA, Box 11, folder 2, self-survey 1959.
143. CSWR/UofA, Box 11, folder 5, Basic Institutional Data 1969 (historical review).
144. Keleher collection, file 13342, trust bond indenture between the Saint Joseph on the Rio Grande Development Corporation and Albuquerque National Bank, 4/20/60.
145. CSWR/UofA, Box 5, folder 17, Annual Report of the St. Joseph library, 1959-1960.
146. Simmons, op. cit., pp. 366-370; Wood, Robert Turner. *The*

Postwar Transition of Albuquerque, New Mexico 1945–1972. Santa Fe: Sunstone Press, 2014, pp. 63-71; population.us/nm/Albuquerque, macromedia.net/cities.
147. CSWR/UofA, Box 6, folder 1, Board of Trustees minutes, April 22, 1960; CSWR/Box 11, folder 2, NCA review report, 11/23-24/59.
148. Ibid; Hall, Ruth K., op. cit., p. 27; *Albuquerque Journal*, 4/2/60, p. 13.
149. CSWR/UofA, Box 7, folder 4, faculty meeting minutes, 11/11/60.
150. CSWR/UofA, Box 6, folder 1, Board of Trustees minutes, 10/13/60.
151. CSWR/UofA, Box 7, folder 4, faculty meeting minutes, 9/6/60.
152. CSWR/UofA, Box 5, folder 31, *New Mexico Independent*, 9/3/76, p. 2.
153. CSWR/UofA, Box 4, folder 31, University Scholars Program brochure, n.d.
154. *Albuquerque Journal*, 10/29/62, p. 8.
155. *Albuquerque Journal*, 12/23/62, p. 44.
156. CSWR/UofA, Box 7, folder 3, faculty meeting minutes, 2/2/60.
157. CSWR/UofA, Box 7, folder 4, faculty meeting minutes, 10/10/62.
158. *Albuquerque Journal*, 2/11/63, p. 19.
159. McCord, Richard. *No Halls of Ivy*. Winona, MN: Lasallian Christian Brothers, 2013, p. 168.
160. CSWR/UofA, Box 7, folder 4, faculty meeting minutes, 3/9/62.
161. CSWR/UofA, Box 4, folder 7, "Growing with New Mexico—A Report on the Achievements and Opportunities of the College of St. Joseph," Spring 1962.
162. *Albuquerque Journal*, 2/22/63, p. 48, 4/18/63, p. 2.
163. *Albuquerque Journal*, 6/2/64, p. 2.
164. *Albuquerque Journal*, 8/18/63, p. 40.
165. Michael Keleher interview, 2020.
166. CSWR/UofA, Box 7, folder, 4, faculty meeting minutes, 9/7/63.
167. *Albuquerque Journal*, 9/21/63, p. 16.
168. www.theresians.org. Note that St. Therese church on north Second Street in Albuquerque is also dedicated to St. Therese of Lisieux.
169. CSWR/UofA, Box 15, *Focus*, Vol. 7, No. 2, 10/23/63, p. 1.
170. CSWR/UofA, Box 7, folder 4, faculty meeting minutes, 4/14/61.
171. CSWR/UofA, Box 7, folder 4, faculty meeting minutes, 12/12/62.
172. CSWR/UofA, Box 7, folder 4, faculty meeting minutes, 4/10/63.

173. CSWR/UofA, Box 7, folder 5, faculty meeting minutes, 5/12/61.
174. *Albuquerque Journal*, 1/25/59, p. 5.
175. Ibid; *Albuquerque Journal*, 6/21/64, p. 3, 12/29/64, p. 29.
176. Cordova, op. cit., p. 106; CSWR/UofA, Box 7, folder 5, faculty meeting minutes, 1/14/64.
177. *Albuquerque Journal*, 7/4/64, p. 23; CSWR/UofA, Box 7, folder 5, faculty meeting minutes, 1/14/64.
178. Keleher collection, file 13342, Indenture Trust between College of St Joseph on the Rio Grande Development Corporation and Bank of New Mexico, 9/30/65.
179. *Albuquerque Journal*, 8/16/64, p. 25, 9/4/64, p. 51, 11/15/64, p. 2.
180. *Santa Fe New Mexican*, 11/25/65, p. 28.
181. *Albuquerque Journal*, 11/6/64, p. 2; *Deming Headlight*, 9/30/65, p. 8.
182. *Deming Headlight*, 9/30/65, p. 8.
183. Keleher collection, file 13339, letter from Koch to Jenkins, 12/2/74, letter from Kahn to Pfefferhorn, 4/15/75.
184. CSWR/UofA, Box 9, folder 2, Faculty Senate minutes, 1/22/81.
185. CSWR/UofA, Box 4, folder 7, special supplement to *The Observer*, 1980, p. 6.
186. *Santa Fe New Mexican*, 1/14/65, p. 13; *Albuquerque Journal*, 4/25/65, p. 40.
187. "Field of Dreams," enwikipedia.org.
188. CSWR/UofA, Box 7, folder 5, faculty meeting minutes, 3/9/65.
189. CSWR/UofA, Box 8, folder 8, faculty meeting minutes, 11/11/65.
190. Keleher collection, file 13318, New Mexico State Corporation Commission certificate, 1/7/66.
191. CSWR/UofA, Box 8, folder 1, Official Record of the Faculty Senate Determinations, 5/23/66.
192. CSWR/UofA, Box 9, folder 12, Letter from Sister Luella to Rev. Schneider, 5/24/67.
193. CSWR/UofA, Box 8, folder 1, Faculty Senate Determination, 10/26/66.
194. CSWR/UofA, Box 9, folder 10, minutes, 3/24/67 and 2/21/68.
195. CSWR/UofA, Box 10, folder 7, minutes of the Academic Affairs Committee, 10/6/66, 12/19/66, 5/19/67.
196. CSWR/UofA, Box 10, folder 7, letter from John Barrett to Sister Marilyn, 3/18/68.
197. Davis, op. cit., p. 194.
198. CSWR/UofA, Box 7, folder 5, faculty meeting minutes, 1/23/66;

Box 6, folder 1, Board of Trustees minutes, April 22, 1960.
199. *Albuquerque Journal*, 2/10/66, p. 34, 1/12/66, p. 29.
200. Keleher collection, file 14648, agreement between the University of Albuquerque and Vista Sandia Hospital, 11/11/78. Vista Sandia Hospital, originally called Nazareth Hospital, became Valle North Caring Center which closed in 2008 (*Albuquerque Journal*, 10/17/2011 @ abqjournal.com). See also Alexander, Francelle. *Albuquerque's North Valley—Vol II—Alameda and Los Ranchos*. Los Ranchos: Rio Grande books, 2018, p. 201.
201. *Albuquerque Journal*, 5/2/66, p. 2.
202. CSWR/UofA, Box 11, folder 18, Self-Study report, 10/1/79.
203. *Albuquerque Journal*, 7/14/66, p. 35.
204. According to Michael Keleher, Concha Kleven, a former state legislator and advocate for bilingual education and women's rights, taught an etiquette course for girls, many of whom came from rural New Mexico (Keleher collection, file 00572; Keleher memoir, 5/1/91).
205. Cordova, op. cit. p. 33.; *Arizona Daily Sun*, 2/8/66; *Albuquerque Journal*, 12/28/66, p. 18; *Albuquerque Tribune*, 1/27/66, p. 1.
206. Keleher collection, file 9020, Summary of Planning Workshop, 1/21/67.
207. CSWR/UofA, Box 14, College of St. Joseph on the Rio Grande catalog, 1950-1951.
208. CSWR/UofA, Box 11, folder 2, self-survey 1959; Paul Krause, "The Thomistic Roots of Vatican II Humanism," Vogelin View, 12/2/19, vogelinview.com.
209. John Shook, "Christian Humanism, Religious Humanism, and Secular Humanism," Center for Inquiry, 12/8/09 (centerforinquiry.com).
210. CSWR/UofA, Box 9, folder 11, Summary Report on the workshop on Planning, 3/4/67.
211. CSWR/UofA, Box 9, folder 12, Memo to Faculty Senate containing a Proposal for the Institute of Southwestern Studies, 1966.
212. Interview with Ray John de Aragon, 8/21.
213. CSWR/UofA, Box 8, folder 1, Faculty Senate Determination, 12/18/66; Facts and Figures 1967 for the University of Massachusetts at Amherst, p. 122.
214. University of New Mexico Board of Regents minutes, 6/10/66.
215. CSWR/UofA, Box 8, folder 1, Faculty Senate Determination, 12/19/66.

216. CSWR/UofA, Box 2, folder 21, Report of the Christian Commitment Committee, 1/67.
217. CSWR/UofA, Box 2, folder 21, letter from Brown to committee, 3/31/67.
218. CSWR/UofA, Box 2, folder 21, letter from Brown to committee, 1/5/68.
219. CSWR/UofA, Box 11, folder 2, self-survey 1959; Paul Krause, "The Thomistic Roots of Vatican II Humanism," Vogelin View, 12/2/19, vogelinview.com.
220. CSWR/UofA, Box 2, folder 21, Recommendations of the Committee, 5/29/68.
221. CSWR/UofA, Box 10, folder 7, letter from Foss to various, 4/4/68.
222. CSWR/UofA, Box 10, folder 7, letter from H. Davis to Ted Foss, 4/10/68.
223. CSWR/UofA, Box 6, folder 1, Board of Trustee meeting May 19, 1967; *Albuquerque Journal*, 5/24/67, p. 2; Keleher collection, file 9021, letter from Keleher to Viatora, 5/24/67.
224. *Albuquerque Journal*, 8/16/64, p. 25, 5/29/69, 5/25/69, p. 22; Keleher collection, file 9021, letter from Keleher to Doiron, 5/24/67.
225. CSWR/UofA, Box 6, folder 1, Board of Trustee meeting, 10/22/63.
226. *Albuquerque Journal*, 5/5/67, p. F11.
227. *Albuquerque Tribune*, 4/8/67, p. 13.
228. CSWR/UofA, Box 10, folder 7, 4/4/68.
229. The Student Council became the Student Senate with the issuance of a new constitution and by-laws in 1968 (CSWR/UofA, Box 9, folder 10, Student Senate minutes, 5/9/68).
230. CSWR/UofA, Box 9, folder 6, Student Senate minutes, 2/27/67.
231. Correspondence with Ray John de Aragon, 8/21.
232. CSWR/UofA, Box 9, folder 10, Student Senate minutes, 3/11/67.
233. CSWR/UofA, Box 6, folder 1, Board of Trustees meeting, 5/19/68.
234. CSWR/UofA, Box 6, folder 1, Board of Trustee meetings, 7/26/68, 9/20/68.
235. *Albuquerque Journal*, 5/24/67, p. 9.
236. *Albuquerque Journal*, 5/23/67, p. 8.
237. *Albuquerque Tribune*, 4/10/67, p. 19 and www.sportscasting.com.
238. *Albuquerque Journal*, 8/13/67, p. 52; *Albuquerque Tribune*,

9/13/67, p. 29.
239. *Albuquerque Tribune*, 9/19/67, p. 2.
240. CSWR/UofA, Box 10, folder 1, memo from Mazzio to Sister Marilyn, 3/20/68.
241. CSWR/UofA, Box 10, folder 2, Analysis of Problems and Recommended Solutions, 3/25/68.
242. CSWR/UofA, Box 10, folder 2, President's Executive Council minutes, 3/10/69.
243. CSWR/UofA, Box 11, folder 5, Basic Institutional Data, Spring 1969.
244. CSWR/UofA, Box 9, folder 10, faculty meeting minutes, 10/22/68.
245. *Albuquerque Journal*, 11/29/68, p. 5.
246. McCord, op. cit., pp. 183-185.
247. Keleher collection, file 9022, letter from Doiron to Klene, 10/6/69.
248. *Albuquerque Journal*, 1/27/68, p. 5.
249. *Albuquerque Journal*, 10/20/68, p. 46; CSWR/UofA, Box 4, folder 7; Buddeke, Martha. "How the University of Albuquerque Can Make the Grade." *New Mexico Magazine*, May 1977, pp. 44-49.
250. CSWR/UofA, Box 10, folder 2, Presidential Executive Council minutes, 3/24/69.
251. CSWR/UofA, Box 16, item 1, *Ambassador*, Vol. 1, No. 1, 10/69.
252. CSWR/UofA, Box 16, folder 2, *El Proclamador*, Vol. 2, No. 6, p. 1, 5/73.
253. CSWR/UofA, Box 16, folder 2, *El Proclamador*, Vol 3. No. 1, 9/73.
254. CSWR/UofA, Box 10, folder 2, memo from Kleinhenz to Doiron, 5/20/68.
255. CSWR/UofA, Box 10, folder 2, President's Executive Council, 9/17/69.
256. CSWR/UofA, Box 10, folder 2, memo from Kleinhenz to Doiron, 5/20/68.
257. CSWR/UofA, Box 8, folder 8, Faculty Senate minutes, 4/23/69.
258. CSWR/UofA, Box 6, folder 2, University of Albuquerque Development Alternatives, July 1969.
259. Keleher collection, file 9022, correspondence.
260. CSWR/UofA, Box 10, folder 2, President's Executive Council minutes, 4/2/69.

261. Keleher collection, file 9022, Board of Trustee minutes, 5/21/69.
262. *Albuquerque Journal* 12/12/68, p. 39, 1/2/69, p. 30.
263. CSWR/UofA, Box 7, folder 4, faculty meeting minutes, 9/5/62.
264. Cordova, op. cit., p. 39.
265. *Albuquerque Journal*, 12/13/68, p. 64.
266. *Albuquerque Journal*, 12/20/68, p. 21.
267. Ibid.
268. *Albuquerque Journal*, 5/29/64, p. 4.
269. *Albuquerque Tribune*, 7/4/69, p. 17.
270. CSWR/UofA, Box 10, folder 2, minutes of the President's Executive Council, 2/21/69 and 4/23/69.
271. CSWR/UofA, Box 11, folder, 7, Report of Visit to the University of Albuquerque by NCACSS, 3/2-4/69.
272. Correspondence with Ray John de Aragon.
273. *Albuquerque Tribune*, November 20, 1968, p. 45.
274. *Albuquerque Tribune*, 5/29/69, p. 30 and 1/3/69, p. 23.
275. *Albuquerque Journal*, 8/17/68, p. 14.
276. CSWR/UofA, Box 11, folder 5, Basic Institutional Data, Spring 1965.
277. *Albuquerque Journal*, 8/17/69, p. 46.
278. CSWR/UofA, Box 6, folder 2, letter from Burns to Doiron, July 29, 1969.
279. *Albuquerque Journal*, 12/24/69, p. 2.
280. *Albuquerque Journal*, 8/17/69, p. 48.
281. CSWR/UofA, Box 9, folder 10, Student Senate minutes, 4/1/69.
282. CSWR/UofA, Box 2, folder 9, Martinez letter.
283. *Albuquerque Journal*, 1/ 26/70, p. 2, 7/19/70, p. 41, 12/24/70, p. 5.
284. Davis, op. cit., p. 228, quoting Huntington.
285. CSWR/UofA, Box 9, folder 10, Student Senate minutes, 9/23/69 and 5/12/70.
286. Interview with James McGovern, student 1969-1971.
287. CSWR/UofA, Box 9, folder 10, Faculty Senate minutes, 7/23/69.
288. CSWR/UofA, Box 10, folder 2, President's Executive Council, 9/24/69.
289. *Albuquerque Journal*, 10/14/69, p. 1.
290. CSWR/UofA, Box 9, folder 10, Faculty Senate minutes, 10/7/69.
291. CSWR/UofA, Box 10, folder 2, President's Executive Council, 10/16/69.

292. CSWR/UofA, Box 15, *Sand Trumpet*, Vol. 3, 10/15/69.
293. CSWR/UofA, Box 8, folder 1, Copeland letter, 5/8/70.
294. CSWR/UofA, Box 8, folder 1, Copeland letter, 5/8/70; Box 10, folder 2, President's Executive Council minutes, 5/6/70.
295. CSWR/UofA, Box 8, folder 5, letter from Sister Marilyn to the Board, 1/19/70, giving an effective date of 1/26/70.
296. *Albuquerque Journal*, 1/20/70, p. 1.
297. Ibid; *Albuquerque Journal*, 1/21/70, p. 27, 1/22/70, p. 5.
298. CSWR/UofA, Box 16, Item 1, *Ambassador*, Vol. 1, # 2, 1/70, p. 2.
299. *Albuquerque Journal*, 1/21/70, p. 27, 1/22/70, p. 5.
300. *Albuquerque Tribune*, 1/21/70, p. 4.
301. *Albuquerque Journal*,1/21/70, p. 27, 5/16/70, p. 1, 8/16/70, p. 57; CSWR/UofA, Board of Trustees minutes, 5/15/70.
302. Keleher collection, file 00572, Keleher memo, 5/1/91.
303. CSWR/UofA, Box 8, folder 5, Report to the Faculty Senate on the Performance of the Fiscal Policies Committee from 4/68-4/69, n.d.
304. *Albuquerque Journal*, 1/26/70, p. 2.
305. *Albuquerque Journal*, 8/16/70, p. 57.
306. CSWR/UofA, Box 6, folder 1, Board of Trustee minutes, 10/13/60.
307. Keleher collection, file 11448, letter from Niederberger to Harrell, 9/11/73.
308. *Albuquerque Journal*, 2/1/71, p. A-2.
309. *Albuquerque Journal*, 7/28/70, p. 14.
310. *Albuquerque Tribune*, 3/20/70, p. 2.
311. *Albuquerque Journal*, 1/7/71, p. 1; Keleher collection, file 11448, Board of Trustee minutes, 2/19/71; *Albuquerque Tribune*, 5/29/74, p. 2.
312. *Albuquerque Journal*, 12/13/70, p. C-2.
313. CSWR/UofA, Box 15, for example *Sand Trumpet*, Vol. 8, No. 4, 11/26/70.
314. CSWR/UofA, Box 8, folder 2, Faculty Senate Executive Committee minutes, 2/15/71.
315. CSWR/UofA, Box 8, folder 2, undated *Faculty News Bulletin*.
316. *Albuquerque Journal*, 3/24/71, p. 5.
317. *Albuquerque Tribune*, 3/26/71, p. 1.
318. CSWR/UofA, Box 15, *Focus*, Vol. 9, No. 5, 3/24/66, p. 7; *Albuquerque Journal*, 3/27/71, p. 4.
319. CSWR/UofA, Box 8, folder 5, letter from Ted Foss to Sister Barbara Ann, 3/31/70; letter from Frank Kleinhenz to Rolf Lindquist,

5/20/70.
320. *Albuquerque Journal*, 8/22/70, p. 25.
321. Keleher collection, file 11448, minutes of Executive Committee of the Board of Trustees meeting.
322. *Albuquerque Journal*, 10/20/70, p. 19.
323. CSWR/UofA, Box 8, folder 1, Faculty Senate Resolution, 3/20/70.
324. *Albuquerque Journal*, 10/28/70, p. 1, 11/20/70, p. 16.
325. *Albuquerque Journal*, 3/21/71, p. 34.
326. *Gallup Independent*, 4/28/71, p. 2.
327. *Albuquerque Journal*, 6/6/71, p. 25, 6/9/71, p. 19.
328. *Albuquerque Journal*, 8/24/71, p. 24, 9/4/71, p. 2, 9/10/71, p. 32.
329. Keleher collection, file 10954, lease, 9/1/71; letter from Keleher to John Deme, 5/30/75.
330. CSWR/UofA, Box 8, folder 1, Faculty Senate Legislation, 5/24/70.
331. CSWR/UofA, Box 6, folder 2, Board of Trustee minutes 4/23/71.
332. CSWR/UofA, Box 6, folder 1, Board of Trustee minutes, 4/22/60.
333. *Albuquerque Journal*, 8/3/71, p. 4.
334. Ibid.
335. *Albuquerque Tribune*, 10/8/71, p. 25.
336. *Albuquerque Journal*, 6/20/71, p. 2, 8/15/71, p. 56, 3/39/71, p. 18, 6/20/71, p. 2, 11/30/71, p. 18; *Valencia County News-Bulletin*, 8/9/71, p. 1.
337. *Valencia County News-Bulletin*, 6/17/71, p. 1.
338. CSWR/UofA, Box 6, folder 2, Board of Trustee minutes, 10/29/71.
339. *Valencia County News-Bulle*tin, 11/1/71, p. 1.
340. *Albuquerque Journal*, 12/16/68, p. 11, 6/20/71, p. 2; Burr, Baldwin G., et. al., *Notable and Notorious Neighbors in Valencia County History*. Valencia County Historical Society, 2018.
341. CSWR/UofA, Box 6, folder 2, Balance sheet, 12/31/71.
342. *Albuquerque Journal*, 9/17/71, p. 55, 4/15/72, p. 1.
343. *Albuquerque Journal*, 2/13/72, p. 66.
344. CSWR/UofA, Box 8, folder 5, *Sand Trumpet*, 4/24/72.
345. *Albuquerque Journal*, 4/30/72, p. A-1 and 5/1/72, p. A-2.
346. Facebook responses from Matthew Jaramillo and Debra Dionisi to Richard Melzer, 3/16/20.
347. *Albuquerque Journal*, 5/1/72, p. 1; Keleher collection, file 11448, Executive Committee of the Board of Trustees minutes, 5/19/72.

348. Keleher collection, file 11448, Executive Committee of the Board of Director minutes, 9/8/72.
349. CSWR/UofA, Box 11, folder 11, Institutional Profile, 1972.
350. CSWR/UofA, Box 11, folder 13, Report of NCA visit, 5/3-4/72.
351. CSWR/UofA, Box 11, folder 14, Self-Study Report, 12/4/73.
352. CSWR/UofA, Box 8, folder 3, Faculty Senate minutes, 5/9/75.
353. CSWR/UofA, Box 8, folder 4, Academic Grievance Procedures, 4/77; CSWR/UofA, Box 9, folder 1, letter from Cochran to Smith, 4/29/77.
354. CSWR/UofA, Box 8, folder 5, letter from Kleinhenz to Desaulniers, 12/5/72.
355. CSWR/UofA, Box 8, folder 5, letter from Sister Winifred to Zanetti, 11/15/74; letter from Zanetti to Stephanson, 2/14/75.
356. Keleher collection, file 11448, letter from Norman Burns to Frank Kleinhenz, 8/3/72.
357. *Albuquerque Journal*, 10/8/72, p. 20.
358. Keleher collection, file 11448, Board of Trustees minutes, 1/28/72; *Albuquerque Journal*, 2/20/72, p. 26.
359. *Valencia County News-Bulletin*, 11/5/70, p. 10.
360. *Albuquerque Journal*, 5/16/72, p. 59.
361. *Albuquerque Journal*, 7/2/72, p. 5, 8/13/72, p. 59.
362. Keleher collection, file 9020, memo from Kosky, 2/9/73.
363. Wood, op. cit., pp. 359-361.
364. Keleher collection, file 11448, letter from Baxter to Kleinhenz, 4/24/73.
365. CSWR/UofA, Box 6, folder 3, Board of Trustee minutes, 7/5/73.
366. CSWR/UofA, Box 10, folder 7, memo, 3/9/73.
367. en.wikipedia.org, ww2.ed.gov.
368. *Albuquerque Journal*, 7/9/69, p. A-3.
369. Elsie Scott interview, 8/16/21; email from Elsie Scott to John Taylor, 9/20/21.
370. Keleher collection, file 11448, Board of Trustees minutes, 6/28/72.
371. *Albuquerque Journal*, 12/16/73, p. 109.
372. CSWR/UofA, Box 2, folder 4, letters, 9/26/75.
373. CSWR/UofA, Box 5, folder 24, "Title III Proposed Development Program," October 1973.
374. CSWR/UofA, Box 5, folder 26, Board of Trustees minutes 7/12/76.

375. *Albuquerque Journal*, 7/2/72, p. 5.
376. *Albuquerque Journal*, 2/1/73, p. 10.
377. CSWR/UofA, Box 10, folder 3, planning assumptions, 1/31/73.
378. Keleher collection, Public Affairs file, memo documenting "University of Albuquerque Final Master Plan—Phase A—Summary of Recommendations," 12/73.
379. *Albuquerque Journal*, 9/6/71, p. 13.
380. Keleher collection, file 13324, University of Albuquerque Foundation Articles of Incorporation.
381. Keleher collection, file 1463, Special Resolution of the Board of Trustees of the University of Albuquerque, 3/9/73, also the large compendium of deeds and appraisals in this same file.
382. Keleher collection, file 11448, Board of Trustee minutes, 6/6/73; *Albuquerque Journal*, 5/10/73, p. 40; *Silver City Daily Press*, 6/8/73, p. 6.
383. Keleher collection, miscellaneous file, memo to Board of Trustees from Frank Kleinhenz, 6/6/73.
384. *Albuquerque Journal*, 8/5/73, p. 6; *Santa Fe New Mexican*, 8/5/73, p. 8.
385. *Rio Rancho Observer*, 8/24/73, p. 2.
386. Matthew 5:14.
387. *Rio Rancho Observer*, 8/24/73, p. 2.
388. Note that, other than during intramural contests, UofA never fielded a football team.
389. *Albuquerque Tribune*, 1/22/74, p. 6.
390. *Albuquerque Journal*, 7/20/73, B-4, 8/11/73, p. 8; *Albuquerque Tribune*, 8/15/86, p. A-1.
391. Keleher collection, letter from Ray Padilla to Zanetti, 3/11/74.
392. CSWR/UofA, Box 15, *Sand Trumpet*, Vol. 8, No. 1, 1/1/74.
393. Note that George Anderson was somewhat infamous in local collegiate circles. He was accused of being a "plant" by the Board, of being an agitator, and that he had CIA, FBI, or police training (Keleher collection, file 11447, George Anderson file).
394. CSWR/UofA, Box 15, *Sand Trumpet*, Vol. 8, No. 2, 2/15/72.
395. CSWR, Box 15, *Sand Trumpet*, 4/25/75, No. 7, p. 7.
396. CSWR/UofA, Box 16, item 4, *Black Focus*, Vol. 1, p. 2, 3/75.
397. Keleher collection, file 14648, Center for Law Enforcement, Corrections, and Social Services annual report 1973-1974, June 1974.
398. *Albuquerque Journal*, 11/6/73, p. 27.

399. CSWR/UofA, Box 5, folder 17, makeup of the student body—fall 1975.
400. CSWR/UofA, Box 8, folder 1, Faculty Senate Legislation 4/26/74.
401. *Albuquerque Journal*, 10/17/73, p. 12
402. Email from Brad Moore to John Taylor, 1/27/20.
403. *Albuquerque Journal*, 6/26/70, p. 22.
404. *Albuquerque Journal*, 7/10/70, p. 34.
405. *Albuquerque Journal*, 5/23/69, p. 1, 7/10/70, p. 34.
406. CSWR/UofA, Box 6, folder 5, letter from Summers to Smith.
407. *Albuquerque Journal*, 6/15/69, p. 55.
408. *Albuquerque Tribune*, 4/30/69, p. 4.
409. *Albuquerque Journal*, 6/15/69, p. 55.
410. CSWR/UofA, Box 6, folder 2, Board of Trustee minutes, 5/29/68.
411. Keleher collection, file 520/22, open letter from Smith and Killorin to members of the State Legislature, 1/23/73.
412. Keleher collection, Box 7, folder 13337, letter from Ackeren to Killorin, 6/7/75.
413. CSWR/UofA, Box 8, folder 3, Memo from University Academic Policies Committee to Faculty Senate, 3/8/76.
414. Keleher collection, file 13320, letter from Keleher to Killorin, 1/11/77; CSWR/UofA, Box 5, folder 26, Board of Trustees minutes, 5/10/77.
415. CSWR/UofA, Box 4, folder 7, Buddecke, op. cit., quoting Zanetti. UNM had actually established a General College in 1935 to help direct incoming students and to provide remedial assistance (Davis, op. cit., p. 153).
416. *Albuquerque Journal*, 2/5/77, p. 4.
417. *Albuquerque Journal*, 2/16/77, p. 14.
418. *Farmington Daily Times*, 5/6/77, p. 23.
419. CSWR/UofA, Box 6, folder 5, press release from the Office of the Governor, February 9, 1977.
420. *Farmington Daily Times*, 5/6/77, p. 23.
421. *Albuquerque Journal*, 3/29/77, p. 7
422. Ibid.
423. *Clovis News-Journal*, 5/5/77, p. 2.
424. *Albuquerque Tribune*, 10/10/77, p. 29.
425. Keleher collection, file 00572, Keleher memoir, 5/1//91.
426. *Albuquerque Journal*, 6/15/77, p. 2.

427. *Albuquerque Journal*, 10/13/77, p. 49, 10/16/77, p.1, 11/9/77, p. 2.
428. Keleher collection, file 520/22, letter from Killorin to Apodaca, 1/26/78.
429. Keleher collection, file 12093, minutes of Board of Trustees meeting 3/7/78; *Albuquerque Journal*, 2/21/78, p.1; *Albuquerque Journal*, 7/31/78, p. 10.
430. CSWR/UofA, Box 6, folder 6, Board of Trustee minutes, March 7, 1978; *Albuquerque Journal*, 9/10/76, p. 1.
431. *Albuquerque Journal*, 9/13/78, p. 1.
432. *Albuquerque Journal*, 9/20/78, p. 3.
433. CSWR/UofA, Box 6, folder 7, Board of Trustees minutes, 2/8/79.
434. *Albuquerque Journal*, 3/6/74, p. B-4, 3/13/74, p. 18, 3/29/74, p. 9.
435. *Albuquerque Journal*, 5/4/74, p. 6.
436. Keleher collection, file 11448, minutes of the Executive Committee of the Board of Trustees meeting, 3/27/74.
437. *Albuquerque Journal*, 3/30/74, p. 1.
438. *Albuquerque Journal*, 3/30/74, p. 7.
439. CSWR/UofA, Box 8, folder 3, Faculty Senate minutes, 2/15/75.
440. Some estimates gave tuition, room, books, and fees 94 percent of the total revenue (Keleher collection, file 11448, Board of Trustee minutes, 3/21/75).
441. Keleher collection, file 11448, Board of Trustee minutes, 3/29/74.
442. CSWR/UofA, Box 8, Folder 3, General Guidelines for the Administration of Scholarships and Financial Aid, n.d.
443. *Albuquerque Journal*, 11/16/74, p. 1.
444. *Albuquerque Journal*, 4/20/74, p. 14.
445. *Albuquerque Journal*, 9/17/74, p. 9.
446. *Albuquerque Journal*, 11/27/70, p. 66.
447. CSWR/UofA, Box 5, folder 25, Bilingual-Multicultural Education at the University of Albuquerque: Native American Component, 1976.
448. *Albuquerque Journal*, 8/11/77, p. 53.
449. CSWR/UofA, Box 6, folder 4, Board of Trustee minutes, 1/31/73; *Albuquerque Journal*, 1/7/75, p. 17.
450. *Albuquerque Journal,* 3/5/74, p. B-4.
451. Keleher memoir, 5/1/91.
452. *Albuquerque Journal*, 3/22/75, p. 12.
453. Keleher collection, file 11448, memo from Powell to Board of

Trustees, 4/21/74.
454. CSWR/UofA, Box 6, folder 4, staff newsletter, 4/23/75; *Albuquerque Journal*, 4/24/75, p. 13.
455. Keleher collection, file 11465, memo to staff, 4/23/75; *Albuquerque Journal*, 8/15/76, p. 49.
456. *Albuquerque Journal*, 5/20/76, p. 20.
457. Ibid.
458. Keleher collection, file 11559, Board of Trustees minutes, 7/14/75; *Albuquerque Journal*, 7/15/75, p. 3, p.10.
459. Keleher collection, file 11448, Board of Trustees minutes, 7/26/74; *Albuquerque Tribune*, 7/28/75, p. 20.
460. *Albuquerque Journal*, 7/25/74, p. 43.
461. Personal interview, Richard Melzer, 12/20.
462. *Albuquerque Journal*, 8/1/75, p. 60.
463. CSWR/UofA, Box 6, folder 4, Board of Trustee minutes, July 14, 1975.
464. Interview with Theresa Carson, 10/21/20.
465. CSWR/UofA, Box 10, folder 2, President's Executive Council, 9/25/74.
466. Ibid.
467. *Albuquerque Journal*, 7/17/75, p. 14.
468. CSWR/UofA, Box 2, folder 5, letter from Tillet to Huling, 8/19/75.
469. CSWR/UofA, Box 6, folder 4, minutes of special Board of Trustees meeting, 9/5/75.
470. CSWR/UofA, Box 6, folder 4, letter from Riordan to Zanetti, 5/16/75.
471. Keleher collection, file 14648, special Board of Trustee minutes, 9/5/75; *Albuquerque Journal*, 9/6/75, p. 23.
472. *Albuquerque Journal*, 9/30/75, p. A-12; CSWR/UofA, Box 5, folder 26, Board of Trustees minutes, 9/29/75.
473. Ibid; Keleher collection, file 13327, memorandum from Keleher to file, 11/21/75.
474. Keleher collection, file 11449, offer for sale of Monroe Junior High, 3/18/74; letter from Cordova to Stapleton, 2/26/76; *Albuquerque Journal*, 12/13/75, p. 10; CSWR/UofA, Box 8, folder 5, letter from Stephenson to Cordova, 2/18/76.
475. Keleher collection, file 11465, letter from Killorin to Smith, 5/20/76; CSWR/UofA, Box 6, folder 6, letter from Killorin to Smith.

476. Ibid.
477. *Albuquerque Journal*, 5/8/76, p. 2; Keleher collection, file 11465, letter from O'Connell to Keleher, 6/14/76.
478. *Albuquerque Journal*, 5/8/76, p. 2.
479. Keleher collection, file 12092, Board of Trustees minutes, 7/1/76.
480. *Albuquerque Journal*, 7/5/76, p. 4.
481. *Albuquerque Journal*, 8/15/76, p. 33.
482. *Albuquerque Journal*, 8/15/76. p. 41.
483. CSWR/UofA, Box 10, folder 9, fall 1996 summary.
484. CSWR/UofA, Box 8, folder 3, cash flow statement, 11/30/76.
485. Keleher collection, file 00572.
486. *Albuquerque Journal*, 12/1/76, p. 12.
487. CSWR/UofA, Box 11, folder 15, Self-Study Report, 12/3/76.
488. Keleher collection, file 13323, University of Albuquerque Self-Study Report Prepared for the North Central Association of Colleges and Secondary Schools, 12/3/76.
489. Ibid.
490. Ibid.
491. *Albuquerque Journal*, 2/2/77, p. 1.
492. CSWR/UofA, Box 6, folder 5, Proposed Budget Guidelines – 1977-1978.
493. CSWR/UofA, Box 8, folder 4, A Report to Division and Program directors on Scheduling for Fall Semester, 5/6/77; *Albuquerque Journal*, 5/12/77, p. 11.
494. CSWR/UofA, Box 8, folder 4, Faculty Senate minutes, 5/6/77.
495. CSWR/UofA, Box 9, folder 1, report by Carey to Division and Program Directors on scheduling for the Fall Semester, 5/5/77.
496. CSWR/UofA, Box 5, folder 17, Center for Learning Resources Annual Report, 1976-1977.
497. CSWR/UofA, Box 9, folder 1, Faculty Senate minutes, 4/1/77.
498. CSWR/UofA, Box 6, folder 5, Statistical Survey from Students Faculty, Staff, and Administration Concerning the University's Future Options, May 1977.
499. CSWR/UofA, Box 11, folder 17, Report on 1977 NCA visit.
500. Keleher collection, file 520/22, "A Plan to Remain Private," 6/18/77.
501. CSWR/UofA, Box 3, folder 21, letter to Sisters of St. Francis from Faculty Senate, 10/27/78.
502. *Albuquerque Journal*, 9/4/77, p. 54.
503. CSWR/UofA, Box 9, folder 1, letter from Smith to Faculty

Senate, 9/9/77.
504. *Albuquerque Journal*, 3/13/77, p. 2.
505. *Albuquerque Journal*, 5/18/86, p. B-3.
506. *Albuquerque Journal*, 3/13/77, p. 2.
507. *Albuquerque Journal*, 10/8/78, p. 18.
508. Keleher collection, file 12093, minutes of the Board of Trustees meeting, 4/12/78.
509. CSWR/UofA, Box 11, folder 18, Self-Study Report for 1979.
510. CSWR/UofA, Box 6, folder 7, press release, 10/23/78.
511. Keleher collection, file 520/22, letter from T. Keleher to M. Keleher dated 9/20/78. St. Francis Gardens is a senior care facility in Albuquerque that was operated by the Sisters of St. Francis.
512. Keleher collection, public affairs file, letter from Keleher to Van Ackeren, 10/9/78.
513. CSWR/UofA, Box 9, folder 1, statement of Julius Cranston to the Board of Trustees re letter to Sister Eileen, 10/23/78.
514. Keleher collection, public affairs file, letter from Killorin to Van Ackeren, 11/15/78.
515. Keleher collection, public affairs file, minutes of special meeting of the Board of Trustees, 12/12/78.
516. *Albuquerque Tribune*, 10/24/78, p. A-14.
517. *Albuquerque Journal*, 1/9/79, p. 1.
518. *Albuquerque Journal*, 12/19/78, p. 1.
519. *Albuquerque Journal*, 12/20/78, p. 9.
520. CSWR/UofA, Box 8, folder 4, letter from Faculty Senate to Sisters, 10/27/78.
521. CSWR/UofA, Box 8, folder 5, letter from Cranston to Board of Trustees, 11/28/78.
522. *Albuquerque Journal*, 12/22/78, p. 10.
523. At this point in time, the University was owned by the University of Albuquerque Corporation.
524. CSWR/UofA, Box 6. Folder 7, A Proposal for Divestiture, 12/78.
525. CSWR/UofA, Box 4, folder 9, Board proposal.
526. CSWR/UofA, Box 8, folder 4, interoffice memo from Milford to faculty members, 9/21/79.
527. CSWR/UofA, Box 9, folder 1, Faculty Senate minutes, 9/21/79.
528. Keleher collection, public affairs file, letter from Faculty Senate (Cranston) to Van Ackeren, 2/12/79; CSWR/UofA, Box 4, folder 9, statement by Cranston at Faculty Senate meeting 10/23/78, letter from

Faculty Senate to Sisters, 10/27/78, memo from Juanita Martinez (Student Senate) to Board, n.d., memo from law firm of Toulouse, Krehbiel, and Delayo on injunctive relief relative to sale, 2/21/79; *Albuquerque Journal*, 11/1/78, p. A-5.
529. CSWR/UofA, Box 8, folder 6, letter from Cranston to Killorin, 2/13/79; letter from Killorin to Van Ackeren and the Provincial Council, 2/12/79.
530. Ibid.
531. CSWR/UofA, Box 8, folder 6, letter from Cranston to Van Ackeren, 1/25/79.
532. CSWR/UofA, Box 8, folder 6, letter from Van Ackeren to Cranston, 1/30/79.
533. CSWR/UofA, Box 8, folder 6, letter from Cranston to Van Ackeren, 2/3/79; telegram from Faculty Senate to Van Ackeren, 2/2/79.
534. *Albuquerque Journal*, 2/1/78, p.3
535. *Albuquerque Journal*, 2/2/79, p. 3
536. *Albuquerque Journal*, 2/8/79, p. 6.
537. CSWR/UofA, Box 8, folder 6, letter from Wirth to Milford, 4/25/80.
538. Keleher collection, public affairs file, letter from M. Keleher to T. Keleher, 2/8/79.
539. CSWR/UofA, Box 11, folder 18, Self-Study Report for 1979, 10/1/79.
540. CSWR/UofA, Box 6, folder 7, letter from T. Keleher, 3/6/79.
541. CSWR/UofA, Box 4, folder 9, memo from Sisters, 3/16/79.
542. CSWR/UofA, Box 6, folder 7, Board of Trustee minutes, 2/8/79.
543. CSWR/UofA, Box 9, folder 1, Faculty Senate minutes 2/9/79; *Albuquerque Journal*, 2/3/79, p. 1, 2/9/79, p. 1.
544. Keleher collection, Public Affairs file, minutes of Board of Trustees meeting 2/8/79.
545. *Albuquerque Journal*, 3/1/79, p. 1.
546. *Albuquerque Journal*, 3/2/79, p. 1.
547. *Albuquerque Journal*, 3/16/70, p. 6.
548. Keleher collection, public affairs file, memo from Smith to Killorin, 3/15/79.
549. Keleher collection, memberships and publications file, memo by Keleher, 6/30/78.
550. CSWR/UofA, Box 6, folder 7, minutes of Board meetings, 7/12/78 and 11/12/79.

551. Keleher collection, public affairs file, letter from T. Keleher to M. Keleher dated 3/6/79, letter from M. Keleher to T. Keleher, 3/12/79.
552. Keleher collection, Public Affairs file, letter from Juanita Martinez to Board of Trustees, n.d.
553. Keleher collection, file 13323, report to the Board, 3/15/79.
554. CSWR/UofA collection, Box 6, folder 7, Board of Trustee minutes, 3/16/79.
555. Ibid.
556. Ibid; *Albuquerque Journal*, 3/17/79, p. 1.
557. *Albuquerque Journal*, 3/22/79, p. 1, 3/23/79, p. 1.
558. CSWR/UofA, Box 9, folder 1, Faculty Senate special meeting minutes, 3/23/79; CSWR/UofA, Box 6, folder 7, Board of Trustees minutes, 6/4/79.
559. *Albuquerque Tribune*, 3/23/79, p. A-7.
560. *Albuquerque Tribune*, 3/7/79, p. A-1.
561. *Albuquerque Journal*, 2/17/79, p. 1, 3/31/79, p. 1, 4/17/79, p. 14; Keleher collection, public affairs file, letter from T. Keleher to M. Keleher, 3/29/79.
562. CSWR/UofA, Box 8, folder 4, Special Faculty Senate meeting minutes, 4/6/79.
563. *Albuquerque Journal*, 4/17/79, p. 1.
564. CSWR/UofA, Box 9, folder 1, Faculty Senate meeting 4/20/79; *Albuquerque Journal*, 4/18/79, p. 3.
565. *Albuquerque Journal*, 4/25/79, p. 35.
566. CSWR/UofA, Box 9, folder 1, letter from Smith to Albuquerque businesses and community leaders, 5/4/79.
567. *Albuquerque Journal*, 6/6/79, p. 1.
568. *Albuquerque Journal*, 5/11/79, p. 37.
569. *Albuquerque Journal*, 4/17/79, p. 14, 6/6/79, p. 1.
570. *Albuquerque Journal*, 6/6/79, p. 1.
571. CSWR/UofA, Box 8, folder 4, interoffice memo from Milford to faculty members, 9/21/79.
572. CSWR/UofA, Box 8, folder 4, Statement of the Faculty Senate Executive Committee to all University of Albuquerque students, n.d.
573. CSWR/UofA, Box 17, folder 1, *UofA Newslines*, 11/1/79.
574. CSWR/UofA, Box 11, folder 18, Self-Study Report, 10/1/79.
575. *Albuquerque Journal*, 11/13/79, p. 1.
576. CSWR/UofA, Box 6, folder 7, Board of Trustee minutes, 9/18/79, 11/12/79.

577. *Albuquerque Journal*, 3/11/80, p. 24.
578. *Albuquerque Journal*, 7/26/79, p. 3.
579. *Albuquerque Journal*, 3/11/80, p. 24, 6/19/80, p. 8.
580. *Albuquerque Journal*, 4/24/80, p. 39; CSWR/UofA Box 6, folder 10, minutes of special meeting of Board of Trustees, 4/17/79.
581. *Albuquerque Journal*, 8/23/79, p. 1.
582. *Albuquerque Journal*, 5/15/80, p. 6.
583. CSWR/UofA, Box 9, folder 1, minutes of special meeting of the Faculty Senate, 8/18/80.
584. McCord, op. cit., p. 200.
585. CSWR/UofA, Box 8, folder 4, Faculty Senate minutes, 10/17/80; *Albuquerque Journal*, 10/1/80, p. 1.
586. *Albuquerque Journal*, 10/1/80, p. 1.
587. *Albuquerque Journal*, 11/12/80, p. 17; CSWR/UofA, Box 17, *UofA Newslines*, 2/22/80.
588. *Albuquerque Journal*, 7/20/81, p. 7.
589. CSWR/UofA, Box 5, folder 21, Faculty Advisory Committee report to the Faculty Senate on merit pay, 11/21/80.
590. *Albuquerque Journal*, 11/21/80, p. 46, 11/23/80, p. 74.
591. *Albuquerque Journal*, 2/21/81, p. 17.
592. CSWR/UofA, Box 4, folder 4, letter to faculty from Diana Steigler, 5/5/81.
593. *Albuquerque Journal*, 8/18/81, p. 11.
594. CSWR/UofA, Box 8, folder 6, letter from Faculty Affairs Committee to Board, 9/14/81.
595. CSWR/UofA, Box 8, folder 6, note from Faculty Senate to Presidential Search Committee, 7/24/81.
596. *Albuquerque Journal*, 8/27/81, p. 3.
597. *Albuquerque Journal*, 9/1/81, p. 15.
598. *Albuquerque Journal*, 9/16/81, p. 23.
599. CSWR/UofA, Box 2, folder 1, "Strategies for Improving the University of Albuquerque," 9/18/81.
600. CSWR/UofA, Box 3, folder 22, "President's Report to the Faculty Senate," 11/81; *Albuquerque Journal*, 10/23/81, p. 23, 11/21/81, p. 1.
601. CSWR/UofA, Box 3, folder 22, "Faculty Report to the President," 12/1/81.
602. CSWR/UofA, Box 9, folder 2, report of the Faculty Affairs Committee, 10/7/81.
603. CSWR/UofA, Box 8, folder 4, memorandum from Faculty Affairs Committee on Faculty Salaries and Teaching Load, 10/7/81.

604. *Albuquerque Journal*, 12/2/81, p. 1, 12/10/81, p. 2.
605. CSWR/UofA, Box 10, folder 10, letter from Gibson to Noble, 12/18/81.
606. *Albuquerque Journal*, 11/13/82, p. 38.
607. *Albuquerque Journal*, 1/23/82, p. 5.
608. CSWR/UofA, Box 10, folder 10, Brown presentation to Faculty Senate, 2/26/82.
609. CSWR/UofA, Box 10, folder 10, letters from Eddy (3/3/82), Gibson (3/18/82), Brown (3/82), Wagner (3/5/82), Lucas (3/15/82), Johnson (4/2/82).
610. CSWR/UofA, Box 10, folder 10, letter from Noble to Roberts, 3/29/82.
611. CSWR/UofA, Box 10, folder 10, letter from Roberts to Noble, 4/82.
612. CSWR/UofA, Box 10, folder 10, letter from Parajon to Budagher, 3/25/82.
613. CSWR/UofA, Box 10, folder 10, letter from Parajon to Sisters, 4/1/82.
614. *Albuquerque Journal*, 2/18/81, p. 13.
615. CSWR/UofA, Box 5, folder 18, CLAIR council meeting minutes, 1/20/82.
616. *Albuquerque Journal*, 12/19/81, p. 19.
617. CSWR/UofA, Box 16, item 6, *Alumni News*, Vol. 2, No. 2, p. 2, 12/81.
618. CSWR/UofA, Box 9, folder 2, Amendment to Faculty Grievance Procedure, 11/20/81.
619. *Albuquerque Journal*, 1/12/82, p. 15.
620. CSWR/UofA, Box 8, folder 6, letter from Noble to faculty, 1/6/82.
621. CSWR/UofA, Box 8, folder 6, memo from Stephenson, 1/18/82.
622. *Albuquerque Journal*, 11/3/82, p. 16.
623. CSWR/UofA, Box 8, folder 6, letter from Sister Viatora to Ted Foss, 4/26/82.
624. CSWR/UofA, Box 8, folder 6, letter from Sisters to Robert, 4/30/82.
625. CSWR/UofA, Box 8, folder 6, letter from Noble to Thrash, 4/30/82; letter from Cranston to Knight, 4/5/82.
626. *Albuquerque Journal*, 7/25/80, p. 3.
627. CSWR/UofA, Box 8, folder 4, Faculty Senate minutes, 4/18/80

(entire presentation recorded and transcribed).
628. CSWR/UofA, Box 5, folder 28, notes from president of UUPNM, 8/21/80.
629. *Albuquerque Journal*, 7/25/80, p. 3, 4/3/61, p. 1.
630. CSWR/UofA, Box 8, folder 6, letter from Robert to Noble, 5/10/82.
631. CSWR/UofA, Box 8, folder 6, letters from Schumacher, Patero, Tennant, Mathews, Office of Records, Loiacons, et al., 5/10/82.
632. *Albuquerque Journal*, 2/27/82, p. 6.
633. CSWR/UofA, Box 9, folder 2, Faculty Senate minutes, 2/26/82.
634. *Albuquerque Journal*, 4/6/82, p. 1.
635. *Albuquerque Journal*, 4/8/82, p. 21.
636. CSWR/UofA, Box 3, folder 22, letter from Eleanor Noble to Faculty Senate, 3/7/82.
637. CSWR/UofA, Box 9, folder 2, Statement of University-wide concerns, 3/1/82.
638. *Albuquerque Journal*, 4/8/82, p. 21.
639. CSWR/UofA, Box 13, Essay by Connie Meyers in "Essays and Observations," 7/21/82.
640. *Albuquerque Journal*, 4/17/82, p. 17.
641. The UofA had had both individual members and an off-again-on-again chapter of AAUP since the mid-1960s (CSWR/UofA, Box 10, folder 8, individual member listing, 4/29/70).
642. *Albuquerque Journal*, 4/17/82, p. 17.
643. CSWR/UofA, Box 17, folder 3, UofA press release, 4/16/82.
644. CSWR/UofA, Box 16, folder 3, *Today at UofA*, various editions.
645. CSWR/UofA, Box 9, folder 2, Faculty Senate minutes, 5/7/82.
646. *Albuquerque Journal*, 5/8/82, p. 20.
647. CSWSR/UofA, Box 13, *Sister Lode*, November/December 1982.
648. *Albuquerque Tribune*, 12/12/81, page A-2.
649. Davis, op. cit., various pages.
650. Davis, op. cit., pp. 260-263.
651. *Alamogordo Daily News*, 5/11/82, p. 3.
652. *Albuquerque Journal*, 5/11/82, p. 1.
653. *Albuquerque Journal*, 6/25/82, p. 16.
654. *Albuquerque Journal*, 7/15/82, p. 3.
655. *Albuquerque Journal*, 9/1/82, p. 13.
656. A papal nuncio is an ecclesiastical diplomat, serving as an envoy or a permanent diplomatic representative of the Vatican to a country or

to an international organization.
657. Ibid; *Albuquerque Journal*, 10/6/82, p. 17.
658. This was, of course, an incorrect assertion since Frank Kleinhenz had balanced the budget during his administration.
659. *Rio Rancho Observer*, 10/7/82, p. 6.
660. *Albuquerque Journal*, 12/7/82, p. 1.
661. *Albuquerque Journal*, 12/30/82, p. 13.
662. *Albuquerque Journal*, 12/5/82, p. 6. (He was convicted in a trial on 2/24/83—*Albuquerque Journal*, 2/25/83, p. A-1.)
663. In December 1983, in a somewhat ironic turn of events, Frank Welch, made an offer to buy the Parks College in Albuquerque, the very institution that had tried to buy the UofA only a few years earlier. In fact, his purchase actually happened in January 1984 (*Albuquerque Journal*, 12/6/83, p. 1, 1/11/84, p. 13).
664. *Albuquerque Journal*, 1/11/63, p. 1, 2/2/83, p. 2.
665. *Albuquerque Journal*, 2/17/83, p. 49.
666. *Albuquerque Journal*, 2/16/83, p. 1.
667. *Albuquerque Journal*, 2/15/83, p. 2.
668. *Albuquerque Journal*, 3/4/83, p. 11.
669. CSWR/UofA, Box 9, folder 2, address to Faculty Senate, 4/22/83.
670. *Rio Rancho Observer*, 1/12/84, p. 13.
671. *Albuquerque Journal*, 3/21/83, p. 1.
672. *Albuquerque Journal*, 3/29/85, p. 13.
673. Keleher collection, file 11448, Executive Committee of the Board of Trustee minutes, 9/8/72.
674. *Albuquerque Journal*, 3/21/83, p. 1.
675. *Albuquerque Journal*, 5/31/83, p. 13.
676. *New Testament, New Jerusalem Bible*. New York: Doubleday and Company, 1966; *Albuquerque Journal*, 8/13/83, p. 17.
677. CSWR/UofA, Box 9, folder 5, letter from Brooks to Faculty, 9/16/85.
678. CSWR/UofA, Box 9, folder 2, memoir from McBride to Faculty, 6/20/83.
679. *Albuquerque Journal*, 8/7/83, p. 34.
680. *Albuquerque Journal*, 9/30/83, p. 23.
681. *Albuquerque Journal*, 10/14/83, p. 1.
682. *Albuquerque Journal*, 10/15/83, p. 1.
683. *Albuquerque Journal*, 12/22/83, p. 1.
684. Interview with Larry Larrichio, 8/6/21.

685. *Albuquerque Journal*, 10/14/83, p.13, 2/16/84, p. 1, 8/12/84, p. 122.
686. *Albuquerque Journal*, 10/21/83, p. 13, 11/29/83, p. 17; CSWR/UofA, Box 5, folder 18, CLAIR council meeting minutes, 1/20/82.
687. *Albuquerque Journal*, 1/10/84, p. 13.
688. *Rio Rancho Observer*, 3/1/84, p. 11.
689. *Albuquerque Journal*, 4/10/84, p. 13. Sister Stephanie received an honorary degree from UofA during the 1984 commencement exercises.
690. *Albuquerque Journal*, 9/11/84, p. 11.
691. *Albuquerque Journal*, 7/20/84, p. 13.
692. *Albuquerque Journal*, 1/10/85, p. 3.
693. Interview with Esther Shir, 7/28/20.
694. *Albuquerque Tribune*, 2/8/84, p. A-11.
695. CSWR/UofA, Box 15, item 8, *Alumni News*, Vol. 3, No. 2, p. 3, 9/84.
696. Keleher collection, file 18194, letter from McBride to Quinn, 7/17/84.
697. Elsie Scott interview, 8/16/21.
698. CSWR/UofA, Box 11, folder 20, Self-Study report, 12/84.
699. Elsie Scott interview, 8/16/21.
700. Interview with Theresa Carson, 10/21/20.
701. *Albuquerque Tribune*, 3/1/85, p. A-3; *Albuquerque Journal*, 3/1/85, p. 1.
702. Ibid.
703. Keleher collection, file 18194, letter from "One Who Has Been Badly Hurt" to Mrs. Loyd McKee, 2/5/85. Given the circumstances, a good guess would be that "One Who is Hurt" was a member of either the faculty or the staff.
704. Interview with Larry Larrichio, 8/6/21.
705. Elsie Scott interview, 8/16/21.
706. *Albuquerque Journal*, 3/10/85, p. 1.
707. *Albuquerque Journal*, 3/23/86, p. 21.
708. *Albuquerque Journal*, 3/27/85, p. 1.
709. *Albuquerque Journal*, 3/28/85, p. 1.
710. *Albuquerque Journal*, 3/29/85, p. 13.
711. Elsie Scott interview, 8/16/21.
712. Interview with Larry Larrichio, 8/6/21.
713. *Rio Rancho Observer*, 4/10/85, p. 1.
714. Elsie Scott interview, 8/16/21.

715. *Albuquerque Journal*, 4/3/85, p. 1.
716. *Albuquerque Journal*, 4/30/85, p. 8.
717. *Albuquerque Journal*, 6/6/85, p. 47, 6/17/85, p. 47, 6/21/85, p. 13.
718. CSWR/UofA, Box 9, folder 5, Faculty Assembly minutes, 8/22/85.
719. *Albuquerque Journal*, 7/9/85, p. 1.
720. CSWR/UofA, Box 9, folder 4, letter from McBride to Thrash, 8/28/85.
721. *Albuquerque Journal*, 8/11/85, p. 169.
722. *Albuquerque Journal*, 11/17/85, p. 70.
723. *Albuquerque Journal*, 2/6/86, p. 45.
724. *Albuquerque Journal*, 12/20/85, p. 74.
725. CSWR/UofA, Box 9, folder 5, Faculty Assembly minutes, 10/17/85.
726. CSWR/UofA, Box 9, folder 5, Faculty Forum minutes, 10/3/85.
727. CSWR/UofA, Box 9, folder 4, Faculty Assembly minutes, 12/5/85.
728. *Albuquerque Journal*, 2/4/86, p. 3.
729. *Rio Rancho Observer*, 2/26/86, p. 5.
730. *Albuquerque Journal*, 2/12/86, p. 1.
731. CSWR/UofA, letter from McBride and Mounton to UofA students, 3/3/86.
732. *Albuquerque Tribune*, 5/2/86, p. A-19
733. *Albuquerque Journal* 2/18/86, p. 13, 2/19/86, p. 1.
734. CSWR/UofA, Box 9, folder 5, Faculty Assembly minutes, 2/27/86.
735. CSWR/UofA, Box 9, folder 5, Minutes of the meeting of the Faculty Committee for Closing the University of Albuquerque, 3/5/86.
736. CSWR/UofA, Box 9, folder 5, minutes of meeting with the Transition Committee, 3/5/86.
737. *Albuquerque Journal*, 5/17/86, p. A1, 10/19/86, p. 4.
738. Interview with Esther Shir, 7/28/20.
739. *Santa Rosa News*, 5/8/86, p. 4.
740. Interview with Theresa Carson, 10/21/20.
741. *Albuquerque Journal*, 10/19/86, p. 4.
742. *Albuquerque Journal*, 4/18/86, p. 19.
743. An earlier institution calling itself the College of Santa Fe had been established in 1826 by Franciscan Father Sebastian Alvarez. Mondragon and Stapleton, op. cit., p. 9.

744. CSWR/UofA, Box 16, item 1, *Ambassador*, Vo. 2, #1, 3/71, p. 2.
745. Keleher collection, file 13327, letter from Powell to Saueressig, 4/18/73.
746. *Albuquerque Journal*, 2/13/86, p. 1, 3/5/86, p. 16.
747. CSWR/UofA, Box 9, folder 5, letter from McBride and Mounton to student body, 3/3/86.
748. McCord, op. cit., p. 269.
749. CSWR/UofA, Box 9, folder 5, Faculty Assembly minutes, 3/13/86.
750. CSWR/UofA, Box 17, folder 2, *Newslines*, Vol. 1, No. 11, 4/7/86.
751. McCord, op. cit., p. 270.
752. *Albuquerque Journal*, 12/4/86, p. 1.
753. Ibid.
754. *Albuquerque Journal*, 8/1/58, p. 22.
755. *Albuquerque Journal*, 12/4/86, p. 1.
756. McCord, op. cit.. In two interesting coincidences, both CSF and UofA survived for about the same length of time (~60 years) and both had their brief periods of financial success when they hired their first lay presidents—James Fries at CSF and Frank Kleinhenz at UofA.
757. Interview with Esther Shir, 7/28/20.
758. *Albuquerque Journal*, 12/4/86, p. 1.
759. District Court Case D-202-CV-1986-04059.
760. *Albuquerque Journal*, 5/15/86, p. 10.
761. *Albuquerque Journal*, 10/16/86, p. 1; 6/14/86, p. 21.
762. *Albuquerque Journal*, 8/2/86, p. 20.
763. District Court Case D-202-CV-1986-04059.
764. Keleher collection, Imrik files.
765. CSWR/UofA, Box 9, folder 5, Faculty Assembly minutes, 5/1/86.
766. *Albuquerque Journal*, 8/30/86, p. 6.
767. www.norbertines.org/mcbride.
768. *Albuquerque Journal*, 12/19/02, p. 1.
769. Keleher collection, file 00572, Keleher memoir, 5/1/91.
770. Keleher collection, file 18194, letter from Grady to M. Keleher, 4/3/86.
771. CSWR/UofA, Box 8, folder 4, Faculty Senate minutes, 9/21/79.
772. Keleher collection, file18194, "Key Moves and Steps to be taken for increasing general purpose endowment funds," 1983.
773. Keleher collection, file 18194, letter from McBride to Keleher, 1/19/85.

774. *Albuquerque Journal*, 6/14/86, p. 6, 11/14/86, p. 6.
775. *Albuquerque Journal*, 3/25/86, p. 15, 3/29/86, p. 22, 5/15/86, p. 1, 10/15/86, p. 1.
776. *Albuquerque Journal*, 11/21/86, p. 1.
777. *Albuquerque Journal*, 9/20/86, p. 1.
778. Interview with Esther Shir, 7/28/20.
779. *Albuquerque Journal*, 9/2/40, p. 7.
780. CSWR/UofA, Box 7, folder 2, minutes of Faculty Meeting, 2/3/56.
781. CSWR/UofA, Box 7, folder 3, faculty meeting minutes, 5/1/59.
782. *Albuquerque Journal*, 8/3/71, p. 4.
783. Keleher collection, file 13323, University of Albuquerque Self-Study Report Prepared for the North Central Association of Colleges and Secondary Schools, 12/3/76.
784. CSWR/UofA, Box 6, folder 7, press release, 10/23/78.
785. *Albuquerque Journal*, 5/31/83, p. 13.
786. *Albuquerque Journal*, 5/18/86, p. B-3.
787. Keleher collection, file 13323, University of Albuquerque Self Study Report Prepared for the North Central Association of Colleges and Secondary Schools, 12/3/76.
788. According to the National Association of Governing Boards of Colleges, a president should be in office for a minimum of seven years in order to accomplish effective and lasting change without major disruption to the operation of the school. (*Albuquerque Journal*, 5/18/86, p. B-3).
789. CSWR/UofA, Box 7, folder 3, faculty meeting minutes, 2/2/60; *Albuquerque Journal*, 5/18/86, p. B-3.
790. Richard Melzer Facebook solicitation, July 2020.
791. Judith Taylor interview, 7/17/20.
792. Theresa Carson interview, 10/21/20.
793. Elsie Scott interview, 8/16/21.

Bibliography

Primary Sources:

University of New Mexico, Center for Southwest Research and Special Collections, University of Albuquerque Collection (University of Albuquerque Archives—MSS 507 and PICT 000-507).
    Box 1, Annual Reports—Catholic Teachers College, Annual Reports—College of St. Joseph on the Rio Grande, Correspondence.
    Box 2, Administrative files.
    Box 3, Administrative files
    Box 4, Administrative files.
    Box 5, Administrative files.
    Box 6, Board of Trustee materials.
    Box 7, Faculty/Faculty Senate materials.
    Box 8, Faculty/Faculty Senate materials.
    Box 9, Faculty Senate/Miscellaneous Committee Reports.
    Box 10, Miscellaneous Reports.
    Box 11, Self-Study reports and Miscellaneous Data.
    Box 12, Miscellaneous reports.
    Box 13, Miscellaneous donations, artifacts, and newspaper clippings.
    Box 14, University of Albuquerque school catalogues.
    Box 15, Incomplete editions of *C.T.C. Chimes, Focus, Mesa Messenger, Yucca, El Luminario, Sand Trumpet, The Don*.
    Box 16, Incomplete editions of *The Ambassador, El Proclamador, The Signum, Black Focus, Dialog, Spirit of the 80s, Alumni News, One St. Joseph Place*.
    Box 17, Miscellaneous Publications including *Newslines* and *Today at UofA*.

Box 18, Yearbooks: *La Herencia, El Volcan, La Luz* (selected copies of editions, not a full collection).
Box 19, scrapbooks (mostly news clippings).
Box 20, scrapbooks (mostly news clippings).
Box 21, scrapbooks (mostly news clippings).
Box 22, scrapbooks (mostly news clippings).
Box 23, scrapbooks (mostly news clippings).
Box 24, scrapbooks (mostly news clippings).
Box 25, Miscellaneous materials including librettos and ledgers.
Photo Box 1: Miscellaneous photos.
Photo Box 2: Miscellaneous photos.
Photo Box 3: Miscellaneous photos.
Photo Box 4: Miscellaneous photos.

Michael L. Keleher collection. This collection consists of seven boxes with 67 files folders and some loose documents. This collection has been donated to the Center for Southwest Research, but has not been cataloged as of the date of this publication.

Albuquerque Journal, various dates.
Albuquerque Tribune, various dates.
Valencia County News-Bulletin, various dates.
Santa Fe New Mexican, various dates.
Other New Mexico Newspapers (*Deming Headlight, Las Vegas Optic, Clovis News-Journal, Rio Rancho Observer*, etc.,) various dates.

Interviews and Social Media Sources:

Aragon, Ray John de. Student, interview and correspondence, 8/21.
Baca, Mathias "Matt." Student, interviews, 7/25/20, 10/9/20.
Carson, Theresa. Student, interview, 10/21/20.
Cooney, James. Former Vice President for Development at the College of Santa Fe, interview 7/24/20.
Jay, Wendy, Student, interview 8/29/21.
Keleher, Michael L., former University attorney, interviews and correspondence.
Larrichio, Larry. Former admissions counselor, interview 8/6/21.
McGovern, James. Former student, interview 7/24/20.

Melzer, Richard A. Personal interviews and responses to Facebook query dated 3/16/20.
Moore, Brad. T-VI administration, email to John Taylor, 1/27/20.
Scott, Elsie. Administration, 8/17/21.
Shir, Esther (Kris Warmouth). Former librarian, interview 7/25/20.
Taylor, Judith A., RN. Former Associate Professor of Nursing, interview 7/17/20.

Secondary Sources:

Alexander, Francelle. *Albuquerque's North Valley—Vol II—Alameda and Los Ranchos*. Los Ranchos: Rio Grande books, 2018.
Avant, Louis. *The History of Catholic Education in New Mexico*. University of New Mexico Master's Thesis, 1940.
Barney, Robert K., *Turmoil and Triumph*. Albuquerque: San Ignacio Press, 1960.
Buddeke, Martha. "How the University of Albuquerque Can Make the Grade." *New Mexico Magazine,* May 1977, pp. 44-49.
Burr, Baldwin G., et al. *Notable and Notorious Neighbors in Valencia County History*. Tome: Valencia County Historical Society, 2018.
Chavez, Fray Angelico. *But Time and Chance*. Santa Fe: Sunstone Press, 1981.
———. *Two Hundred and Fifty Years Before Lamy*. Archdiocese of Santa Fe, nd.
Cordova, Rudy. *The History of the University of Albuquerque as Reflected in its Athletic Program, 1947-1969*. Self-published, 1981.
Davis, William E. *Miracle on the Mesa—A History of the University of New Mexico, 1889-2003.* Albuquerque: University of New Mexico Press, 2006.
Defouri, Reverend James. *Historical Sketch of the Catholic Church in New Mexico*. San Francisco: McCormick Brothers, 1887.
French, Sister Florita. "The History of Saint Vincent Academy." University of New Mexico Master's Thesis, 1942.
Hall, Ruth K. "Young and Dynamic College." *New Mexico Magazine*, Vol. 31, August 1964, pp. 24-27, 40.
Hau, Sister M. Honora, OSF and Sister M. Rayneria Willison, OSF. "A Brief History of the Congregation of the Sisters of Saint Francis of Perpetual Adoration," an unpublished and undated paper.

Hewitt, Raymond G. "Facts and Figures 1967—University of Massachusetts Amherst Office of Institutional Studies." January 1968.

Horgan, Paul. *Lamy of Santa Fe*. New York: Farrar, Straus, and Giroux, 1975.

McCord, Richard. *No Halls of Ivy*. Winona, MN: Lasallian Christian Brothers, 2013.

Melzer, Richard A. *Captain Maxmiliano Luna—A New Mexico Rough Rider*. Los Ranchos de Albuquerque: Rio Grande Books, 2019.

Mondragon, John B and Ernest Stapleton. *Public Education in New Mexico*. Albuquerque: University of New Mexico Press, 2005.

New Testament, New Jerusalem Bible. New York: Doubleday and Company, 1966.

Schuller, Sister M. Viatora, OSF. "A Brief History of the University of Albuquerque," unpublished and undated paper. CSWR/UofA, Box 1, folder 7.

Simmons, Marc. *Albuquerque*. Albuquerque: University of New Mexico Press, 1982.

Taylor, John M. *Dejad a los Niños Venir a Mi—A History of the Parish of Our Lady of Guadalupe in Peralta* (third edition). Albuquerque: LPD Press, 2005.

———. *Catholics Along the Rio Grande*. Charlestown: Arcadia Press, 2011.

Tórrez, Robert J., "El primer y principal ramo: An Examination of the Status of Education in the Mexican Era New Mexico," unpublished manuscript, 2021.

Wood, Robert Turner. *The Postwar Transition of Albuquerque, New Mexico 1945–1972*. Santa Fe: Sunstone Press, 2014.

Index

A

Academic Affairs Committee 74, 119, 194
Academic Policies Committee 139
Accreditation 33, 52, 53, 55, 56, 62, 68, 78, 95, 96, 98, 114, 116, 150, 157, 160, 161, 181, 182, 183, 184, 201, 202, 204, 223, 224, 246, 254fn62
Adult Education Program 154, 206, 224
Aerospace Program 120, 121
African Studies Institute 74
Agnes Dei (pet lamb) 216
Albuquerque Athletic Committee 77
Albuquerque Bus Company 43
Albuquerque Chamber of Commerce 84, 106, 127, 134, 141, 142, 205, 247
Albuquerque City Commission 69, 70, 134
Albuquerque Civic Auditorium 54
Albuquerque Convention Center 11, 181, 228
Albuquerque Economic Forum 221
Albuquerque High School 60
Albuquerque Journal 44, 64, 107, 111, 113, 126, 153, 155, 164, 172, 213, 229, 232, 245
Albuquerque National Bank 60
Albuquerque Police Academy 106
Albuquerque Police Department 98, 212, 213
Albuquerque Public Schools 119, 127, 133, 247
Albuquerque Federal Savings and Loan 181
Albuquerque Tribune 64, 96
Albuquerque University 73
Alumni affairs 61, 88, 90, 128, 148, 150, 196, 203, 204, 212, 228
Alumni News (alumni newsletter) 212

Alvarez, Father Sebastian, OFM 280fn743
The Ambassador (alumni newsletter) 90
Ambrose, Vic 96
American Association of University Professors (AAUP) 102, 198, 201, 202
American College Testing (ACT) 71, 119, 146, 210
Anderson, George H. 130, 267fn293
Anderson, Senator Clinton P. 64, 110
Apodaca, Governor Jerry 140, 142
Aragon, Ray John de 83, 129, 130
Archdiocese of Santa Fe 11, 16, 20, 21, 26, 27, 30, 33, 34, 64, 67, 69, 163, 167, 170, 171, 175, 181, 207, 211, 212, 214, 215, 225, 227, 232, 234, 235, 236, 237, 240, 242, 243
Archdiocese of St. Louis 11
Aristotle 45, 59
Armstrong, Louis 54
Arson 113
Associates Program in Hospitality 120, 224
Assumption Hall 47, 71
Athletics 36, 47, 53, 54, 55, 63, 64, 71, 76, 77, 84, 91, 93, 94, 96, 108, 128, 148, 154, 174, 187, 191, 203, 204, 230, 238
Avant, Louis 14

B
Baca, Chris 116
Baca, Felicita Sachs 31, 254fn58
Baca, Mathias " Matt," PhD 49, 56, 57
Bailey, Floyd 112
Bank of New Mexico 71
Barney, Robert K. 25
Barnhardt, Reverend Dr. Hyacinth 26, 27, 250
Basil, Brother 14
Baxter, Jill 118
Belen Branch 40, 106, 111, 112, 117, 150, 151
Benavidez, Fray Alonso de 14
Bennett, Secretary of Education William 220
Bernard, Father Edward 54

Bintner, Sister M. Catherine Ann, OSF 44, 64, 84
Bishop, Luis 117
Bismarck, Chancellor Otto von 18
Black Focus 130
Board of Trustees 11, 34, 63, 70, 74, 75, 80, 83, 90, 91, 92, 103, 104, 105, 108, 109, 113, 114, 115, 118, 119, 122, 123, 124, 125, 126, 129, 130, 131, 134, 135, 136, 137, 139, 140, 141, 142, 143, 144, 145, 146, 149, 150, 151, 152, 153, 156, 158, 159, 161, 162, 164, 165, 166, 167. 168, 169, 170, 171, 172, 173, 174, 175, 176, 177, 178, 180, 181, 182, 184, 185, 186, 187, 191, 192, 194, 195, 196, 197, 198, 199, 200, 202, 203, 205, 206, 210, 211,212, 214, 219, 220, 221, 225, 226, 227, 228, 230, 232, 235, 245, 246
Bonzel, Aline (see Bonzel, Mother Maria Theresia, OSF)
Bonzel, Mother Maria Theresia, OSF 17, 18
Box, Bobby 83
Boyle, Betty Gayle, RN 214
Boyle, Patricia 184
Boyle, Sister M. Mathias, OSF 23, 24, 250
Bradbury and Stamm 62, 116
Bradley, Father William 27, 30, 33, 34, 250
Branch Community College Act 141
Braun, Sister M. Barbara Ann, OSF 80, 105
Bridge International School 188
Brown, Arthur 134, 135
Brown, Professor Bob 111
Brown, Professor Eugene 63, 79, 195, 199, 200
Brunswick, Erma 150
Budagher, State Senator John A. 19
Burke, Frank 94
Byrne Hall 71, 73, 186
Byrne, Archbishop Edwin Vincent 29, 30, 31, 32, 33, 34, 44, 45, 64, 67

C
Campbell, Governor Jack 73
Campos, Ricardo 183
Candelaria, Neil 205

Cano, Javier 224
Carey, Dean J. Peter 162
Carnegie Commission on Higher Education 133
Carson, Theresa 151, 217, 218, 249
Catholic Teachers' College of New Mexico 11, 14, 27, 30, 33, 34, 38
Catholic University (Washington, DC) 27, 33, 53, 206
"The Caucasian Chalk Circle" (play) 229
Center for Law Enforcement, Corrections, and Social Services 106, 130, 131
Center for Learning and Information Resources (CLAIR) 118
Center for Southwest Research and Special Collections 5, 10, 71, 240
Central New Mexico Community College (CNM) 143
Chavez, Rudy 144, 146
Chavez collection 27, 240
Chavez, Senator Dennis Jr. 71, 72, 240
Cheating 68, 69
Chi Gamma Iota fraternity 45, 163
Christian Angelology 17, 18
Christian Brothers 17, 27, 212, 230, 231
Christian commitment 77, 78, 79, 118, 119, 124, 131, 132, 137, 144
Chum, Ed 224
Cicuye 14
CIT Corporation 71
Civil Defense 40
Clovis News-Journal 32
Cole, Judge Gerald 200
College of Artesia 110
College of Santa Fe 185, 212, 230-233, 234, 235, 240, 281fn756
College of St. Joseph 33-73
College of St. Joseph on the Rio Grande (see College of St. Joseph)
College of St. Thomas (St. Paul, Minnesota) 219
Colorado Springs Branch 111
Colorado Springs Motherhouse 51, 61, 66, 89, 92, 144, 166
Committee on Curriculum 54
Committee on Honors and Discipline 69
Community college issue 92, 110, 122, 133-143, 144, 161, 164, 167, 174, 182, 189, 213, 214, 216, 233, 247

Community Counseling Services 232
Computer science 58, 71, 113, 118, 210, 211, 243
Concho, Carlotta 151
Congregation of the Poor Sisters of Saint Francis Seraph of the Perpetual Adoration 17
Congregational Church 31
Coniga, Grace 33
Connelly, Governor Henry 14
Continental Airlines 187
Conway, State Superintendent of Public Education John V. 20, 33
Cooney, James 233
Cooper, David 216, 217
Coors Boulevard 43, 44, 71, 87
Coors, Judge Henry George III 43
Copeland, Joe 100, 101, 110
Cordova, Rudy 35, 26, 47, 48, 63, 76, 77, 93, 130
Cordova, Gil 145, 147, 148, 149, 151, 152, 174, 248, 250
Coronado, Francisco Vasquez de 13
Corrales (village) 143, 206
Corrales Road 43
Cosden, Professor Ruth 228
Cranston, Dean Julius "Jack" 167, 172, 185, 186, 206, 250

D
Daeger, Archbishop Alfred Thomas, OFM 19, 23, 24, 25
Davis Hall 68, 110, 120, 213
Davis, Archbishop James Peter 67, 68, 73, 100
Davis, William Eugene "Bud" 134
Dawson, Christopher 79
Daly, John 105
Deferrari, Roy, PhD 27, 33
Defoe, Professor George 84
Defouri, Reverend James 16
DeLayo, Leonard 178
Dennis Chavez Memorial Library 21
Department of Ecumenical Studies 80
Desaulniers, Professor Lawrence 74, 116, 124, 144, 187, 235

Deuble, Frank 110
Diocese of Durango, Mexico 16
Dionisi, Debra 114
Divini Illius Magistri (papal encyclical) 40, 41
Doiron, Sister M. Marilyn, OSF 49, 81, 82, 83, 86, 88, 89, 90, 92, 94, 95, 97, 98, 101, 102, 103, 104, 174, 234, 250
Domenici, Senator Peter V. 11, 53, 127, 128, 134, 249
Dominguez, Zoile 84
The Don (campus newsletter) 37
Dons (athletic team) 48, 53, 94, 187
Dormitory issues (see also Byrne Hall, Davis Hall, Madonna Hall, St. Clare Hall, room and board) 20, 21, 23, 60, 66, 68, 71, 73, 75, 76, 81, 82, 83, 86, 87, 92, 94, 95, 113, 177, 180, 214, 215, 221, 247
Downell, Carlos Wayne 130
Drama Department 64, 65, 94, 116, 117, 147
Dreshman, Ward 152
Duffy, Bill 238
Dunphy, Father 82
Dwenger, Bishop Joseph Gregory 18

E
Earthquakes 106, 107, 114
Eastern New Mexico University 114, 135
Eglington, William 184
Ellenberger, Norm 203, 204
Ellerbe Corporation 122
El Luminario (campus newsletter) 43
El Mac Court 71
Employment Security Commission 165
Encinias, Professor Miguel 147
Engle, Mary 245, 246
Enrollment issues 22, 23, 28, 29, 31, 44, 52, 53, 55, 57, 58, 60, 61, 62, 64, 65, 68, 76, 81, 82, 84, 86, 88, 91, 92, 94, 97, 99, 110, 111, 114, 115, 118, 119, 122, 131, 136, 146, 152, 153, 154, 159, 162, 170, 172, 175, 176, 182, 185, 190, 191, 206, 207, 209, 210, 211, 213, 214, 219, 221, 222, 224, 225, 228, 232, 243, 244, 247, 248
Escalona, Fray Luis de 13, 14

Espelage, Bishop Bernard 24, 250
Executive Committee of the Board of Trustees 108, 126, 144, 182, 200

F
Faculty Assembly 224, 225, 227, 235
Faculty Advisory Committee 187
Faculty Forum 211, 224, 225
Faculty Handbook 195, 200, 201, 222, 225, 234
Faculty News Bulletin (faculty newsletter) 107
Faculty salaries 78, 83, 86, 94, 98, 156, 161, 188, 193, 227
Faculty Senate 74, 100, 101, 105, 108, 109, 110, 115, 116, 118, 144, 145, 160, 162, 167, 169, 171, 172, 182, 185, 188, 190, 191, 192, 193, 195, 197, 198, 199, 200, 202, 203, 206, 211, 222
Falls, D. W. 70, 75, 83, 135
Farrell, Mary Jane, RN, PhD 214
Federal Education Facilities Act of 1963 71
Federal Office of Equal Opportunity 83
"Field of Dreams" (movie) 73
Fine Arts Center 110, 111, 206, 229
Fioke, Brother Clarence 230, 231, 232
First National Bank of Albuquerque 179, 181
Flora, Sister Jo-Ann, SND 210, 211, 219, 221, 222, 223
Foss, Ted 108
Franciscan Order 13, 14, 16, 17, 23, 24, 25, 26, 27, 35, 240, 243, 251fn1, 252fn20, 280fn743
Franciscan Province of the Holy Gospel 13
Franco-Prussian War 18
Funk, Hugh 75

G
Gabaldon, Raymond 113
Garcia, Assistant Dean of Students Jose 78
Garcia, Monsignor 34
Garihee, Marcia 54
German, Lawrence 142, 143
Gerken, Archbishop Rudolph Aloysius 26, 27, 29, 30, 31
GI Bill of Rights 29, 116

Gibson, Professor Joan 194, 199
Glover, Randall 212
Gonzales, James R. 90
Grady, William B. "Bing" 222, 224, 236
Graham, Jack 81
Great Depression 25, 40
Great Society 89
Gregory I, Pope 18
Grey Nuns 25
Grievance procedures 115, 196, 197

H
Hall, Ruth 44
Hartmann, Reverend Julius 27
Hau, Sister M. Honoria, OSF 35
Heim, Richard 82
Hernandez, Edmundo 49
Higher Education Facilities Act of 1963 65, 122
Hill, Joe 151
Hilton Foundation 99
Hinshaw, Valerie 220, 221
Hoehn, Father Roger 51
Hogan, Father Thomas 216
Hogg, Sarah 163
Holy See (see Vatican)
Horizon Corporation 99, 111, 112, 117, 126, 187
Hospitality Industries Program 120, 224
House Bill 541 181
Household Finance Corporation 83
Hoye, Monsignor Daniel 235
Huff, Robert, PhD 150
Humanism 77, 80, 132, 144, 145, 157, 210, 244, 245, 249
Humphreys, Roberta 212
Hunt, Sister Marjorie 110
Huntington, Samuel 99
Hygein Foundation 64

I

IBM Corporation 71, 132, 254fn50
Immaculate Conception church (Albuquerque) 20, 21
Immaculate Heart of Mary Province 18
Imrik, Professor Andrew 71, 84, 145, 190, 233, 234, 235
Independent Community College Act 142
International Franciscan College (Rome) 23
Institute of Southwestern Studies 74, 78

J

"J" (on Volcon) 48, 49, 107
James Marshall Distinguished Service Award 234
James Monroe Middle School 152, 153
Jaramillo, Matthew 113
Jehensen, Professor Yvonne 130, 206
Jenkins, Myra Ellen, PhD 72
Jennings, Kathleen 72
Jesuit Order 17, 21, 27, 81, 253fn24
John Paul II, Pope 235, 236
Johnson, President Lyndon B. 49, 65 89, 99, 119
Johnson, Yvonne 130
Jones, Bob 152
Jones, Joel 139

K

Kao, Simon, PhD 68, 71
KDEF radio 110
Keleher and McLeod, PA 1
Keleher, Loretta 41
Keleher, Margaret "Peggy" 1
Keleher, Michael L. 1, 42, 92, 108, 139, 149, 152, 166, 173, 174, 175, 176, 233
Keleher, Timothy 143, 166, 169, 173, 175, 176, 178, 179, 187
Keleher, William A. 1, 28, 41
Kennedy, President John F. 48, 65, 107
Kenney, Dan 163
Kent State University 100

KGGM radio 65
Killorin, James 136, 137, 138-143, 149, 150, 167, 168, 169, 170, 171, 173, 174, 175, 177
King, Governor Bruce 175
Kinney, Carol 108, 122,123, 214
Kinney, Mayor Harry 222
Kirk, John 180
Kirtland Air Force Base (see Kirtland Air force Base Branch)
Kirtland Air Force Base Branch 40, 55, 84, 86, 110, 151, 232
Kiva Auditorium 11, 228
Klein, Samuel, PhD 64
Kleinhenz, Francis A. "Frank" 89, 90, 91, 94, 95, 97, 104, 105, 106, 108, 110, 111, 112, 114, 116, 117, 118, 119, 126, 127, 135, 150, 154, 174, 221, 222, 224, 225, 234, 236, 244, 246, 248, 250
Klene, Donald 89
Knode, Dean J. C. 33
Korean War 40, 47, 63
Kosky, Eugene, PhD 118
Krahe, Reverend Daniel 34
Krbec, Dean Kirby 113
Kugler, Mother M. Basilia, OSF 34, 35, 38, 39, 246, 250
Kulturkampf 18
KZIA radio 110

L
La Herencia (yearbook) 216
Lamy, Archbishop Jean Baptiste 16, 17
Landon, Susan 8, 213
Lanier, Charles 77, 78
Lattanza, Roger 91, 105
League of United Latin-American Citizens (LULAC) 128
Lee, Joe 168, 178, 180, 182
Lee, Professor Warren 170, 178, 185, 199, 219, 221
Legacy Campaign 222, 224, 236
Legislative Finance Committee 187
Legoza, Rick 130
Lemke. Charles 42

Lewis, James 151
Library (see also Center for Learning and Information Resources) 22, 28, 41, 53, 56, 60, 61, 66, 71, 72, 73, 95, 96, 97, 111, 115, 118, 160, 161, 216, 240
Los Ranchos de Albuquerque 57
Lourdes Hall 76, 111, 113, 232
Lucas, Professor John 206, 224
Lujan, Representative Manuel 11, 128
Luna, Maureen 143

M
Madonna Hall 60, 62, 73, 213, 221
Madrid, Nick 36
Maio, John 221
Makin, Right Reverend Benjamin T., O. Praem. 207
Maloof, Judy 84
Management, Inc. 182
Mandalari, Father Alphonso, SJ 20
Maria Theresia, Mother (see Bonzel, Mother Theresia, OSF)
Marriott Corporation 224
Martinez, Don Antonio Jose ("Padre") 13
Martinez, Juanita 176
Martinez, Professor Nancy 197, 210
Martinez, Robert 78, 98, 99
Martinez, Ted 140, 143
Master Planning Committee (see planning)
Mazzio, Frank 86, 87
McBride, Father Alfred, O. Praem. 11, 206-223, 224, 225, 226, 231, 234, 235, 236, 246, 248, 250
McCaffrey, Fred 103
McCarthy, Reverend Edward T. 33, 34
McCarty, Frankie 8, 118
McConnell, William R., PhD 133
McGrath, James 54, 68
McKee, Gena 184, 196, 206, 214, 219, 220, 235
McKinzie, Gloria 95
McReynolds, Sister Stephanie, OSF 8, 205, 207, 214, 215

Mendoza, Christy 229
Mercure, Alex 139
Merritt, John 149
Mesa Messenger (campus newsletter) 52
Mesa Road 42
Mescall, Judge Tom 214
Mexican-American War 16
Middle Rio Grande Council of Governments 137
Milford, Professor Homer 173, 182
Miller, A. Otto 108, 109, 126
Mindorf, Father Claude, OFM 23
Monroe, John K. 41
Montoya, Senator Joseph 108, 128
Moots, Sister Giotta 237
Moratorium Day 99, 100
Morgan, Don 184, 185
Morley, Professor Jim 64
Morris, Congressman Tom 71
Morrison, Father 69
Mounton, Brother Donald 230, 231
Multi-Cultural Education Enrichment Program (MEP) 147

N
National Association for the Advancement of Colored People (NAACP) 152
National Association of Intercollegiate Athletics (NAIA) 54, 76, 77
National Center for Hispanic Culture and Studies 210
National Collegiate Athletic Association (NCAA) 76, 84, 93, 96, 204
National Defense Student Loan Program 58
National Institutes of Health 88, 106, 146, 147
National Labor Relations Act of 1935 198
National Labor Relations Board 198, 199
National Labor Relations Board vs. Yeshiva University 198
National Science Foundation 71, 99
National Vietnam Moratorium Committee 100
Nazareth Hospital 260fn200
Neutzling, Pat 94

Newman, Cardinal John Henry 54
New Heritage Program 105
New Mexico Highlands University 129, 235
New Mexico Hotel and Motel Association 224
New Mexico Independent College Association 56, 132
New Mexico State Board of Education 27, 33
New Mexico State Board of Educational Finance (BEF) 133, 140
New Mexico State Corporation Commission 73, 74
New Mexico State Legislature 142, 175, 187, 225, 247
New Mexico State Records and Archives Center 72
New Mexico Territory 14, 16, 17, 19, 20
Newslines (campus newsletter) 202
Niederberger, Professor Walter 106
Nixon, President Richard M. 100, 106, 145
Noble, Professor Eleanor 190, 191, 195, 197, 200
Norbertine Order 206, 207, 212, 236
North Central Association of Colleges and Secondary Schools 33, 52, 53, 56, 59, 61, 81, 95, 97, 118, 150, 157, 161, 181, 182, 184, 198, 223, 224
Nursing Program 74, 75, 84, 88, 93, 96, 106, 111, 117, 131, 160, 161, 185, 191, 204, 205, 214, 215, 232, 249

O
O'Brien, Father Albert, OFM 24, 25
Office of Economic Opportunity 119
Office of Education 110
Olivas, Sabino 184
Operation Bootstrap 58, 110
Ortega, Joaquin, PhD 56
Ortiz y Pino de Kleven, Concha 75, 76, 260fn204
Otero, Rosalie 222
Our Lady of Guadalupe chapel (Old Town) 237
Our Lady of Lourdes High School 32, 33, 242
Our Lady of Lourdes Seminary 32

P

Padilla, Fray Juan de 13
Padilla, Rafael 152
Padilla, Ray 129
Padilla, Sosimo 184
Palmisano, Coach Leon 187
Papal Nuncio 205, 278fn656
Paradise Hills 70, 91, 134, 236
Parajon, Professor 195
Parenti Field 237
Parks College Incorporated 167, 168, 169, 171-178, 180, 182
Partners in Progress 196
Pecos (see Cicuye)
Peña Blanca 19
Pfeiffer, Charles, PhD 147
Pfeiffer, Ralph, PhD 132
Piccirilli, Joseph and family (Piesrasanta, Italy) 45
Pima Medical Institute 233
Pitival, Archbishop John Bautiste 21
Pius IX, Pope 16
Pius XI, Pope 40, 41, 77
Pius XII, Pope 29
Planning 77-79, 82, 86, 90, 92, 108, 109, 112, 115, 122, 123, 124, 153, 154
Plato 45, 63
Police Science 94, 98, 106, 117
Popejoy, Tom 84, 133, 247
Powell, Ray 109, 126, 129, 146, 149, 230
Pratt, State Representative Judith 175, 181
Price, V. B. 226
Professional Salespersons of America 224
Provincial Council of the Sisters of St. Francis 165, 171
Prussia 17, 18
Public Service Company of New Mexico 42, 149
Purcell, Doria 78

Q
Quivera 13, 14

R
Ravel Brothers Feed Store 83
Reagan, President Ronald 230
Reece, Dan 154
Regina Hall 74, 75, 84
Regina School of Nursing 74
Recordsgate 212
Richardis, Sister M., OSF 54
Rihm, Sister Alma 74
Rio Grande Center (see Belen Branch)
Rio Grande Development Corporation 60
Riordan, Guy 204
Robert, John 194, 195, 198, 201, 203, 204, 214
Roney, Brother Cyprian Luke 185
Room and board (see also dormitory issues) 84, 94, 180, 184
Route 66 43, 69
Royal Court 71
Ryan, William 92

S
Saavadra, Louis 141
Sacred Congregation for Religious and Secular Institutions 188, 205
Sagrada Art School (Old Town) 237
Salas, Sister Agnes de 32, 250
Salazar, Loretta 90
Salazar, Nika 31
Sanchez, Beatrice 25
Sanchez, Archbishop Robert 170, 171, 187, 205, 213, 222, 228, 232
Sandia Laboratories (later Sandia National Laboratories) 40, 55, 61, 90, 109, 126, 127, 129
Sand Trumpet (campus newsletter) 100, 107, 129, 130
San Felipe Pueblo Branch 111
Santa Cruz de Cañada 14
Scholastic Aptitude Test (SAT) 210

Saueressig, Harold 230
Schaefer, Sister M. Luella, OSF 109
Schaefer, Margaret, RN 204
Schneider, Father Marcian 102
Schoenfeld, Professor Elise 147
Schoeppner, Reverend Clarence C. 27, 34
Scholarships 61, 71, 91, 92, 93, 94, 146, 209, 221
School symbols (song, flag, logo, colors) (see also "J" on Volcon) 17
Schuller, Sister M. Viatora, OSF 11, 34, 35, 51, 52, 56, 58, 62, 68, 73, 76, 77, 80, 81, 197, 246, 250
Scoggins, Lieutenant Lee 49
Scott, Elsie 8, 119, 120, 217, 222, 249
Sears Roebuck Corporation 83
Searson, James W., PhD 20
Searson-Martin reading series 20
Second Vatican Council 77, 80, 82
Seraphim (plural of seraph) 17, 18
Servicemen's Readjustment Act of 1944 (see GI Bill of Rights)
Shambaugh, Clyde 57
Shared Management Services, Incorporated 181
Shaw, Harriet 14, 15
Shaw, Reverend John Milton 14, 15
Sheets, Howard 42
Shir, Esther 216, 240
Signum (alumni newsletter) 150
Simmons, Marc 29
Simms, Governor John 113
Singer, Robert 184
Sister Lode 203
Sisters of Charity 17
Sisters of Loretto 17
Sisters of Mercy 25
Sisters of St. Francis and Daughters of the Most Holy Hearts of Jesus and Mary 17
Sisters of St. Francis (also Congregation of the Poor Sisters of St. Francis Seraph of the Perpetual Adoration, Sisters of St. Francis Seraph of the Perpetual Adoration, Sisters of St. Francis Seraph, Sisters of

the Third Order Regular of St. Francis) 11, 17, 20, 22, 23, 24, 27, 28, 34, 35, 38, 39, 41, 42, 51, 53, 63, 64, 66, 68, 73, 86, 87, 88, 91, 94, 95, 102, 103, 104, 105, 109, 110, 118, 122, 123, 124, 131, 135, 136, 137, 139, 142, 143, 144, 146, 150, 152, 156, 161, 162, 165-181, 184, 186, 187, 195, 196, 197, 205, 206, 214, 215, 217, 240, 242, 243, 245, 246, 247, 248

Sloan, E. H. 41

Sloan, Maxine 41

Slusher, Deputy District Attorney Steve 213

Smith, Reverend Clifford 178, 179, 180, 181, 182, 184, 185

Smith, Coach Ernie 94, 187

Smith, Laurence C., PhD 134, 140, 142, 143, 153, 154, 165, 172, 174, 178

Smoker, Dave 140

Southern Association 201

Southwest College 113

Southwest Indian Polytechnic Institute 160

Sperry Corporation 221

St. Anthony's Orphanage 18, 20-23, 25, 28, 29, 31, 32, 34, 51, 56, 254fn60, 254fn61

St. Augustine 45

St. Bonaventure College (New York) 24, 25, 27

St. Cecilia chapel (UofA) 240

St. Charles Borromeo church (Albuquerque) 237

St. Clare Hall 71, 73

St. Francis Gardens 166

St. Francis Hall 47, 106, 107

St. Francis Normal School for Catholic Sisters of St. Francis 20-23

St. Francis Seminary (Cincinnati) 23

St. Francis Summer College 24-26

St. Joseph (statue) 43, 44, 50, 238, 239, 256fn94

St. Joseph Chapel (Assumption Hall) 47

St. Joseph Hospital 38

St. Joseph on the Rio Grande church (Albuquerque) 241

St. Joseph on the Rio Grande College 11, 38-73, 81, 88, 107, 127, 133, 134, 217, 237, 242

St. Joseph on the Rio Grande Development Corporation 60

St. Joseph on the Rio Grande High School 213
St. Joseph Province 18
St. Mary's College (California) 56, 127
St. Mary's School (Albuquerque) 34, 60, 213, 240
St. Michael's College 240
St. Norbert Abbey 206, 236
St. Pius X High School 9, 47, 53, 92, 111, 153, 213, 234, 237-241, 256fn94
St. Pius X High School Branch 111
St. Therese of Lisieux 68, 258fn168
St. Thomas Aquinas 45, 58, 59
St. Vincent Academy 92
Starline Corporation 126, 222
Steigler, Diana 188
Stoffel, Reverend Jules N. 27, 30, 34, 250
Student Assembly 36
Student Choice Act 216
Student Council 43, 68, 82, 96, 261fn229
Student Senate 77, 82, 83, 96, 98, 99, 100, 101, 108, 109, 112, 129, 144, 146, 152, 176, 205, 261fn229
Sullivan, Father 58, 243, 244
Summers, Reverend Harry 134
SunWest Bank 222

T
Taylor, Judith, RN 249
Technical-Vocational Institute (Albuquerque) 83, 84, 111, 122, 133-136, 139-143, 225, 233
Ten-Year Development Program 73
Theresians 658, 258fn168
Thomism 48, 58, 59
TIAA-CREF 78
Tijerina, Reyes Lopez 83
Tillet, Steve 151, 152
Tingley Coliseum 34
Today at UofA (campus newsletter) 202
Topp, Michael 152

Trivett, Gene 71
Tuition 64, 65, 66, 78, 83, 85, 94, 95, 110, 1112, 123, 136, 145, 146, 149, 150, 152, 153, 156, 159, 162, 173, 180, 184, 187, 192, 208, 210, 216, 220, 221, 247, 248, 269fn440

U
Ulibarri, Sabina 83
United States Department of Health Education and Welfare 52, 88, 106
United States Housing and Home Finance Administration 68
United States Veterans' Administration 116
United University Professors 198, 199
University Center 11, 76, 84, 87, 106, 107, 117, 240, 241
University of Albuquerque Committee of the West Side Association 134
University of Albuquerque Foundation 125
University of Albuquerque Legacy Campaign 222, 224, 236
University of Albuquerque Rio Grande Center (see Belen Branch)
University of New Mexico 8, 10, 27, 28, 33, 34, 56, 72, 74, 78, 84, 99, 111, 133, 134, 135, 139, 140, 141, 142, 149, 150, 163, 184, 188, 190, 202, 203, 204, 214, 217, 225, 226, 233, 240,
University Scholars Program 63, 64
Upward Bound Program 119

V
Valle North Caring Center 260fn200
Van Ackeren, Sister M. Eileen, OSF 136, 137, 138, 150, 165, 166, 167, 171, 172, 174, 177, 184
Vander Meer, Jo, RN 204, 205, 249
Vasquez de la Cueva, Don Fernando, Duke of Alburquerque 257fn133
Vatican 77, 80, 82, 188, 205, 212, 214, 236, 244, 245, 278fn656
Veterans 29, 58, 63, 89, 98, 99, 116, 155, 163
Veterans Education and Training Program (VETAP) 116
Vicariate Apostolic of New Mexico 16
Vietnam Protest Day 100
Vietnam War 76, 88, 89, 99, 100, 163, 248
Vista Sandia Hospital 74, 260fn200
Volcano Cliffs 126

Volcon 48, 29, 107
Voss, Monsignor Elwood C. 68

W
War on Poverty 119
Ward, Lydia, RN 204, 205
Warmoth, Kris (see Esther Shir)
Webster Grove University 92
Weidman, Lonnie 84
Weiser, Alan 184, 185
Welch, Frank, PhD 188-206, 214, 222, 244, 248, 250
Weisenberg, PhD 188, 189
Wesenenberg, Jack 184
West Mesa 9, 41, 43, 49, 57, 108, 127, 190, 237, 242
White, Fred 41
White, Mildred 41
Wich, Sister Rose Therese 213
Wilken, Reverend Robert, OFM 35, 36, 37, 250
Williams, Professor Richard 202
Willison, Sister M. Rayneria, OSF 33, 35, 41
Wirth, Robert 173
Women's Recreational Association 34
World War II 28, 40, 189, 236
Wylie Brothers 43

Y
Yale University 72
Yip, Cheung Lung 96
Young, Martha, PhD 154
Yule, Dennis 107
Yslas, Dean Mucio 112, 116, 128, 129, 130, 144, 148

Z
Zanetti, Joseph 116, 126-129, 135, 138, 142, 144, 146, 147, 148, 149, 151, 174, 250
Zens, Professor 64
Zozobra (band) 83

www.ingramcontent.com/pod-product-compliance
Lightning Source LLC
Chambersburg PA
CBHW021338230426
43666CB00006B/338